The Leave-No-Crumbs Camping Cookbook

RICK GREENSPAN & HAL KAHN

The Leave-No-Crumbs Camping Cookbook

150 Delightful, Delicious,
and Darn-Near Foolproof Recipes
from Two Top Wilderness Chefs

RICK GREENSPAN & HAL KAHN

 Storey Publishing

The mission of Storey Publishing is to serve our customers by publishing practical information that encourages personal independence in harmony with the environment.

Edited by Dianne M. Cutillo and Carey L. Boucher
Cover design by Steve Hughes
Art direction and interior design by Meredith Maker
Text production by Karin Stack and Melanie Jolicoeur
How-to illustrations by Brigita Fuhrmann
Photographs on pages 47 and 159 courtesy of YMCA Camp Belknap, Wolfeboro, NH. Mess kit photograph on page 155 by Lisa Clark. Family camping photographs courtesy of Deborah Balmuth, Caroline Burch, Laurie Figary, Elinor Goodwin, and Ilona and Jim Sherratt.
Indexed by Nan Badgett/Word•a•bil•i•ty

Storey books are available for special premium and promotional uses and for customized editions. For further information, please call 1-800-793-9396.

Printed in the United States by Banta

10 9 8 7 6 5 4 3 2 1

Library of Congress Cataloging-in-Publication Data

Greenspan, Rick.
  The leave-no-crumbs camping cookbook : 150 appetite-satisfying recipes
for the great outdoors / Rick Greenspan and Hal Kahn.
      p. cm.
      ISBN 1-58017-500-7 (pbk. : alk. paper)
  1. Outdoor cookery. I. Kahn, Hal, 1930- II. Title.
TX823 .G75 2004
641.5'78—dc22
                                              2003014939

CONTENTS

Acknowledgments

As we neared the end of this book, we began to fidget about acknowledgments. Rick said, "Flat out, my fridge comes first." Hal countered with his stove, and things spiraled out of control from there, ending with a grateful nod to a spatula here, a garlic press there. The human component got lost in the shuffle, until the animal component was broached.

One of us brought up the guinea pigs — the friends and family who actually taste-tested our fare as we stirred our cauldrons and mixed our batters. A finger in the frosting, a sip of salsa, teenage poaching of an experiment in puddings at midnight, a threat of lawsuits if one more miscreant fish stew appeared on the supper table: These were the reports we got back from the trenches. (Though in all honesty, we've never seen a guinea pig in a trench.) We

are delighted to announce that through it all, loyalty trumped discretion, and those of us who began together have ended together.

Rick's daughters Sherri and Nicole missed not a day of school despite their father's nightly importuning to try the latest version of Cornstarch Supreme or whatever was bubbling in his retort. And their mother, Mary, held the line against the more explosive chutneys, protecting her brood and the family's three dogs from further harm. Thanks, gang.

Hal's friend and mate Maureen smiled politely whenever he appeared with another Asian dipping sauce, retreating wisely to the Chardonnay before venturing a taste and an opinion. M's opinions are famous in her line of work. Ta, luv.

Our mutual friend and backpacking co-conspirator Steve Horowitz has an

iron stomach and a gourmet's instinct for what will work, and he lets us know at every turn whether we've got it right or wrong. And he's given us his famous lentil recipe as well. What a guy. Ed Jaramillo, another of our backpacking pals, has even given up his beef jerky to make room for some of our wilder concoctions. Talk about sacrifice . . .

Lydia Itoi, the food writer, inspired us to try to make a book from our years cooking on the trail. Rita Abraldes and Gabriela Salas kindly sent us a recipe from their San Francisco restaurant Charanga. Tobie Meyer-Fong set us straight about *jiaozi*, and Sujata Halarnkar allowed us to use her prizewinning cabbage salad. We'll send you copies of the book with our gratitude inscribed therein.

Whoever heard of a couple of scruffy backpackers with a posh New

York agent? Well, we've got one, Stacey Glick, and she never makes a comment about our clothes or puns. At least to our faces. We've put Hal's old trail boots in the mail to you, Stace, and Rick's grease-stained bandana. We know no higher praise. And Carey Boucher and Dianne Cutillo, our editors, have allowed us to stay reasonably untamed while making sure we got our home-

work done. They've tolerated most of our talk-back as they sit in western Massachusetts while all we've had to do is stay out of the California sun. Thanks team.

Nobody writes a book anymore without help from a computer maven, and ours is just that, an expert's expert. Marc Schmitter compressed This and merged That, formatted to the right

when we were heading left, spaced lines while we spaced out. We'll pay your phone bill and probably call a hundred times more before the second edition appears. Thanks for saving our butts.

— HK and RG
Summer 2003

Introduction

Try this: turn your back on your kitchen and walk out.

Get far enough away so that you can't go back for a spatula, a recipe file, the fridge, the pepper grinder and sea salt, all those pots and pans and molds and fish-poachers and food processors and blenders. The barbecue on the deck doesn't count. It's too close and you're too dependent on what's left in the pantry. Nope. Farther. Say to a picnic stop at the local state park. Or to a campsite 10,000 feet up in the Third Mono Creek Recess in the high Sierras. Or up a lazy river on a canoe, out of sight, out of mind. Good. Now try to feed the family or friends or your lover or just yourself as you would at home — with imagination, delight, a sense of

adventure and taste. That's what this book is about.

Note the stipulations — imagination and adventure. If your idea of wilderness fare is the stuff that comes in freeze-dried packets or out of a can, or is limited to prepackaged pancake mix, ballpark franks, and a flank steak over the grill, you're reading the wrong book. You won't like what follows, and we hope you disapprove. If, however, you think that fine cooking can be done no matter where you are; if improvisation is part of your culinary vocabulary; if, in a word, you think it's possible and desirable to begin a day at your campsite with fruit crêpes, wrap poached trout in a

sushi roll, celebrate the Sabbath (whatever day of the week it is) with a braided challah, wow the woodlands with a homemade pizza, or make dumplings for your casserole or for your Chinese dim sum, then stick around. We'll show you how.

The mind-set required in all this is to regard an outing of any length as a holiday, a time out of mind, during which a campfire or stove is an invitation to the imagination. You won't care if your hands get dirty, the yeast rises faster than you're used to, or the homedried strawberries need rehydrating before you can proceed with the cobbler. You'll be willing to scramble up a boulder field to get the last snow of summer for the snow cones or rename the trout that's fallen off the grill — it's now "Cajun black" — then fetch it out of the ashes and keep on cookin'. And if you're in your car, you'll avoid the fast food joints near the park or campground. The pleasure principle is at work here. No kvetching allowed.

Our job is to prove that no kvetching is necessary. Take our friend Lydia, for example. She's never been backpacking, barely been camping. Yet when we challenged her to come up with an outdoor dish of her own, she appeared at the fire pit in the local park with a chicken stew that formerly contained dumplings — they'd disappeared in the process of dehydrating. Unfazed, she made do with some powdered egg whites, flour, baking powder, a little oil, and a pinch of paprika she found in her parka. She used these ingredients to make six or seven tiny dumploids. Fifteen minutes later, we were eating like those overstuffed clubmen in late Victorian novels. The only problem was determining who was more proud, she or we.

OUR PROMISE TO YOU

If we do our job right, we'll make you the pride of your own personal wilderness. This is a promise. You will have more — and more interesting — recipes to take over the river and through the woods than any other source (except perhaps your grandmother) has put on the table for you. You don't need to be an expert, just an enthusiast. But we'll push the envelope, just for the sheer pleasure of it. You don't need a chocolate cake, iced and layered, out there, but, well, in fact you do. It's the ultimate aphrodisiac, and if you don't believe us, just try it. You provide the partner, we'll provide the recipe. Call us in the morning.

We are not going to waste your time with a lot of portentous culinary philosophy. You want recipes, not dialectics, a user's manual for good eating in the great out-of-doors. In these pages, you'll find all the information you need to manage campfires and campstoves, bake without an oven, measure things without traditional measuring spoons and cups, clean a fish, make a soufflé, eat vegetarian or carnivorous from the same basic recipes, and search the Internet for foodstuffs that for unknown reasons your local market has ignored. We'll even scream on occasion, "Don't forget the matches!"

Whatever kind of trip you're planning (at least in the culinary sense), you'll find recipes here for the taking. Hiking a fast 15 miles a day and only have time and fuel for a pot of boiling water before the sun goes down? Excellent. We have more recipes here for home-dehydrated one-pot meals than any backcountry cookbook in history. Spending a couple of days hanging out at a mountain lake with friends and lovers? Excellent. This is a veritable user's manual on improv cooking over, in, and under coals or on a camp stove. Taking the six-year-old on her first overnight trek — all of half a mile? Excellent again. Let her do the cooking. There's plenty here for young as well as old hands. Hauling a six-burner Dynasty range with two convection ovens into the outback on a flatbed truck? You probably need Julia Child more than us, but all of our recipes are upscale-compatible too.

HOW WE'RE ORGANIZED

We have organized the book into nine culinary chapters and a tenth in which we take care of the nuts and bolts: stoves and fuels, trip planning, and cooking techniques. The culinary chapters group old friends together, like Soups & Stews (including chilies, curries, lentils, dal, and, we would never forgive ourselves if we left it out, Picadillo Cubano) and Noodles & Dumplings (replete with the indispensable matzo balls and Chinese steamed and boiled dumplings). Trout flounder by themselves in their own chapter, and tofu shares space with Fruits & Vegetables, and why not, we say. Grains comprise a big chapter, where you'll find risottos, pilafs, polentas, and other grains you never dreamed of. Check out the appendix for lists that will help you through the seemingly daunting tasks of shopping and packing for your trip, as well as for resources.

Along the way, you may encounter a language problem. These things happen in cosmopolitan markets, and we're here to help. There you are, hip deep in Sauces & Schmeers and you've left your Yiddish dictionary at home. Schmeers are spreads, as in jams and frostings. Pancakes, Crêpes & Soufflés is a natural "pairing" even if we can count to three. Breads & Cakes sets up shop cheek by stuffed jowl with Pies, Quiches, Cobblers & Pizzas, enough of a mouthful to keep us all fat and happy till breakfast.

Measurements & Terminology

You won't have Pyrex and a standard set of dry measures (like we use at home) at your campsite. You don't need 'em. Approximations, guesses, and tasting is what we're after here. You won't starve. Honest. In all of our at-camp instructions, these are the terms we use:

Pot. We use three nesting pots that fit one inside another for easy transport. Each has a bail handle and a tight-fitting lid with a handle of its own. The lids can do double duty as small pans when needed. Our small pot holds 4 cups (liquid or dry), our medium pot holds 8 cups, and our large pot holds 12 cups.

A sierra cup is lightweight, stackable, and heat-resistant.

Sierra Cup. Our recipes were developed with 9-ounce Sierra cups, which are equivalent to a bit more than 1 cup in kitchen measurements. Sierra cups are lightweight cups made specially for camping. They stack easily and, when drinking hot liquids, you are less likely to burn your lips than if using an ordinary metal cup because the rims are made of a heat-resistant alloy. They're available at camping supply stores and on the Internet (see Resources on pages 224–225).

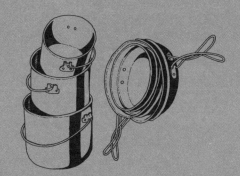

Nesting pots can be transported easily. The lids also serve as small pots.

Fry Pan. Ours is a 10½-inch Teflon-coated pan with a folding (and removable) handle.

Spoon. A standard camping-kit spoon, about soup-spoon size, a fraction less than a standard tablespoon measure.

Helpful Ratios

TO MAKE	START WITH (powdered/ uncooked)	ADD WATER	MAKES	RATIO (water to item)
Buttermilk	2 spoons	1 Sierra cup	1 Sierra cup	8 to 1
Milk	2 spoons	1 Sierra cup	1 Sierra cup	8 to 1
Egg whites	1 spoon	2 spoons	1½ egg whites	2 to 1
Eggs (whole)	1 spoon	2 spoons	1 egg	2 to 1
Bulgur	½ Sierra cup	¾ Sierra cup	1 Sierra cup	1.5 to 1
Couscous	½ Sierra cup	¾ Sierra cup	1 Sierra cup	1.5 to 1
Lentils	½ Sierra cup	1 Sierra cup	1 Sierra cup	2 to 1
Quinoa	½ Sierra cup	¾ Sierra cup	1 Sierra cup	1.5 to 1
Rice (white)	½ Sierra cup	1 Sierra cup	1½ Sierra cups	2 to 1

GUIDE TO SYMBOLS

Every recipe is marked by a symbol indicating where you'll be doing most of the preparation for the dish.

means you'll be slicing, dicing, cooking, and dehydrating at home, and you'll just need to rehydrate at camp (there are a few recipes that don't even require rehydration). If you're planning to reach a campsite as the sun goes down, these are the recipes you'll want.

means that you'll be mixing and fixing at camp, although of course you'll need to purchase and pack the ingredients at home. If you're leaving on your trip at six o'clock tomorrow morning and you're just now heading to the grocery store, these recipes are for you.

recipes require both home and camp prep time.

If all this information doesn't do it for you, just open the book at any page and start cooking. We'll be there to help.

[Chapter 1]

Fruits & Vegetables

We're hopelessly addicted to local farmers' markets. Rick often shows up early, before the booths are even set up, to get first crack at the ripe persimmons and the most luscious figs. Hal, on the other hand, likes to be there when the farmers are packing up. That way, he can buy the unsold produce for pennies on the dollar. In either case, as we head back to our cars, it isn't unusual for people to stop us in the street to ask, "Excuse me, but what restaurant are you buying this for?" Clearly these folks don't have home dehydrators operating around the clock as camping season approaches. Nor do they daydream all winter long of exotic vegetable purées and mouthwatering fruit-roll combinations for next summer. Leftover dehydrated fruit and veggie recipes, by the way, make great snacks all year round.

Fresh Vegetables in the Wild

When we first started camping, back in the Neolithic age, there was no such thing as freeze-dried food. We'd never heard of dehydrators. On his early trips, Rick hauled potatoes, canned clams, and canned brown bread in his army-surplus pack. The only fish that Hal ate as a student trekking through Scandinavian forests were sardines in olive oil. Somehow, we survived.

Over the years, our legs and shoulders have grown weary of 50-pound packs, and we've found lighter tents, packs, sleeping bags, and, of course, foods. Yet while we no longer carry whole spuds or sardine tins on our trips, we consider a couple of cloves of fresh garlic to be as vital as our compass.

So, if you crave fresh vegetables and don't mind the extra weight, we have a few suggestions. Be careful with vegetables like cauliflower and tomato: Cauliflower molders and tomato turns to tomato sauce as you hike. Some veggies will survive in a pack, however. Here are a few that will last 3 to 7 days, are easy to cook, and don't produce a lot of waste (seeds, core, and skin): cabbage, carrots, eggplant, garlic, green beans, onions, potatoes, and zucchini.

Bean Sprouts

If you find yourself craving fresh food after a few days in the wilderness, there's a simple solution: Grow your own. Mung bean sprouts make a great trail snack, and they can be added to soups, rices, soufflés, and crêpes.

½ cup dry mung beans

1. Fill a plastic bag with water and soak the beans overnight. In the morning, drain the water. Close the bag and keep it in a dark, cool place during the day (inside a small pot works well).

2. Rinse the beans thoroughly with fresh water once or twice a day to keep them moist, but not wet. They'll sprout in about 3 days.

3. Once the beans sprout, use them within a day or two, or they may start to molder.

Makes ¾–1 cup

Dehydrated Fruit 🏠

When shopping for fruit to dehydrate, buy the sweetest and ripest fruit you can find. Don't worry about looks; concentrate on flavor. We find that apples, apricots, bananas, blackberries, cantaloupes, figs, mangoes, nectarines, papayas, peaches, persimmons, pineapples, plums, raspberries, strawberries, and even watermelons taste great when dehydrated.

6–8 pounds fresh fruit

Cooking oil, if necessary

1. Remove the inedible parts of the fruits, including cores, seeds, and tough skins. If the fruit is wet or sticky, spray a little nonstick oil on the tray before laying out the fruit.

2. Slice the fruit ¼ inch to ⅜ inch thick. Make the slices as thick as they can get without bumping into (and sticking to) the stacked tray above in the dehydrator.

3. Dehydrate 12 to 24 hours till hard and leathery. There is no need to turn the fruit over. If you remove it too soon — when it is still soft and pliable — it may go moldy while you are camping.

𝒩ote: For more information on dehydrating, see pages 215–217.

Makes 1½–2 pounds dehydrated fruit

DEHYDRATING

Four pounds of fresh fruits or vegetables yield approximately 1 pound of dehydrated fruits or vegetables. The dehydrating process may take anywhere from 12 to 24 hours, depending on the make of your dehydrator and the food's density, water content, ripeness, and thickness. Not to worry. You can't overdry fruits and vegetables, so leave them on as long as you want or until your electricity bill tops the S&P 500. For more information on dehydrating, see pages 215–217.

BLANCHING

Broccoli, carrots, cauliflower, green beans, and potatoes need to be softened a little before dehydrating. Otherwise, they dry so hard they could stand in for Stonehenge. They'll never rehydrate. Blanching is the answer to the question, "So whadda we do?" Blanching means dropping the sliced vegetables into boiling water for a minute or two, then plunging them into cold water for a minute or two. Once blanched, vegetables dehydrate just like fruit. For really tough vegetables, such as carrots and potatoes, it works best to grate or julienne them (that is, slice 'em real thin), and then blanch them before dehydrating on lined trays.

Dehydrated Vegetables 🏠

If you dehydrate your dinners, you'll already have lots of vegetables in your dehydrated meals. We bring just a few handfuls of dehydrated vegetables — bell peppers, eggplant, Japanese eggplant, leeks, scallions, mushrooms, onions, pumpkin, summer squash, chard, spinach, tomatoes, bok choy, Napa cabbage, and zucchini are our favorites — to add to pizzas, quiches, crêpes, and other dishes we plan to make at camp. These vegetables can all be dehydrated exactly like fruit, and they don't require any special preparation before dehydrating.

1–2 pounds of vegetables
Cooking oil, if necessary

1. Remove the inedible parts of the vegetables. If the veggies are wet or sticky, spray a little nonstick oil on the tray before laying them out.

2. If possible, slice the veggies ¼ inch to ⅜ inch thick. Make the slices as thick as they can get without bumping into (and sticking to) the stacked tray above in the dehydrator.

3. Dehydrate 12 to 24 hours. There is no need to flip. The veggies are done when they're hard and leathery.

If you remove them too soon — when they are still soft and pliable — they may go moldy when you are camping.

Notes: For even better flavor, soak the absorbent veggies (such as eggplant and mushrooms) in soy sauce, teriyaki sauce, or your favorite marinade before dehydrating. One word of warning: Dehydrate onions on the back porch, or your kitchen will smell like a pizzeria on steroids. For more information on dehydrating, see pages 215–217.

Makes ¼–½ pound dehydrated veggies

Banana–Persimmon Roll 🏠

Rick's kids are fruit smoothie junkies. They start with sweet fruit, fresh from the farmers' market, add a few ice cubes, a little milk, and some sugar, and blend till creamy. The only problem: After two or three blenders' worth, what do you do with the leftovers? Usually Dad finishes them. But one day, when Rick was too full to swallow another gulp, he spotted an empty dehydrator tray. Smoothie rolls were born.

2 ripe bananas

2 Fuyu persimmons, quartered

½ cup milk (or fruit juice of your choice)

2–4 tablespoons sugar

SUGAR

Fruits take longer to dehydrate when sugar is added. For best results, flip the fruit roll over about halfway through the drying process.

1. Blend the bananas, persimmons, and milk or juice into a thick mixture in a blender — the thicker, the better. Add the sugar to taste. Depending on the sweetness of the fruit, you may not need any sugar.

2. Spread on lined trays and dehydrate 15 to 24 hours, till leathery.

3. Remove from the dehydrator trays, fold in half or in quarters, and seal in airtight bags.

Makes 1 roll; serves 2 well-tempered children or 1 determined teenager

FRUIT ROLLS

There are two ways to get a fruit-based mixture thick enough to pour on your dehydrator trays. The first way is to stew it. Start with fruit, sugar, and perhaps some lemon; add as little water as necessary to make the mixture a liquid (depending on the fruit, you may not need any at all); and slowly heat the mixture. As it heats, the flavors will blend, the water will boil and evaporate, and it will naturally thicken. The texture should be that of a thick, warm jam — something you can spread on the dehydrator trays (or your body; we're easy) with a rubber spatula or the back of a large serving spoon. That's when it's ready to dehydrate.

The second way is to just throw the ingredients into a blender, blend the mixture to a homogeneous consistency, and pour the resulting "smoothie" onto lined dehydrator trays. Some fruits, such as rhubarb, taste better when cooked before blending; others, such as banana, work well without cooking. Feel free to experiment with your favorites.

Candied Orange 🏠

Yes, we know all about blood sugar and the ineffectual sugar rush, but when we're schlepping over a boulder field off trail in the August sun, taking a break with a couple of cookies or a tab of semisweet chocolate feels great. This, too, makes our list of essential nonnutritional supplements.

  2 medium or large juice or navel oranges, washed

½–⅔ cup sugar

1. Cut the oranges into ¼-inch-thick slices.

2. Spread the sugar on a flat plate. Press the orange slices onto the sugar on one side; flip and repeat.

3. Dehydrate 7 to 10 hours, till the oranges are crisp and hard.

Serves 4

Peach–Apricot Rolls 🏠

In season, half the peaches and apricots from northern California's orchards can be found in Rick's kitchen — and bedroom, both bathrooms, and the garage — ready for eating, cooking, and, yes, dehydrating. Here's why.

  2 pounds ripe peaches, pitted and quartered

  2 pounds ripe apricots, pitted and halved

1½ cups sugar

  2 cups water

     Juice of about ¼ lemon (1–2 teaspoons)

1. Mix the fruit slices thoroughly with the sugar in a large bowl. Place the mixture in a nonreactive pot.

2. Add the water and bring the mixture to a boil. Stir occasionally to prevent sticking, keeping the heat moderately high.

3. Cook till the fruit mixture begins to thicken, about 20 minutes. Remove from the heat.

4. Add lemon juice to taste. Spread on lined trays and dehydrate 12 to 15 hours, till the fruit feels leathery. If the top feels sticky, lift off the trays, turn over, and continue drying 4 hours or more.

5. When finished, just pull the rolls off the trays, fold in half or quarters, and seal in airtight bags.

Makes 2 rolls; serves 4 adults or Rick by himself

Rhubarb–Strawberry Rolls 🏠

The Chinese once threatened to cut off the rhubarb trade with England. This would constipate every Brit from South End to Liverpool. We don't know about the English, but we would have caved in to Chinese demands immediately. After all, can anybody do without rhubarb and strawberries? This has nothing to do with digestion, just unmitigated pleasure.

2 pounds rhubarb

2 pints strawberries, sliced in half

1½ cups water

2 cups sugar

Juice of about ¼ lemon (1–2 teaspoons)

1. Wash the rhubarb and slice it crosswise. Slice the strawberries and set aside.

2. Place the rhubarb in a large nonreactive pan and add the water. (Rhubarb is loaded with water, so don't fret if it looks like there's not enough.)

3. Bring to a rolling boil, then lower the heat to simmer. Add 1 cup of the sugar. Stir very gently once during cooking to immerse the top pieces in the boiling water. Cook till the rhubarb is soft, 5 to 7 minutes.

4. Just before the rhubarb begins to get soft, in 3 to 4 minutes, add the sliced strawberries.

5. Two minutes before removing from heat, add the remaining 1 cup of sugar. Rhubarb is tart and usually needs more sugar than you'd like to use.

6. When the rhubarb is soft, remove the pan from the heat. Add the lemon juice to taste. Spread on lined trays and dehydrate 15 to 24 hours, till leathery.

7. Remove from the dehydrator trays, fold in half or in quarters, and seal in airtight bags.

Makes 2 rolls; serves 4 adults or all of Liverpool in a tight squeeze

VEGETABLE PURÉES

Two of our favorite authors once said this about vegetable purées: "We used to think [they] were baby food for adults. Were we wrong! They're the perfect camping fare, easy to make, easy to dry and pack, easy on the eye, nose, and throat, easy on the wallet, nutritious as hell, light as a fare-thee-well, and, if you didn't quite catch the point, terrific." Okay, we admit it: We wrote this ode to the veggie smoothie ourselves. Vegetable purées are so good that they inspire self-reference.

The mechanics of purées are simple: Lightly sauté the vegetables to fix the flavors, then slowly braise or bake them in a broth till tender. Process in a blender until the mixture reaches the consistency of a smoothie. Finally, dehydrate. Following are some of our favorites, as well as some new ones to cover all the bases.

Leek & Potato Purée

This purée is a medal winner in wilderness cooking, comfort food division.

4 tablespoons butter

1 bunch (about 1 pound) leeks, washed, drained, and sliced into ¼-inch rounds

1 potato (about ½ pound), peeled and diced

3 celery stalks (about ½ pound), chopped fine

2 cups chicken or vegetable stock (see pages 26 and 27), plus more to blend if necessary

Salt and freshly ground black pepper

2 teaspoons dried mint leaves, or 1 tablespoon fresh mint

1–2 Sierra cups water, to rehydrate

at home

1. Melt the butter in a heavy-bottomed saucepan. Sauté the leeks, potato, and celery to fix the flavor, about 10 minutes.

2. Add the stock, salt and pepper to taste, and mint. Cover and simmer slowly 15 to 20 minutes, till the vegetables are very soft.

3. Purée in a blender or food processor till smooth. Add more stock if necessary to achieve the consistency of a thick fruit smoothie.

4. Spread on lined trays and dehydrate 15 to 24 hours, till leathery. Freeze in airtight bags. On the trail, it will last 1 week to 10 days.

at camp

5. Rehydrate with the water to cover. Cook, stirring, till reconstituted as the purée you loved to taste-test at home.

Serves 2 as a main course or 4 as a side dish

Celery Root & Pear Purée

This was inspired by a recipe in Julee Rosso and Sheila Lukins's The New Basics Cookbook, *though we've taken so many liberties with it that they would probably disown it unless they were lost, cold, and hungry in the Marble Mountains and stumbled into our campsite.*

The celery root, also called celeriac, *may be the ugliest vegetable in the market. It looks like something Bert and Ernie from* Sesame Street *might have invented on an off day. But looks are deceiving. Taste, and become a believer.*

3 pears

1 large celery root

1 tablespoon butter

1 tablespoon olive oil

2–3 cups chicken or vegetable stock, to cover (see pages 26 and 27), plus more to blend if necessary

Juice of about ¼ lemon (1–2 teaspoons)

1 tablespoon sugar

½ teaspoon cardamom

Freshly ground black pepper

2 tablespoons chopped parsley

2–3 Sierra cups water, to rehydrate

at home

1. Peel and core the pears, and chop into bite-sized pieces. Peel the celery root and chop into bite-sized pieces.

2. Melt the butter and heat the olive oil in a heavy-bottomed saucepan. Sauté the celery root and pears till lightly browned, about 5 minutes.

3. Add the stock, lemon juice, sugar, cardamom, and pepper to taste. Bring to a boil. Decrease the heat to a slow simmer, cover, and cook till the celery root is fork soft, 15 to 20 minutes.

4. Add the parsley and remove from the heat. Allow to cool slightly. Purée in a blender or food processor till smooth.

If necessary, add more stock to achieve the correct consistency, which is halfway between extremely smooth mashed potatoes and a thick but pourable smoothie.

5. Spread the purée on a lined dehydrator tray and dry 15 to 24 hours, till it feels leathery.

at camp

6. Rehydrate with the water to cover. Cook, stirring, till you get a soft, reconstituted purée. It will taste almost like that Thanksgiving stuffing you thought you'd never eat on the trail.

Serves 2 as a main course or 4 as a side dish

Fennel & Onion Purée

Hal thinks fresh anise, licorice, and fennel all taste the same. Rick doesn't even know what they are. But both of them like the results of this dish, and so do their relatives and other demanding critics.

2 fennel bulbs

1 large onion

2 tablespoons butter

2–3 cups chicken or vegetable stock, to cover (see pages 26 and 27), plus more to blend if necessary

2 tablespoons dry sherry or white wine

Salt and freshly ground black pepper

2–3 Sierra cups water, to rehydrate

at home

1. Remove the stems and bulbs from the fennel. Chop the remainder fine. Roughly chop the onion.

2. Melt the butter in a heavy-bottomed saucepan. Sauté the fennel and onion till glazed and just turning golden, 3 to 5 minutes. Add the stock, sherry, and salt and pepper to taste. Simmer, covered, till soft, 15 to 20 minutes.

3. Purée in a blender or food processor till smooth. Add more stock if necessary, no more than ¼ cup at a time. If you're out of stock, water will do. Dehydrate on lined trays 15 to 24 hours, till leathery.

at camp

4. Rehydrate with the water to cover. Cook, stirring, till the purée is soft and most of the water is gone.

5. Do a blindfold test. Is this fennel? Anise? Licorice? Keep track when someone gets it right.

Serves 2 as a main course or 4 as a side dish

Variation: Add braised spinach 5 minutes before the fennel and onions are done. To braise the spinach, heat a mixture of olive oil and butter in a large skillet, place 1 to 2 bunches of washed and trimmed spinach leaves in the pan, and cook, constantly turning the leaves over so that they all get exposed to the heat. The leaves will reduce in size and soften to a dark, lustrous green. No need to chop the leaves before or after.

Carrot & Squash Purée 🏠

Mix and match whatever's fresh in the market. Most vegetables like each other and are more compatible in the blender than a lot of our friends are in their personal relationships. (We've never psychoanalyzed a carrot, but it's a thought… .) Carrots are common, but squashes can be exotic. No matter: Ask no questions. Any type of squash and any sort of carrot will marry for life.

3 large carrots, sliced ¼ inch thick (no need to peel)

2–3 cups vegetable stock (see page 27) or water (both taste great), plus more to blend if necessary

4 tablespoons butter

2 summer squashes, sliced ½ inch thick

1 onion, chopped fine

2 tablespoons orange juice

1 teaspoon cinnamon and sugar mixture (1 part sugar to 8 parts cinnamon)

Salt and freshly ground black pepper

2–3 Sierra cups water, to rehydrate

at home

1. Boil the carrots in the stock in a medium-sized saucepan, till just soft, about 10 minutes. Drain.

2. Melt the butter in a large skillet or heavy-bottomed saucepan. Sauté the squash and onion in butter till just soft, 5 to 7 minutes.

3. Add the boiled carrots, orange juice, and cinnamon and sugar. Stir to glaze the veggies and allow the liquid to cook down till slightly thickened, 4 to 5 minutes. Add the salt and pepper to taste.

4. Purée in a blender or food processor till smooth. If necessary, add more stock or water in ½-cup increments to provide a thick yet pourable "smoothie."

5. Dehydrate on lined trays for 15 to 24 hours, till leathery.

at camp

6. Rehydrate with the water to cover. Cook, stirring, till the texture is smooth and thick, 5 to 10 minutes.

Serves 2 as a main course or 4 as a side dish

VARIATIONS

- Add ½ cup slivered almonds during the last 4 minutes of cooking.
- Flavor with cardamom instead of cinnamon.
- Flavor with 2 tablespoons fresh chives, 2 teaspoons grated fresh ginger, and 2 tablespoons chopped cilantro.
- Omit the onion.

INVENT PURÉES

Go ahead, invent your own purées. Try some of these combinations:

- Broccoli rabe, spinach, and red chard
- Red and yellow beets
- Spinach and potatoes
- Parsnips and roasted eggplant (see Chinese Cold Noodles for roasting eggplant, page 67)

Add wild mushrooms or grated Swiss cheese to any of the above to vary texture and flavor.

Spinach & Chard Purée

This may be the simplest purée of all to make, but it's as good as any of the others. The mixture is versatile, for it can be eaten as-is or combined with other purées just before pouring onto dehydrator trays. The dehydrated purée can be combined with other purées during rehydration, too.

1 bunch green or red chard, stems removed, trimmed

1 onion, chopped fine

2 cloves garlic, chopped fine

1 bunch spinach, stemmed

2 tablespoons olive oil

Freshly ground black pepper

Pinch nutmeg

½–1 cup chicken or vegetable stock (see pages 26 and 27), plus more to blend if necessary

1–1½ Sierra cups water, to rehydrate

at home

1. Cut off the stems of the chard, and then tear the leaves away from the white spine that runs up the middle. Chop the chard into rough slices.

2. Sauté the onion and garlic in a large skillet till the onion is translucent, about 3 minutes. Add the chard and spinach, turning constantly so that all sides hit the heat. As the vegetables soften, add the pepper to taste and the nutmeg. Continue cooking and stirring till very soft, about 7 minutes.

3. Place the mixture in a blender or food processor and purée till smooth. If necessary, add stock in ¼-cup increments to reach the right consistency.

4. Spread on lined dehydrator trays and dry 5 to 10 hours, till the mixture flakes to the touch.

at camp

5. Rehydrate with the water to cover. Bring to a light boil, stirring constantly till smooth and thickened.

Serves 2 as a main course or 4 as a side dish

Jicama & Plantain Purée 🏠

Somebody made the mistake of giving Hal a food processor halfway through the writing of this book. We haven't been able to get him away from the thing, and he keeps coming up with ever more exotic combinations. "Just testing," he tells us. Once in a while he comes up with a winner, and this is one. Jicama (pronounced "HICK-a-ma") is one of those nutty-tasting bulb plants that people mostly eat uncooked in salads or sliced and salted.

3   plantains

2   Anaheim chiles (see Handling Hot Chiles for precautions, page 37)

½   jicama

¼   cup vegetable oil

    Salt

½   tablespoon sugar

½–1 cup tomato or orange juice

1–1½ Sierra cups water, to rehydrate

at home

1. Peel the plantains and slice them lengthwise. Slice the Anaheim chiles lengthwise and seed them. Peel the jicama, and finely chop or grate it.

2. Heat the oven to 400°F.

3. Brush the plantains with some of the vegetable oil; sprinkle with the salt to taste. Brush the chiles with the remaining vegetable oil and set on a baking tray together with the plantains.

4. Roast in the oven till soft, about 20 minutes.

5. Purée the roasted vegetables, jicama, and sugar in a food processor. Add the juice as necessary to create a textured purée: that is, a purée that is not thoroughly smooth. You want a bit of the jicama's nutlike texture to remain.

6. Spread on a lined dehydrator tray and dry 5 to 10 hours, till mealy in texture and thoroughly dried.

at camp

7. Rehydrate with the water to cover. Bring to a light boil, stir, and simmer till thick and smooth. Sing songs of old Mexico. Doff your sombrero. Pay homage to the food processor.

Serves 2 as a main course or 4 as a side dish

Plantains 🏠🔥

"Yes, we have no bananas… ." Ah, that old refrain. But wait, we've got plantains, and it's high time you included them in your larder or pantry or backpack. Plantains are to bananas as pomelos are to grapefruit or sherbet is to ice cream: a member of the family seen less often at the banquet table. The plantain is your cooking banana, and that's what we plan to do with these plantains. Serve them as a side dish with Picadillo Cubano (page 52) or in place of (or with) rice and beans.

When shopping for plantains, look for those with very dark, even black, skins. They will be the ripest. But light-skinned plantains will also work just fine. Plantains have very little flavor if you taste them uncooked, but don't worry, the flavor develops in the cooking.

3 large plantains

2–2½ Sierra cups water, to rehydrate

4–6 tablespoons vegetable oil or clarified butter (see page 99)

Salt and freshly ground black pepper

at home

1. Peel the plantains and slice them into rounds, as you might a banana, or in lengths.

2. Place on dehydrator trays and dry 10 to 15 minutes, till hard and leathery.

at camp

3. Rehydrate in the water to cover. Boil in a medium-sized saucepan till the plantain slices are soft when pierced by a fork, about 10 minutes. Drain. (If you wish, reserve the cooking liquid. It can be used to rehydrate stews and risottos, or in the batter of banana pancakes.)

4. When the plantain slices are fairly dry (you can set them in the sun for 10 to 15 minutes or pat them dry with that extra toilet paper you brought along),

sauté them in the oil. Add generous salt and pepper to bring out the flavor. Cook for only a few minutes on each side.

5. Serve with the rest of your dinner or eat as a snack.

Serves 3 as a side dish

Variation: Plantains can also be served sweet. Sauté them, preferably in clarified butter, with a coating of sugar or sugar and cinnamon. This makes a great quick dessert or snack.

Sujata's Zesty Cabbage Salad

A couple of years ago, we were invited to judge an outdoor cooking contest at the famous outdoor store, REI, in Berkeley, California. Each of the five finalists had to prepare a dish that contained only eight ingredients, transported easily, and took less than 30 minutes to prepare. The store provided them each with a two-burner Coleman stove and an apron. Somebody blew a whistle. We went around sniffing and tasting, nodding sagely, and writing cryptic messages to ourselves. The winner was as obvious as the piquant spices in her recipe. Sujata Halarnkar won hands down, and she has kindly let us reproduce her recipe with some modifications for backpackers.

3 Sierra cups finely shredded green cabbage

½ Sierra cup chopped dry-roasted peanuts

1 green chile, chopped (optional)

2 spoons olive oil

¼ spoon mustard seeds

¼ spoon cumin seeds

Juice of 1½ limes (3 tablespoons)

¼ Sierra cup chopped cilantro

Salt

1. Lightly mix the cabbage, chopped peanuts, and chile in a pot. Set aside.

2. Heat the oil in a fry pan or pot top over medium heat.

3. As soon as the oil is hot, add the mustard seeds.

4. As soon as the mustard seeds begin to pop, add the cumin seeds. Let the seeds crackle for 3 to 4 seconds. Turn the heat off.

5. Immediately add the mustard and cumin seed seasoning to the salad mix. Add the salt to taste and the lime juice.

6. Mix well and garnish with the chopped cilantro. Serve immediately.

Note: Fresh ingredients (cabbage, lime, chile, and cilantro) are not our usual fare when we camp. If you're looking to lighten your load, or if you want to indulge in this salad after 3 or 4 days of hiking, feel free to eliminate the optional chile, substitute bottled lime juice for the fresh lime, and add dried cilantro to the hot oil before pouring it over the cabbage. And for those who know their edible wild greens, such as miner's lettuce, fiddlehead, yellow rocket, or wild spinach (lamb's quarters), leave the cabbage home and forage for yourselves. It will still be delicious.

Serves 4

Sweet & Sour Tofu ⟐

Dry-and-rehy tofu has always been the Holy Grail for vegetarian campers. Try as we might, our many attempts to dehydrate tofu always had the consistency — and flavor — of high-topped sneakers. Luckily, the problem has now been solved. You see, whereas America's food scientists spent the last half-century creating marshmallow-flavored breakfast cereals and low-calorie sweeteners, the Japanese were tinkering with tofu. We still don't understand how it works, but we can say with certainty that instant tofu is the only food we've ever seen that includes a packet labeled "coagulant." If there were a Nobel Prize for achievements in food science, instant tofu would be our nominee. A couple of notes. A single package of instant tofu goes a long way; in fact, it goes a little too far. Half the package is plenty for this recipe. Also, if your backyard is lacking in shiitake mushrooms for you to dehydrate, take heart. The same store that sells the instant tofu is likely to have a good selection of dried Japanese mushrooms as well.

½ package instant tofu, a total of 1–1½ ounces

½ Sierra cup rice

1 Sierra cup water, to cook the rice

8 dried shiitake mushrooms

1 Sierra cup boiling water, to rehydrate the mushrooms

2 spoons sugar

3 spoons Asian rice vinegar

1 spoon low-sodium soy sauce

1 spoon cornstarch

2 spoons cold water, to dissolve the cornstarch

2 spoons cooking oil

1. Prepare the instant tofu according to the package instructions, up to the point that the tofu is sitting in a pot for 20 minutes to harden. The final step (plunging the tofu into cold water) isn't necessary. Just leave it in the pot till you're ready to sauté it.

2. Bring the rice and water to a boil in a medium-sized pot. When the water boils off just to the surface of the rice, try to reduce the heat to a slow simmer, cover, and cook till the rice is soft, 10 to 12 minutes.

3. Meanwhile, rehydrate the mushrooms. Pour the boiling water over the mushrooms, cover, and let sit for about 20 minutes. (If you are low on mushrooms, most any dehydrated vegetable will do.) Once the mushrooms are soft, remove them from the water. Reserve the mushroom broth.

4. Add the sugar, vinegar, and soy sauce to the mushroom broth. If necessary, heat or stir the mixture enough to dissolve the sugar.

5. In another Sierra cup, dissolve the cornstarch in the cold water.

6. Cut the tofu into cubes about ½ inch thick. Heat the oil in a pan, and sauté the tofu till one side is golden brown. Flip the tofu and add the mushrooms. Sauté for about 10 minutes, till the mixture is browned and heated throughout.

7. To make the sweet and sour sauce, add the cornstarch mixture to the mushroom broth and heat, stirring constantly, till the sauce bubbles and thickens.

8. Spoon the mushrooms and tofu onto a bed of rice and smother with the sauce.

Serves 2

Portable Tofu

Can't do without your tofu, yet can't imagine schlepping a tub in water? Here are some dried or processed tofus that work in the wilderness.

- **Japanese soft tofu.** Comes in powdered form with simple "add water" directions. This is what we use in our Sweet and Sour Tofu recipe (facing page).

- **Japanese "freeze-dried" tofu (koya-dofu).** Comes both in dried "cake" form and whole. The whole koya-dofu will last a day or so if packed in airtight bags.

- **Japanese fried bean curd (aburage)** (see page 75). Seal in airtight bags and use on the first or second day of your camping trip.

- **Smoked bean curd.** Looks like a chaw of tobacco. A small piece is easy to pack and can be added to soups, stews, and stir-fries. Available in natural food stores.

- **Chinese tofu skins (doufu pi).** Lightweight sheets of dried tofu. Boil till soft, cut into strips or squares, wrap food in them, and steam or stir-fry.

CONTOOCOOK RIVER PARK, CONCORD, N. H.

Baked Eggplant Parmigiana 🏠🔥

Evolution is a strange and wonderful phenomenon. Take eggplant. As far as we can figure, the sole evolutionary purpose for the eggplant is to provide us with an excuse to eat cheese, garlic, and olive oil. Here's one of our favorite recipes.

1 large eggplant

1 cup tomato sauce

2–4 Sierra cups water, to rehydrate

2 cloves garlic

1 egg or equivalent powdered egg

2 spoons flour

3 spoons olive oil

4–5 ounces (about ½ cup) cheese (traditionally mozzarella and Parmesan), sliced ¼ inch thick

at home

1. Slice the eggplant into eight to ten ½-inch-thick rounds and dehydrate 5 to 10 hours, till dry and hard. If you don't already have dehydrated tomato sauce in your camping pantry (see page 211), dehydrate that as well by spreading the sauce on lined dehydrator trays. In 10 to 12 hours, you'll have a fine tomato sauce "fruit roll." (Hey, tomatoes *are* fruit, aren't they?)

at camp

2. To rehydrate the eggplant, bring the water to a boil, pour enough over the eggplant rounds to cover, and let sit for 10 to 20 minutes. Drain.

3. Rehydrate the tomato sauce using as little of the water as possible. It will not rehydrate to the full cup of sauce that you started out with, but you'll only need 4 to 6 spoons of sauce for the parmigiana.

4. Dice the garlic, keeping the 2 chopped cloves separated.

5. Scramble the egg in a Sierra cup. Pour the flour into a second Sierra cup. In a fry pan, heat 2 spoons of the oil with 1 clove of the garlic.

6. Dredge each slice of rehydrated eggplant in the egg, coat with the flour, and fry in the oil till golden brown on both sides. Set aside.

7. After your first panful of eggplant is done (about half of the eggplant rounds), add the remaining spoon of oil and garlic clove and fry the remaining eggplant rounds.

8. You can bake the parmigiana in a baking pan (like a pizza, pages 217–219) or in aluminum foil (like calzone, page 208). Place half of the eggplant on the bottom, layer the cheese on top, then spread on the tomato sauce, and finish with the remaining eggplant. Bake 10 to 12 minutes, or till the cheese is melted and the flavors mixed.

Serves 2

[Chapter 2]

Soups & Stews

Caspian Lake from the Golf Links, Greensboro, Vt.

Hal's grandfather used to end every Sunday dinner with
a bowl of soup. For him, soup was the coup de maître
of a good meal — its crowning glory. He knew a thing or
two about soup that seems to have been forgotten by the great American public,
for whom soup means something that comes out of a can. We're going to prove
the public wrong and old Pop Slote right. Dive in, the broth's just right. Don't,
however, dive into the stews in this chapter. You'll break your head. They're thick,
the way all stews ought to be, whatever you call 'em. The Irish have a word for
them: gallimaufry; so do the French: ragout; so do the Hungarians: goulash; and
even Japanese sumo wrestlers: chanko-nabe. And if a spoon won't stand up in any
of their bowls, you've been cheated. Complain in the language of your choice.

All of the soup and risotto recipes in this book, and some of the stews and pilafs, call for chicken or vegetable stock. Call it broth, it's the same thing: It's soup before the additions. The canned varieties are okay, but since you're in the kitchen anyway, why not make your own?

Chicken Stock

This one comes from grandmother to mother to son and daughter. One of us is the son.

1 stewing hen, 6–8 pounds, whole

1 onion

1 carrot, sliced into three large chunks

2 celery stalks (plus leaves), sliced in large pieces

1 bay leaf

8 peppercorns

5 sprigs parsley, stemmed

1 teaspoon salt, or more to taste

Cold water to cover

1. Combine all ingredients in a big stockpot. Include the chicken gizzard, liver, heart, and neck (if you're lucky enough to find them still inside the chicken). Cover and bring to a boil. Lower the heat to a slow simmer and cook for 4 to 5 hours, till the chicken is fall-apart soft.

2. Remove the chicken; you may reserve it for other purposes. Discard the vegetables.

3. Pour the stock through a colander into a large bowl.

4. Cool to room temperature. Cover and refrigerate overnight. Remove the layer of fat on top with a slotted spoon.

5. To store, place in airtight 1-quart containers and freeze. The stock will last for up to 3 months. Use the thawed stock within 2 days or, thereafter, bring to a boil and simmer 20 minutes. This will permit another 2 to 3 days' use.

Makes about 4 quarts

Vegetable Stock

This used to be easy. Your granny would toddle down to the grocer and ask for soup greens. She'd come home with a mixed bag of celery leaves, carrot and turnip tops, and chard and spinach in their last days. Now? Forget it. The produce surgeons have cut away the good stuff before it ever gets to market. We are left to fend for ourselves or grow our own vegetables. The rule here is, use whatever's available. Proportions are arbitrary. No need to peel anything. For more intense flavor, brown some of the veggies quickly in oil before creating the stock.

5 scallions, chopped

3 celery stalks and leaves, chopped

2 large carrots, chopped in large chunks

2 zucchini

1 parsnip, chopped

2 leeks, sliced and washed well; include lots of the leek greens

Cooking oil for browning (optional)

1 bay leaf

6 cloves garlic

1 onion, whole

8 sprigs parsley

1 teaspoon salt, or to taste

1 teaspoon freshly ground black pepper, or to taste

Cold water to cover

1. If desired, brown the carrots, celery, parsnip, and zucchini in the oil in a large skillet over medium-high heat for 5 minutes.

2. Combine all ingredients in a large stockpot. Bring to a boil, lower the heat, and simmer, partially covered, about 30 minutes.

3. Strain the broth and discard the veggies. Place the stock back in the pot and reduce by boiling over moderate heat for 15 minutes.

4. Cool to room temperature. Store in airtight 1-quart containers in the freezer for up to 3 months or in the fridge for up to 5 days.

Makes 1½–2 quarts

DRY SOUP MIXES: USE OR ABUSE?

Commercial dry soup mixes have the half-life of *Australopithicus afarensis*, which means they're packed with preservatives and other artificial nuggets. If, however, you've got a good natural foods store in your neighborhood, the soup mixes can be good or great, so if you're not up for making your own, you could do worse. We're talking bulk foods here, which means we can't offer brand names. But here's a list of dry mixes we found we like, discovered in San Francisco's legendary health food emporium, Rainbow Grocery (see Resources, page 224):

wild rice and veggie soup

alphabet veggie soup

32 bean and veggie soup

spring southwestern soup

split pea soup

calico soup blend

curry lentil soup

Chicken Bouillon Cubes

The "quick 'n' easy" comes in the using, not the making, but why buy those tiny chemical-filled nuggets they sell as cubes in the market? Some of our campsite recipes call for chicken stock, and as it's unlikely you're going to find a stewing hen climbing that nearby rock face, you might as well bring these along. Use 1 bouillon cube per 1 Sierra cup of boiling water. If you like, add a pinch of salt and pepper to spice things up.

10 cups chicken stock, fat removed (see page 26)

1. The goal is to reduce the stock from 10 cups to about 1½ cups. Bring the stock to a boil in a large saucepan, stockpot, or Dutch oven. Lower the heat and simmer for about 1 hour 40 minutes. The stock should turn a deep brown color and feel like syrup coming off the spoon. Turn the heat down as low as you can to keep the stock from burning; cook for about 20 minutes longer, at which point the "syrup" will be thicker and the color darker.

2. Pour the stock into a small square baking pan (8 inches square). Cool to room temperature. Cover and refrigerate overnight.

3. Uncover and cut into 14 to 16 squares. Wrap each square individually in plastic. Store in airtight bags in the freezer for up to 3 months, till it's time to head out. Then use within 10 days.

Note: Because these homemade cubes contain no coagulants, they will melt in the sun or a warm pack. Here's what to do. Either keep 'em in a camp cooler or place 'em in a small plastic bottle or pill container before leaving home. They will become a liquid essence but lose none of their clout in the cooking pot.

Makes 14–16 bouillon cubes

The Splatter Effect: Purée and Duck

Let's assume you've never puréed anything in your life. You'd have liked to have puréed your math teacher or the local dolt representing you in Washington, but you'd rather spend time in the wilderness than in Folsom. So. You've read the recipe, and it says to "purée half of the soup," blah blah blah. If you're like Hal, you've got a 23-year-old blender with cracked sides, a gasket that's seen better days, a lid that the Smithsonian has inquired about for its collection. But it works. You don't know to let the soup cool down a bit, and you ladle it three-quarters of the way up the blender jar. And you think, "I don't need the top on this thing… ." Right. And of course you think that the purée button is too slow. Right again. When the scars on your hands and face heal, you'll know better. This stuff's hot, *and* it bubbles up like lava. So, take the following advice:

- Purée a little at a time, no more than half a jar at a time.
- Always close the lid.
- Purée in short pulses rather than in one long blend.
- Halfway through, with the motor off, mix the partly puréed soup with a rubber spatula. This helps get the undone stuff closer to the blender blades.

- Keep your nose out of the jar.
- Don't have a blender? Use a food processor. Don't have a food processor either? Use one of those old food mills, the kind your grandmother still uses to make her applesauce. Don't have that either? Use a big strainer and a large wooden spoon to press the soup contents through into a bowl. Works fine.
- Come see Hal's scars. He writes from experience. Someone just gave him a food processor for the first time, and he made all the mistakes possible (and some that are only probable). Lesson: Read the instruction book. Then proceed with caution.

Barley Soup with Mushrooms 🏠

Campers require comfort food the way couch potatoes require chips and dips. Well, here's a gold-medal winner in the comfort food competition. Wild mushrooms have long been tamed, but this soup feels like it comes right out of the woods. We found the recipe in the New York Times *and have adapted it for the dehydrator and the backwoods.*

½ cup dried mushrooms (porcini or shiitake)

1½ cups boiling water

3 tablespoons vegetable oil

1 carrot, chopped fine

1 onion, chopped fine

3 cloves garlic, minced

½ pound white mushrooms, coarsely chopped

½ pound portobello, oyster, or shiitake mushrooms, coarsely chopped

½ cup pearl barley

6 cups vegetable, chicken (see pages 26 and 27), or beef stock

3 tablespoons dry sherry or Madeira

Salt and freshly ground black pepper

1 tablespoon red wine vinegar

4–6 Sierra cups water, to rehydrate

at home

1. Soak the dried mushrooms in the boiling water for at least 20 minutes. Drain, reserving the liquid. Chop the mushrooms fine. Set aside.

2. Heat the oil in a large, heavy-bottomed pot over medium-high heat. Sauté the carrot and onion in the oil till the onion begins to brown, about 3 minutes. Stir in the garlic and continue cooking for no more than 1 minute. Stir in the fresh mushrooms and cook another 5 minutes, or till the mushrooms begin to release their liquid.

3. Stir in the barley and cook till it begins to color, about 3 minutes. Pour in the stock, sherry, chopped reconstituted mushrooms, and reserved liquid. Season with the salt and pepper to taste. Stir.

4. Simmer for about 45 minutes, till the barley is soft. Remove from the heat. Stir in the vinegar.

5. You have three choices for dehydrating: Spoon the soup onto lined trays; purée in a blender, then spoon onto lined trays; or purée half the soup, mix with remaining soup, then spoon onto lined trays. Each method works well, but puréeing at least part of the soup makes dehydrating a little easier.

6. Dehydrate 12 to 15 hours, till dry and gravelly in texture.

at camp

7. Rehydrate by covering with the water and bringing to a boil in your largest pot. Cook and stir for 5 to 10 minutes, until softened and thickened.

Variation: To make a mushroom spread that can be eaten on or with bread as a meal, reduce the liquid to a minimum once rehydrated. This is also a nice way to use leftovers.

Serves 4

Brazilian Black Bean Soup 🏠

Rick is a vegetarian, Hal is an omnivore. In this case, we'll split the difference. The basic recipe here appeared years ago in the New York Times, *and in the unbiased opinion of the ravening meat eaters in our crowd, it's flat out the best backpacking soup ever invented.*

1 pound dried black beans

¼ pound cured ham (or equivalent Canadian bacon), cut in ½-inch cubes

¼ pound salt pork, cut into ½-inch cubes

¼ cup olive oil

4 cups finely chopped onions

⅓ cup minced garlic

14 cups chicken (see page 26) or beef broth, fresh or canned

Cayenne pepper

Salt and freshly ground black pepper

¼ cup dry sherry

2 tablespoons red or white wine vinegar

½ cup cooked rice (optional)

4–6 Sierra cups water, to rehydrate

1 spoon dried onions (optional)

1 spoon lime juice or lemon juice (optional)

at home

1. Soak the beans in water to cover overnight. Drain before using.

2. Cook the ham and salt pork in a skillet over low heat, about 7 minutes, until the fat is rendered out. Using a slotted spoon, place the ham and pork on paper towels to drain. Set aside.

3. Heat the oil over medium-high heat in a large stockpot or Dutch oven. Sauté the onions and garlic till the onions are translucent, about 5 minutes. Stir in the ham and pork. Add the drained beans.

4. Pour in the broth. Bring to a boil, and lower the heat to a simmer. Season with the cayenne and salt and pepper to taste. (Go easy on the salt.) Partly cover and cook slowly, stirring occasionally, about 4 hours, till the soup begins to thicken and all the flavors are melded.

5. Purée half of the soup and beans in a blender or food processor, till smooth.

Return the soup to the pot and stir to blend with the remaining soup and beans.

6. Pour in the sherry and vinegar; mix well. Stir in the cooked rice, if desired. (The rice is usually served as a garnish, but we're saving steps here.)

7. Ladle onto lined dehydrator trays. Dry 10 to 12 hours, until the soup looks like a cobbled desert floor.

at camp

8. Rehydrate with the water to cover, boiling till the beans are soft, 10 to 12 minutes.

9. Garnish with the dried onions and lime juice, if using.

Serves 6–8

Note: If you don't want to take this many servings on your hike, halve the amount you dehydrate.

Mexican Vegetarian Black Bean Soup ⌂

Every year, our friend Maureen goes to one of those posh spas south of the border. She sometimes forgets her passport. But she never forgets the calorie count or the taste of the food served there. We couldn't count a calorie any more than we could the number of mesons on the head of a pin, but this much we know: This soup's as healthy as it is tasty.

1 cup dried black beans

2 cups chopped onion

6 cups vegetable stock (see page 27)

¾ pound tomatoes, chopped

4 scallions, chopped

1 green bell pepper, seeded and chopped

1 celery stalk, chopped

1 jalapeño chile, seeded and minced

1 tablespoon ground cumin

2 teaspoons fresh oregano, chopped

1 bay leaf

Salt and freshly ground black pepper

3 tablespoons fresh cilantro, chopped

4–6 Sierra cups water, to rehydrate

Yogurt masala (optional) (see page 100)

at home

1. Soak the beans in water to cover overnight. Drain before using.

2. Pour the vegetable stock over the onions in a large stockpot. Bring to a boil.

3. Carefully add the beans. Lower the heat so that the liquid is simmering steadily. Cover and cook about 40 minutes, till the beans are soft but not mushy.

4. Purée half of the mixture in a blender or food processor till thick and smooth. Pour back into the stockpot.

5. Stir in the tomatoes, scallions, bell pepper, celery, jalapeño, cumin, oregano, bay leaf, and salt and pepper to taste. Return to a simmer, cover, and cook for 40 minutes.

6. Stir in the cilantro. Return to simmer and cook for 20 minutes. Remove the bay leaf. If the soup is not thick enough — it should feel "heavy" when stirred — cook down another 15 minutes.

7. Spread on lined trays and dehydrate 10 to 12 hours, till thoroughly dried and the texture of the desert floor you know and love so well.

at camp

8. Rehydrate with the water to cover. Boil until the beans are soft, about 12 minutes.

9. Serve with a dollop of rehydrated yogurt masala, if using.

Serves 4

Leek & Potato Soup 🏠

Keep asking the question, "What's in season?" When you're handed leeks and potatoes and winter vegetables, you're not going to be making a spring bouquet. When it's summer and the tomatoes are ripening on the vine, you're not going to be thinking rutabagas. (Does anybody ever think rutabagas?) What we've got here are leeks and potatoes and a soup to warm the cockles of your heart. The cockles are located left of the right ventricle.

5 slices bacon

2 tablespoons olive oil

2 tablespoons butter

2 cups finely chopped leeks (white parts only)

2 cups finely chopped onion

1 cup diced celery

1 teaspoon dried tarragon

½ teaspoon dried thyme

Salt and freshly ground black pepper

5 cups chicken or vegetable broth (see pages 26 and 27)

3 cups finely diced potatoes

1 bunch spinach, stemmed, washed, and chopped fine

½ cup half-and-half (optional)

4–6 Sierra cups water, to rehydrate

at home

1. Render the bacon in a large stockpot or Dutch oven for about 5 minutes. Remove the bacon. You can eat it as you make the rest of the soup, or chop it up and toss it back in at step 5. (We're after fat here, not the bacon. Yeah, yeah, we know about cholesterol, but forgo some of the cheap cookies and accept this instead. It's all about flavor.)

2. Heat the olive oil and butter with the bacon fat in the stockpot. When the butter is melted, add the leeks, onion, and celery, lower the heat, and cook 10 to 15 minutes, till the veggies are soft but not burned. Season with the tarragon, thyme, and salt and pepper to taste.

3. Slowly pour in the broth and spoon in the potatoes. Cover and simmer till the potatoes are just soft, about 15 minutes.

4. Stir in the spinach and simmer till wilted, about 2 minutes.

5. Purée half the soup in a blender or food processor till thick and smooth. (If you want to include the cooked bacon bits, add them to the blender before you purée.) Return to the pot and pour in the half-and-half, if using. (What you've got here is a smoky, thick, and hearty soup, and at the campsite you're going to feel hearty, thick, and smoky eating it.)

6. Spoon onto lined trays and dehydrate 12 to 15 hours, till thoroughly desiccated.

at camp

7. Rehydrate with the water to cover. Cook down for 10 to 12 minutes, till thick and — have we said this? — hearty.

Serves 4

Basque Salt Cod, Leek & Potato Soup 🏠

Vegetarians and marriage counselors will wish to avert their eyes here. We're dealing with a steamy union of fish and meat, something divorce lawyers would call incompatible and vegans, a mésalliance. The Basques, who practically invented the cod fish and understand the endearments of a good sausage, know better. Humble ingredients + brilliant combinations = a formula for living happily ever after. If you don't agree that this is the most fabulous soup ever served at a campsite, please stay home, lock the doors, and open up a can of alphabet soup. Call us when you want to come out and play. Soaking the cod takes a couple of days, so don't forget to include the extra time in your schedule.

½ pound salt cod

3 large baking potatoes

3–4 leeks

4–5 tablespoons butter

6 cups chicken stock (see page 26)

Salt and freshly ground black pepper

½ pound chorizo (Spanish or Mexican sausage)

4–6 Sierra cups water, to rehydrate

at home

1. To prepare the salt cod, take it out of the freezer and let it sit, still in the box, in the fridge overnight. Open the box and, using a sharp knife, cut the cod in half through the middle. Reserve one half. Wrap the other and return it to the freezer.

2. Place the cod in a large bowl, cover with cold water, and leave uncovered in the fridge. Drain and replace with fresh water 4 to 5 times over the next 2 days. The soaking leaches the salt out of the preserved cod.

3. After 2 days, drain the salt cod. Break it into rough pieces and set aside.

4. To prepare the soup, peel the potatoes and cut into small dice-sized pieces. Cut the root end off the leeks and slice the white parts and some of the light green stem into small rounds. Wash the slices thoroughly (there's always dirt in leeks — beware) and dry roughly in paper towels.

5. In a large, heavy-bottomed pot or Dutch oven, heat the butter. Cook the potatoes and leeks in the butter over medium heat, stirring, for about 10 minutes, until the flavors are released and the veggies are beginning to soften. Don't let the potatoes stick to the bottom of the pot.

6. Pour in the chicken stock. Season with salt and pepper to taste. (There will still be salt left in the cod, so use the salt sparingly.) Bring to a boil, lower the heat, and simmer, covered, for 15 minutes. Stir in the cod and simmer for 7 to 10 minutes longer, till the cod is cooked through. Remove from the heat.

7. Scoop out the solid contents from the soup and purée them in a food processor or blender till smooth. You may have to do this in batches. Pour or spoon the purée back into the soup stock. Mix well and adjust the seasonings to taste.

If you were eating this at home, that's all you'd do till time to serve. At the last moment, you would slice the chorizo (if you had the dried and smoked kind, which doesn't need to be cooked) in small pieces, place them in individual serving bowls, and pour the reheated soup over them. If the chorizo needed cooking, you'd do that first (we'll show you how in the next paragraph) and then spoon it into the empty bowls. But because we're preparing this for the campsite, here's what to do next.

8. If you found dried, smoked chorizo in the market, slice it thin and pour the hot purée over it. Swirl to dissolve the chorizo in the soup. If you bought unpreserved chorizo, slice away the plastic wrapping and sauté the chorizo until cooked through, about 7 to 10 minutes. It will crumble as you cook it. Remove from heat and spoon directly into the hot purée. Swirl to mix in thoroughly. The colors will be beautiful, and the entire thing will look something like one of those abstract paintings by the great Barcelona artist Antoni Tàpies.

9. Spoon onto lined trays and dehydrate 12 to 24 hours, till dry and crumbly. Refrigerate in airtight bags for up to 3 months, till ready to leave on your camping trip. The dehydrated soup will last 2 weeks or more on the trail. Just keep it, along with all of your other foods, out of the sun at the campsite.

at camp

10. To rehydrate, place the contents in a large pot, cover with the water, and cook till the purée comes back to life, about 10 minutes. If it is too thick, add more water. If too thin, cook down till you have the thickness you like. The melding of the cod and chorizo flavors will be unforgettable, and you'll want to add a bunch of x's to your name in honor of the Basque language.

Serves 4

Mexican Lime Soup

Fire in the belly down Yucatán way. Here is a great and unexpected combination of hot serrano chiles and limes, making a mockery of the chicken soup your granny thought was so good. We've taken liberties with the traditional recipe in order to get it thick enough to dehydrate and to account for the fact that you're probably not going to schlep stale corn tortillas and a lot of oil into the wilderness. We also leave out the chicken livers and gizzards because too many of our friends no longer permit them. (Hal has to go out on the back porch to eat them.)

10–15 unpeeled garlic cloves

¼ teaspoon dried oregano

2 chicken breasts

10 peppercorns

Salt

8 cups water or chicken broth (see pages 26 and 27)

1 medium onion, chopped

½ medium green bell pepper, chopped

¼ cup vegetable oil (traditionalists may use lard)

1 large tomato, chopped fine and mashed

Juice of 2 limes (¼ cup)

Zest of 2 limes (4 teaspoons)

Zest of ¼ grapefruit (⅓ cup)

3–4 serrano chiles, finely chopped (see Handling Hot Chiles for precautions, facing page)

6 stale tortillas

4–6 Sierra cups water, to rehydrate

at home

1. Heat an iron skillet or fry pan over medium to high heat, till very hot. Toss in the garlic cloves and let the peels scald on all sides, about 5 minutes, till they begin to blacken. Turn often. Remove from the heat and, when cool enough to handle, strip away the peels. They should come off easily, and the garlic will be soft.

2. Toast the oregano by tossing it gently in a very hot, small iron fry pan for 1 to 2 minutes. Stop when the flavor begins to invade your nostrils.

3. Combine the garlic, oregano, chicken breasts, peppercorns, and salt to taste in a large pot with the water. Bring to a boil, lower the heat, and simmer till the chicken is tender, 20 to 25 minutes. Remove from the heat, remove the chicken and, when cool, shred into small pieces. Reserve the broth.

4. Sauté half of the onions and all of the green peppers in 2 tablespoons of the oil till just soft, about 3 minutes. Stir in the mashed tomato and cook 5 minutes longer.

5. Spoon the tomato mixture into the broth, along with the shredded chicken, lime juice and zest, grapefruit zest, remaining chopped onion, and serranos. (*Note:* Serranos are really hot. Cowards and rational types may wish to remove the seeds and veins before chopping and using.)

6. Put half the soup in a blender and purée. This will thicken the soup and turn it chicken-white. Add the purée back into the soup.

7. Spread on lined trays and dehydrate for 10 to 15 hours, till thoroughly dry.

8. Brush the tortillas lightly with the remaining oil and cut into strips. In a hot iron skillet, brown lightly, 3 to 5 minutes, or till just crisp. Dehydrate separately for 5 to 7 hours, till the

HANDLING HOT CHILES

When handling hot chiles, wear kitchen gloves to keep the caustic juices away from your skin. Avoid contact with eyes or cuts. Wash your hands thoroughly after handling.

texture of jerky. (*Note:* If you're car camping or canoeing and don't need to be mindful of weight, take the tortillas with you, slice into strips, and fry at the campsite. Add them to the rehydrated soup.)

at camp

9. Rehydrate the soup with the water to cover; use more water for a thinner soup. Bring to a boil then simmer 7 to 10 minutes, stirring occasionally, till thickened to your taste. Add the tortilla strips just before serving.

Serves 4

Pumpkin Soup or

If you're ever snowshoeing north of Trondheim, Norway, or, for that matter, just whapping mosquitoes and telling "uff da" jokes at your campsite in the Boundary Waters Wilderness in Minnesota, you're going to need something warm and filling to keep the inner fires burning. Here's what the Norwegians would do. The first method requires mostly home preparation; the second takes more work at the campsite. Alternative ingredient quantities for Method 2, when appropriate, are provided in parentheses.

1 medium-sized pumpkin or large butternut squash, or 2 cans pumpkin purée if using Method 2

3 tablespoons cooking oil, if using Method 1

1 large onion (about ½ pound), chopped

¾ teaspoon ground mace (or more to taste)

½ teaspoon freshly ground black pepper (or more to taste)

5 cups chicken or vegetable broth (homemade or canned) (see pages 26 and 27)

2 cups grated Jarlsberg or Swiss or 1 Sierra cup finely sliced if using Method 2

4–5 Sierra cups water, plus 1 to 2 more if using Method 2, to rehydrate

1–2 spoons cooking oil, or clarified butter (see page 99) if using Method 2

Method 1

at home

1. Preheat the oven to 375°F.

2. Using a sharp knife, halve the pumpkin at the midsection and scrape out the pith and seeds. Place cut side down on a baking sheet and bake till soft to the touch, about 30 minutes depending on the size of the pumpkin. Remove from the heat.

3. Flip over with a spatula and, when cool enough to handle (about 15 minutes), scrape out the pulp and place it in a large bowl. Set aside.

4. Heat the oil in a large heavy-bottomed pot or Dutch oven. Sauté the onion till translucent and soft, about

4 minutes. Add the pumpkin pulp, mace, pepper, and broth; mix well and simmer for 5 to 10 minutes, till the broth is well heated and the pulp is soft. Remove from the heat and add the cheese. Allow to cool for a few minutes.

5. Purée in a blender until very smooth.

6. Dehydrate on lined, lightly oiled trays for 15 to 24 hours, till dry and smooth like a cracked fruit roll. For best results, flip over once about 3 hours from the end of the drying time and continue to dehydrate until completely dry.

Note: Two dehydrator trays' worth of this soup will keep three or four hikers (or one Norwegian 50K cross-country skier) contentedly fueled. Feed the rest to friends at home.

at camp

7. Rehydrate with the water for 10 to 15 minutes and, if you have cheese to spare, slice some and place on the top of the soup when serving.

Method 2

at home

1. Follow step 2 in Method 1 to prepare the pumpkin.

2. Simmer the pulp, mace, pepper, and broth for 5 to 10 minutes, till the broth is well heated and the pulp is soft. Cool, then purée in a blender. Follow step 6 in Method 1 to dehydrate the soup.

3. Slice the onions thin (about ¼ inch) and dehydrate for 10 to 12 hours, till dry and crisp.

at camp

4. Rehydrate the onions in a cup or two of water over low heat for 5 minutes. Remove, and when cool enough to handle, squeeze dry with your hands. Sauté in the oil until just beginning to brown, 3 to 5 minutes.

5. Pour the water in a large pot. Add the sautéed onions and the dehydrated pumpkin. When the water comes to a boil, stir frequently till thickened, about 10 minutes. Remove from the heat.

6. Stir in the cheese till melted into the soup. Serve immediately.

Serves 3–4

WILDERNESS SOUPS

- **Make 'em thick. These aren't first courses; they're the whole meal.**
- **Delicate consommés and broths won't work. If you dehydrate these, they'll disappear.**
- **Fire 'em up. Spicing and flavoring count big in the cool of an evening. Don't spare the palate.**
- **Add dumplings at the campsite. They won't rehydrate if you make them at home.**

Pumpkin–Sage Soup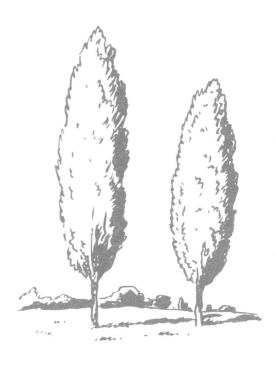

Hal found "Excellent!!" scrawled on the back of an old envelope where he first wrote this recipe down years ago. You may want to add a third exclamation point after making this one.

3 tablespoons butter

1 medium onion, chopped fine

2 pounds pumpkin chunks (*not* purée; canned is okay)

1 cup vegetable or chicken broth (see pages 26 and 27)

1 cup water

Salt and freshly ground black pepper

4–5 sage leaves, torn into rough pieces

¼ teaspoon cayenne pepper

¼ teaspoon dried nutmeg

1 cup milk

1 cup half-and-half or heavy cream

4–6 Sierra cups water, to rehydrate

at home

1. Melt the butter in a heavy-bottomed pot. Sauté the onions for 1 to 2 minutes, till they begin to turn translucent. Add the pumpkin chunks, broth, water, and salt and pepper to taste.

2. Bring to a boil, reduce the heat, and simmer, covered, about 25 minutes, till the pumpkin is fork soft. Remove from the heat.

3. Purée till smooth in a blender or food processor. Pour back into the pot.

4. Add the sage, cayenne, nutmeg, milk, and half-and-half to the purée and stir. Simmer for 10 minutes.

5. Ladle onto lined dehydrator trays and dry till the mixture has the texture of a fruit roll, 15 to 24 hours. You may have to turn the drying roll over once, 2 or 3 hours from "done," to ensure complete dehydration. Store in airtight bags in the freezer for up to 5 months. It will last 2 to 3 weeks on the trail.

at camp

6. To rehydrate, cover with the water, bring to a boil, then simmer, stirring till soft and thickened, 10 to 15 minutes.

Serves 3–4

The Purloined Lentil 🏠

Guilty as charged. We stole this soup — from the great Zuni Café Cookbook (W. W. Norton, 2002). No alibis, hardly any shame. We see no reason to deprive the backcountry community of pleasure and warmth just because a star chef (Judy Rodgers of San Francisco's incomparable Zuni Café) got there first. We would've invented this if Rick wasn't walking three dogs at 5:00 a.m. every day and Hal wasn't constantly being knocked unconscious by the latest 450-page Victorian novel he's reading. All we can say is this: 1) Ta Judy, luv. 2) We've taken so many liberties with the recipe that she probably wouldn't recognize it anyway. 3) If she shows up at the campsite, she gets first dibs.

4 tablespoons olive oil (Judy says extra-virgin, we say trollop)

1 red bell pepper, diced

1 teaspoon peppercorns, crushed in a mortar

½ teaspoon cumin seeds (not powdered), crushed in a mortar

¼–½ cup diced carrot

¼–½ cup diced celery

¼–½ cup diced onion

3 cloves garlic, chopped fine

1 bay leaf

2 sprigs Italian parsley, chopped

1 cup black or green lentils

5 cups chicken or vegetable stock (see pages 26 and 27)

Salt and freshly ground black pepper

4–6 Sierra cups water, to rehydrate

at home

1. Heat 1 tablespoon of the oil in a large, heavy-bottomed pot. Sauté the pepper for about 5 minutes, till just soft. Stir in the peppercorns and cumin seeds and cook 1 minute longer.

2. Stir in the remaining 3 tablespoons oil, carrots, celery, onions, garlic, bay leaf, and parsley. Sauté briefly to fix the flavors, about 3 minutes. Stir in the lentils, 3 cups of the stock, and the salt and pepper to taste.

3. Reduce the heat and cook at a very slow simmer until the lentils are soft and have absorbed most of the liquid, about 15 minutes. Remove from the heat.

4. Purée in a blender or food processor. Return to the pot and, in small increments, add enough of the remaining stock to make a smooth, thick soup.

5. Spread on lined trays and dehydrate 12 to 15 hours, until thoroughly desiccated.

at camp

6. Rehydrate with the water to cover, bring to a boil, then simmer for about 10 minutes, stirring until the soup is soft and thick. Season with additional salt and pepper to taste.

Serves 2–3

Vegetarian Chicken Lemon Grass Soup

Yes, we know that all chickens are vegetarians, but that's not what we mean here. Do the math. Subtract the chicken from Thailand's famous chicken soup, add a nod of thanks to Mollie Katzen and her indispensable book, Vegetable Heaven *(Hyperion, 2000), multiply your options, divide the ingredients, and conquer. Result: VCLGS (Vegetarian Chicken... .) Looks like a lot of work? Well, maybe more than making a burger, but are we keeping time?*

for flavor pack

- 5 stalks lemon grass
- 3 cans coconut milk, 14 ounces each
- 2 cups dry white wine
- 10 cloves garlic, peeled and put through a garlic press
- 10 slices fresh ginger, about ½ inch in diameter, cut ¼ inch thick
- 3 jalapeño chiles cut in half (see Handling Hot Chiles for precautions, page 37)

for soup

- 1 tablespoon peanut oil
- 1 large onion, chopped fine
- 4 cloves garlic, chopped fine
- 1 tablespoon fresh ginger, chopped fine
- 2 teaspoons salt
- 2 cups chopped bok choy or Napa cabbage (or regular cabbage)
- 2 cups cauliflower, separated into small florets
- 1 cup canned baby corn, drained and sliced into 1-inch pieces (optional)
- 7 dried shiitake mushrooms, rehydrated and quartered (or 10 small white mushrooms quartered)
- 1 red bell pepper, sliced into short sticks
- 1 carrot, chopped into dice
- ½ pound tofu, diced
- 2 cups (packed) fresh basil leaves, roughly chopped
- Juice of about ⅓ lemon (1 tablespoon)
- 2–4 pinches cayenne pepper
- 2–3 Sierra cups water, to rehydrate

at home

1. To make the flavor pack, cut the lemon grass into 2-inch pieces and crush them in a mortar or by using the flat of a heavy knife. Combine in a saucepan with all the other flavor pack ingredients. Bring to a boil and remove from the heat. Cover and let stand overnight, or at least 4 hours.

2. To make the soup, pour the oil into a large, heavy-bottomed pot. Sauté the onion, garlic, ginger, and 1 teaspoon of the salt in the oil till the onion is translucent, about 3 minutes. Stir in the remaining salt, bok choy, cauliflower, baby corn, if using, mushrooms, bell pepper, and carrot. Cover and cook 10 to 12 minutes, stirring occasionally to prevent sticking.

3. To combine, pour the flavor pack through a strainer into the soup mix and simmer for 2 to 3 minutes, till the flavors are fully melded. Stir in the tofu, basil, and lemon juice. Remove from the heat and add the cayenne.

4. At this point, you can spoon the soup as-is onto lined dehydrator trays and dehydrate 15 to 24 hours, till thoroughly dried and flaky, or purée the soup in a blender or food processor before dehydrating. This second option, though unorthodox, will preserve more of the coconut milk in the soup.

at camp

5. Rehydrate with the water, barely to cover. Bring to a boil, reduce heat, and simmer for 7 to 10 minutes, stirring often to prevent burning. The soup should be as thick and as undiluted as possible.

Serves 4

Notes: Lemon grass is available in Asian food shops, many farmers' markets, health food stores, and an increasing number of supermarkets. If you can't find it, check the resources on page 224. Baby corn, which tastes nothing like the grown-up kind, is another staple of Asian food shops.

Lydia's Chicken Stew with Herb Dumplings 🏠

Lydia Itoi is one of America's preeminent food writers, but she had never been camping, so we set her a challenge: to come up with a dish that we could dehydrate at home and then reconstitute at a campsite. She went to work and made this dynamite stew with dumplings. Only thing is, the dumplings failed to reconstitute. Unfazed, Lydia got down on the ground in her spanking-new hiking jeans, fiddling and muttering, trying powdered this and lightweight that, loving the puzzle and finding the solution. We also loved it, and so will you. Thanks, Lydia.

2 tablespoons olive oil

6 chicken legs, separated into drumsticks and thighs

4 carrots, coarsely chopped

4 celery stalks, chopped

4 parsnips, peeled and chopped

3 leeks, white parts only, cleaned and sliced

2 russet potatoes, peeled and quartered

1 tomato, chopped

6 cups homemade chicken stock (see page 26) (canned stock will do as a substitute)

2 dried hot chiles or dash of cayenne pepper (see Handling Hot Chiles for precautions, page 37)

Salt and freshly ground black pepper

Lydia's Instant Dumpling mix (page 77)

2 Sierra cups warm water, plus more as needed, to rehydrate

at home

1. Heat the oil in a large Dutch oven. Brown the chicken till golden on all sides, about 5 minutes per piece. Remove the chicken from the pot and discard excess fat, if desired.

2. Place the carrots, celery, parsnips, and leeks in the Dutch oven with some of the remaining fat. Cook 5 minutes, or till the vegetables begin to soften slightly.

3. Return the chicken to the Dutch oven. Add the potatoes, tomatoes,

chicken stock, chiles, and salt and pepper to taste. Bring to a boil, lower the heat, and simmer 20 minutes.

4. Remove the chicken from the pot with kitchen tongs or a fork and let cool until it can be handled. Remove the meat from the bones.

5. Purée the vegetables and stock in a blender or food processor till smooth. Return the purée to the pot.

6. Stir the chicken into the purée and simmer 5 minutes. Season again with generous amounts of salt and pepper.

7. Pour the stew onto lined, lightly oiled dehydrator trays and dry 15 to 24 hours until the stew has turned into flakes. Refrigerate in airtight plastic bags till departure. This will last 5 to 7 days out of the fridge.

8. Measure the ingredients for the dumpling mix and place in a plastic bag. Seal the bag tightly.

at camp

9. To rehydrate, place the stew flakes in pot. Add the water. Let the flakes soak till softened, about 15 minutes. Add more water if the mixture looks dry. Heat the stew, stirring occasionally and adding water as needed. After 5 to 10 minutes, the stew should look almost as it did before dehydration.

10. Prepare the dumplings according to the recipe instructions, then drop them by spoons into the bubbling stew. Cover and cook 12 to 15 minutes without lifting the lid. When done, the dumplings should be fluffy, with no trace of raw-flour taste.

Serves 3–4

ADDING SEASONING

Dehydrating and rehydrating food dulls its flavor a bit. To combat this effect, season rehydrated food aggressively with salt and ground black pepper.

Louisiana Hot Pot 🏠

Yeah, we know. You're going to catch your own fish. You never fail. Or that's what you tell the gullible people who listen to your wilderness tales around the water cooler. So why would you want the recipe for maybe the best Creole fish stew this side of Lake Pontchartrain? So don't listen. This one's for the truth tellers.

4 tablespoons canola or olive oil

2 cloves garlic, chopped fine or pressed

1 large onion, chopped

2 carrots, chopped

2 large celery stalks, chopped

2 large unpeeled potatoes, cubed

2 small green or yellow zucchini, cut into small dice

1 red bell pepper, chopped

2 cups chopped tomatoes

1 bay leaf

¼ teaspoon thyme

3 cups fish stock or water

1 cup tomato juice or ½ cup tomato sauce

4–10 drops Tabasco or red salsa, or to taste

Salt and freshly ground black pepper

2 pounds firm white fish cut into bite-sized pieces (We use a combination of sea bass and monkfish. You use what you can find: largemouth or smallmouth bass, butterfish, cod, grouper, mahi-mahi, or swordfish, for example.)

Juice of 1½ lemons (3–4½ tablespoons)

Handful sun-dried or dehydrated tomatoes

2–3 Sierra cups water, to rehydrate

at home

1. Heat the oil in a large Dutch oven or heavy-bottomed pot. Sauté the garlic and onion over medium heat till just translucent, about 3 minutes.

2. Stir in the carrots, celery, and potatoes. Sauté for about 5 minutes, or till slightly browned. Stir in the zucchini and peppers and continue to sauté for 5 minutes longer.

3. Add the tomatoes, bay leaf, thyme, fish stock, and tomato juice. Reduce the heat and simmer for about 15 minutes, till the veggies are tender but not mushy.

4. Ask those with tender palates to turn their backs, and add the Tabasco to taste. (Rick would add an entire bottle of Tabasco, but he would add an entire bottle of Tabasco to his corn flakes. Those of us with taste buds left will want to go a little lighter. This stew is, however, meant to pack a wallop.) Remember that dehydrating diminishes spicing. Three, four, or five hefty shakes of the bottle will not harm the environment or your digestive tract. Season with the salt and pepper to taste.

5. Heave in the fish and the lemon juice. (Okay, don't heave. Add the fish carefully.) Simmer 5 to 7 minutes (depending on the thickness of the fish) till it is just cooked through; the fish should flake but not collapse into tiny bits and pieces. Don't worry if it seems slightly underdone. You're going to rehydrate it at the campsite and can finish the cooking then.

6. Ladle onto dehydrator trays fitted with fruit-roll liners or plastic wrap. Dry at the highest temperature setting, if your dehydrator has such settings. Otherwise, just dry till you've achieved a flaky, pebbled texture, 15 to 24 hours.

at camp

7. Rehydrate by barely covering with the water. Add the sun-dried tomatoes. Cook for about 10 minutes. Serve with camp-baked wheat bread (pages 166–67) or cornbread (pages 179–81).

Note: This hot pot is often made with fresh shrimp mixed with the fish, but shrimp don't rehydrate well. If you do use shrimp, do this: Shell and devein about ½ pound of small shrimp. Slice them in half or thirds. That way, they will rehydrate a little better. Add 'em when you toss in the fish.

Serves 3–4

Chicken Casserole...

...that never made it to the campsite. *It's true. We've never got that far. Once dehydrated, this dish replaces all other forms of gorp ever imagined. This is trail nosh supreme. Please let us know how it tastes reheated. We can't wait.*

¼ cup seasoned flour (flour mixed with herbs: savory, chives, basil, tarragon, paprika, pepper, and salt)

1 chicken (4 pounds), cut up in large pieces, as for frying

6 tablespoons olive oil, plus more if necessary

1 onion, diced

2 cloves garlic, diced or mashed in a press

3 celery stalks, chopped

1 carrot, sliced into ¼- to ½-inch rounds

1½ cups chicken stock (approximately) (see page 26)

Salt and freshly ground black pepper

1 cup sliced mushrooms

10 pimiento-stuffed olives, halved

3–4 Sierra cups water, to rehydrate

at home

1. Preheat the oven to 350°F.

2. Pour the seasoned flour into a brown paper bag. Throw in the chicken parts, close the bag, and shake vigorously.

3. Pour 4 tablespoons of the olive oil into a large, heavy-bottomed pot or Dutch oven. Brown the dusted chicken in the oil for about 5 minutes per piece. Remove and set aside.

4. Sauté the onion, garlic, celery, and carrot in the same oil, adding more if needed, till the vegetables begin to soften, about 5 minutes.

5. Return the chicken to the pot with the vegetables. Add broth to barely cover. Season with the salt and pepper to taste.

6. Bake, covered, for 1½ hours, or till the chicken is very tender.

7. Meanwhile, sauté the mushrooms in the remaining 2 tablespoons oil in a small pan. Five minutes before the chicken is done, add the mushrooms and olives to the casserole.

8. Allow the casserole to cool. Remove the chicken parts and debone. Return the chicken to the pot, stirring. It's okay if the chicken falls apart into shreds or small pieces.

9. Spread on lined trays and dehydrate 12 to 24 hours, until completely dry and crunchy. Freeze in airtight bags until you're ready to head out. It will last up to 1 week in the wilderness. Do *not* open and eat while driving to the trailhead. Otherwise you may be too full and contented to go any farther.

at camp

10. Rehydrate with the water to cover. Bring to a boil, then simmer for about 20 minutes. The chicken takes a long time to rehydrate, so if you've got the time, let it first sit in a pot of water till ready to heat up for dinner.

Serves 4–6

Variation: Add a cup of cooked rice to the casserole during the last 15 minutes of baking.

The Slow Burn

Casseroles are tolerant. They'll let you get away with anything as long as you've got lots of time. Try some of the following, or invent your own. Dehydrate and rehydrate as you did for Chicken Casserole.

- **Winter veggies** — turnips, chard, parsnips, rutabagas. Spice heavily with dill, tarragon, chives, and mint. Add garlic, more garlic and… toss in some currants or cranberries. Add wine to the stock. Brown the veggies first, then bake slowly in the stock.

- **Burgundy beef.** See Rick and Hal's recipe online. Find the Web site under Resources on page 224.

- **Gumbo.** Follow your favorite recipe. Keep a flask of Tabasco handy. Cook on the stovetop.

- **Pot roast.** Any recipe will do.

- **Baked beans.** Bake in an old bean pot with honey. Dry, rehydrate, root for the BoSox.

If you've got one of those electric slow cookers, set the temperature way down and let any of the these meals burble for the entire day.

Tex–Mex Green Chili 🏠

How many times have you passed those little round green things wrapped in what looks like last year's tissue paper in the produce section? They're tomatillos, Mexico's finest green tomatoes. Make a chili with them and you won't go back to the reds north of the border. Don't be alarmed by the number of serrano chiles we use here. Remember that spicing seems to leach out in the dehydrating process.

1 cup dried pinto beans

3 tablespoons canola or safflower oil, plus more if necessary

1 pound pork shoulder (boneless), diced into 1-inch bites

3 onions, chopped

6 large or 10 small cloves garlic, roughly chopped

5 serrano chiles, seeds and veins included, chopped fine (see Handling Hot Chiles for precautions, page 37)

1 bay leaf

1 teaspoon dried Mexican oregano leaves (if available; otherwise, regular oregano leaves)

2½ pounds tomatillos, quartered

5–7 cups vegetable or chicken broth (see pages 26 and 27)

Salt

2–4 Sierra cups water, to rehydrate

at home

1. Soak the pinto beans in water overnight. Drain before using.

2. Heat the oil in a Dutch oven. Brown the pork in batches so it browns evenly, about 5 minutes per batch. Set aside.

3. Sauté the onions in the same pot until just soft, 3 to 4 minutes, adding more oil if necessary.

4. Stir in the garlic, serranos, bay leaf, and oregano. Continue to stir for 2 to 3 minutes, to mix well. (If you're fussy and love the smell of toasted oregano, heat an iron fry pan and crumble the oregano leaves in it for 30 seconds before combining with the onion mixture. The smokey taste will please knowing palates.)

5. Stir in the tomatillos. Continue to stir for about 5 minutes, to soften them up a bit. Stir in the browned pork and the beans.

6. Cover with the broth; add water if necessary. Bring to a boil, then simmer slowly for about 2 hours. Add more broth as necessary. Stir occasionally. After 1 hour, season with the salt to taste. You end up with a thick chili with softened beans and meat. Discard the bay leaf.

7. Spread on lined, lightly oiled trays. Dehydrate 10 hours at the highest temperature, or till flaky dry.

at camp

8. Rehydrate with the water to cover. Heat, stirring, till the beans and pork are softened, about 10 minutes. They're not going to be as soft as they were before dehydrating, but who's testing?

Serves 4

Cruiser–Weight Vegetarian Chili 🏠

Imagine yourself in a canoe with Arnold Schwarzenegger, "Refrigerator" Perry, and all the ingredients of this cruiser-weight chili. Something'd have to give. Toss Arney overboard. Hand the "Fridge" a PFD (personal flotation device) and whistle him over and out. But save that chili. And keep it from the bears.

1 cup dried red kidney beans

4 tablespoons cooking oil

3 onions, chopped

3 jalapeño chiles, minced (remove the seeds if you want a milder chili) (see Handling Hot Chiles for precautions, page 37)

3 cloves garlic, crushed or minced

1 green bell pepper, diced

1 red bell pepper, diced

2 pounds ripe tomatoes, chopped

1 can (35 ounces) plum tomatoes, drained

2 bay leaves

2 tablespoons chili powder

½ tablespoon ground cumin

1 bottle of beer (12 ounces) (ale or porter is best)

Salt and freshly ground black pepper

1 cup corn (fresh or frozen — do not thaw)

4 tablespoons cilantro, chopped

1 cup Monterey Jack or Cheddar, grated

1 cup sour cream (optional)

4–6 Sierra cups water, to rehydrate

at home

1. Soak the beans overnight; drain and rinse. Simmer the beans in water to cover till just soft, about 1 hour.

2. Heat the oil in a large, heavy-bottomed pot or Dutch oven. Sauté the onions till just translucent, 4 minutes. Stir in the jalapeños, garlic, and peppers and cook till soft, 4 minutes longer. Stir in the fresh and canned tomatoes, bay leaves, chili powder, cumin, beer, and salt and pepper to taste.

3. Bring to a boil. Add the beans and corn and simmer 1 hour, stirring. After 45 minutes, add the cilantro.

4. Immediately after cooking is completed, stir in the cheese to melt and, when the mixture is no longer bubbling, stir in the sour cream (if using) to incorporate.

5. Spread on lined trays and dry 12 to 15 hours or longer, until you've got several trays of dried, pebbly crackle.

at camp

6. Rehydrate with water to cover. Cook down at a simmer until thick and tasty, 15 to 20 minutes, stirring often.

Serves 4–6

Charanga Restaurant's Picadillo Cubano 🏠
(Cuban-Style Ground Beef with Sofrito, Green Olives, and Raisins)

Our friends Rita Abraldes and Gabriela Salas have been feeding Pan-Latin foodies in San Francisco's famous Mission District for more than 5 years, and they kindly offered us this recipe. The name "Charanga" comes from an orchestral style applied to more traditional forms of Cuban dance music, such as danzón and cha cha cha. Traditionally, this dish is served with black beans, rice, and fried sweet plantains (page 20). Sofrito is the quintessential Cuban sauce or paste, used as a base for many dishes.

1½ pounds ground beef chuck

2 tablespoons olive oil

1 medium onion, diced

1 bay leaf

½ green bell pepper, diced

½ red bell pepper, diced

1 tablespoon minced garlic

1 tablespoon dried ground cumin

1 tablespoon dried whole oregano

Salt and freshly ground black pepper

¼ cup sliced pimiento-stuffed manzanilla olives

¼ cup raisins

¼ cup dry white wine

¾ cup canned tomato sauce

2–3 Sierra cups water, to rehydrate

at home

1. In a large, heavy sauté pan or Dutch oven over medium heat, brown the beef, breaking up large chunks with a spoon. Using a slotted spoon, transfer the beef to a bowl. Drain off the fat from the pan.

2. To make the sofrito, heat the oil over medium-high heat in the same pan and stir in, one at a time and in order, the onion, bay leaf, green and red peppers, garlic, cumin, oregano, and salt and pepper to taste. Cook, stirring frequently, till slightly thickened, about 10 minutes.

3. Return the beef to the pan and stir in the olives, raisins, and wine. Cook for 5 to 10 minutes to reduce the wine till it has all but disappeared; add the tomato sauce and stir well. Cover, reduce the heat to a simmer, and cook till slightly thickened and well flavored, about 15 minutes. Adjust the seasonings to taste.

4. Spread on lined dehydrator trays and dry 12 to 15 hours, till you have a dry gravel of hamburger pebbles.

at camp

5. You may never get around to rehydrating this dish because it's almost the perfect snack food. If you can restrain yourself, rehydrate with the water to cover, bring to a boil, and reduce till barely any water is left, about 5 minutes. This is *not* a stew, even though we've included it in this chapter; it should end up moist but not swimming in broth.

Serves 4–6

Spinach & Onion

Here is the simplest recipe so far, but the minimalists were on to something. This is something!

2 pounds spinach

4 tablespoons ghee (or clarified butter) (see page 99)

1 medium onion, chopped fine

2 green chiles (serranos or jalapeños) (see Handling Hot Chiles for precautions, page 37)

2 teaspoons grated fresh ginger

Salt

1 teaspoon sugar

½ cup water

¼ teaspoon garam masala (see recipe, page 58)

1–2 Sierra cups water, to rehydrate

at home

1. Wash the spinach, trim the stems, and cut roughly, horizontally across the bunch. Set aside.

2. Heat the ghee in a large, heavy-bottomed pot over medium-high heat. Sauté the onion, stirring, about 3 minutes, till translucent but not browned.

3. Stir in the spinach, chiles, ginger, salt, and sugar. Stir and cook until the spinach is well wilted, about 5 minutes.

4. Slowly add the water. Bring to a simmer, cover, and cook 10 minutes. Uncover and let most of the liquid boil off, about 5 minutes. Remove from heat.

5. Stir in the garam masala.

6. Spread on a lined tray and dehydrate 5 to 7 hours, till veggies are crumble-dry.

at camp

7. Rehydrate with the water to barely cover. Cook down until the mixture is soft and thickened, about 5 minutes.

Serves 2

Mustard & Cumin Veggies 🏠

Vegetarians suffer the world's blandness. It doesn't have to be that way. This mixed vegetable stew has the kick of a Harley hog. There are many steps, but the prep is easy. Just slice and dice everything first and lay out the spices in the order you'll use them.

Eat with chapati (page 182) or rice with a side dish of chutney (pages 95–98).

8 tablespoons oil

1 pound potatoes, boiled until just soft but not mushy, 10 to 15 minutes

1 small or medium cauliflower, broken into florets

10 cloves garlic, roughly chopped

1 large piece fresh ginger, about 4 inches long, roughly chopped

2 cups plus 4 tablespoons water

1 teaspoon black mustard seeds (or 2 teaspoons white or yellow mustard seeds)

1 teaspoon cumin seeds

¼ teaspoon fennel seeds

¼ teaspoon onion seeds (*kalonji*) (optional)

1 pound tomatoes, chopped fine (or a 14.5-ounce can of tomatoes will do)

2 teaspoons ground coriander

1 teaspoon cayenne pepper, or more to taste

1 teaspoon ground cumin

1 teaspoon salt (optional)

½ teaspoon ground turmeric

2 carrots, peeled and sliced into ¼-inch rounds

¼ pound fresh or frozen peas (no need to thaw if using frozen)

½ teaspoon garam masala (see recipe, page 58)

2–3 Sierra cups water, to rehydrate

at home

1. Heat 2 tablespoons of the oil in a large pan. Fry the boiled potatoes until they just turn golden. Remove and drain on paper towels. Fry the cauliflower florets until they begin to color, using 2 more tablespoons of the oil if necessary. Drain on paper towels.

2. Using a blender or food processor, make a paste of the garlic, ginger, and 4 tablespoons of the water. Remove and set aside.

3. Heat the remaining 4 tablespoons of oil in a large, heavy-bottomed pot or Dutch oven until very hot. Add the mustard and cumin seeds. As soon as the mustard seeds start popping, add the fennel and onion seeds (if using). Stir once or twice, then add the ginger-garlic paste. Stir for 1 to 2 minutes to mix.

4. Add the tomatoes, coriander, cayenne, cumin, salt (if using), and turmeric. Stir well and cook down till the tomatoes are soft and most of the liquid is gone, 3 to 5 minutes.

5. Pour in the 2 cups of water. Stir, cover, and simmer for 8 to 10 minutes, thereby incorporating all the flavors in a thick tomato mixture.

6. Meanwhile, parboil the carrots for 3 minutes, then drain. After the tomato mixture has simmered 8 to 10 minutes, add the carrots and simmer 4 minutes longer.

7. Using a rubber spatula, stir in the peas, potatoes, cauliflower, and garam masala. Mix gently, return to a simmer, and cover. Cook, stirring occasionally, for 8 minutes or till the carrots and cauliflower are fork soft.

8. Place on lined trays and dehydrate 7 to 10 hours, till dry and almost powdery.

at camp

9. To rehydrate, cover with the water and cook down till the veggies are soft and the sauce is beginning to thicken, about 10 minutes.

Serves 4

CURRIES

You won't find the word "curry" in a good Indian cookbook, because all it really means is "sauce" (*kari* in Tamil, a southern Indian language). Once the British raj got done messing with the language, however, it came to mean just about anything hot and spicy from India cooked in a sauce. As we imagine the legendary Indian cricket player Pinnaduwage Aravinda de Silva would have said about curry if he had been in the kitchen with us or at the campsite, "It's the spices, stupid." Our three curry recipes — Spinach and Onion, Mustard and Cumin Veggies, and Lamb with Spinach — are adapted for backpacking from Madhur Jaffrey's fine *Indian Cooking* (Barrons, 1995).

Lamb with Spinach (Saag Gosht)

Only Popeye, the jerk, would eat spinach out of the can. Sheesh, maybe he eats lamb out of the can, too. That's his problem. Yours is trying to get your fair share of this jewel in the crown when the yahoos come back from fishing and head for the stew pot. Civil disobedience may not work.

Serve with chapati (page 182) or rice, with a side dish of chutney (pages 95–98).

8 tablespoons oil

8 cloves

7 cardamom pods (or ½ teaspoon powdered cardamom)

2 bay leaves

½ teaspoon black peppercorns

1 medium onion, chopped fine

8 cloves garlic, peeled and chopped fine

1 piece fresh ginger, 2 inches long, peeled and chopped fine

1½ pounds boneless lamb, cut into small cubes

2 teaspoons ground cumin

1 teaspoon ground coriander

1 teaspoon salt, or to taste

½ teaspoon cayenne pepper

5 heaping tablespoons yogurt, whisked smooth (we use nonfat yogurt, though any will do)

2 pounds spinach, washed and trimmed of large stems, shredded fine (if using fresh; one 10-ounce package of frozen spinach is also okay)

¼ teaspoon garam masala (see recipe on page 58)

3–4 Sierra cups warm or hot water, to rehydrate

at home

1. Heat the oil in a Dutch oven or heavy-bottomed pot. Add the cloves, cardamom pods, bay leaves, and peppercorns; stir quickly, then add the onions, garlic, and ginger. Sauté till the onions just begin to brown, about 3 minutes.

2. Stir in the lamb, cumin, coriander, salt, and cayenne. Stir well while browning the meat, about 2 minutes.

3. Add the yogurt, 1 tablespoon at a time. After each spoon, stir about 1 minute to incorporate.

4. Stir in the spinach till it wilts.

5. Cover the pot and cook at a very low simmer, about 1 hour, till the meat is fork soft.

6. Stir in the garam masala, cooking till most of the water from the spinach is gone, about 5 minutes. The goal is to end up with a thick green sauce. Remove the bay leaves.

7. Place on lined trays — the fruit-roll insert works best — and dehydrate 12 to 15 hours, till leathery hard.

at camp

8. To rehydrate, cover with the water; if time allows, let soak for about 1 hour in the water to help soften the meat. Bring to a boil and slowly cook down to get back to a thick sauce, 10 to 15 minutes.

Serves 2

Note: As meats dry, they take on a dark, almost black color, and look (and taste) like jerky. No harm eating this dish as-is.

Indian Spices: What and Where?

There are almost as many spices used in the great Indian subcontinent as there are people. What do you need and where can you get 'em? Here's a partial list, arranged according to availability.

At your supermarket:

- Cayenne
- Chiles (fresh, green and red)
- Chiles (dried, green and red)
- Cinnamon (stick and powder)
- Cloves (whole)
- Coconut milk
- Coriander (called cilantro in its fresh form)
- Coriander seeds (ground, whole)
- Cumin seeds (ground, whole)
- Fennel seeds
- Ginger (fresh, ground)
- Nutmeg
- Poppy seeds
- Saffron
- Sesame seeds
- Turmeric

At specialty shops, natural food stores, or Indian markets or by the Internet:

- Asafetida (also called *heeng* and *hing*; it's a resin that smells like truffles, looks like seasoned salt when ground, and is more a flavor enhancer than a "taste" of its own. Store the ground or powdered form in a tightly sealed container. It appears to last forever).
- Cardamom pods and seeds
- Coconut (grated, unsweetened)
- Fenugreek seeds
- Garam masala
- Green mango powder
- Onion seeds (*kalonji*)
- Mustard oil

Do it yourself:

- Roasted cumin seeds. (Shake constantly in a dry cast-iron pan over high heat till lightly browned, 1 to 2 minutes.)
- Ground, roasted cumin seeds. (Roast as above, then grind to a fine powder in a coffee or spice grinder, 3 to 4 quick pulses.)
- Garam masala. (See recipe, page 58)

Garam Masala

Just as you won't find curry in a real Indian cookbook, you won't find curry powder either. What you will find in its place is garam masala, literally "hot spice blend." And we mean blend! As many as 14 spices may be in some garam masalas: coriander, chili, cumin, cinnamon, clove and clove leaves, amchur, salt, curry leaves, anistar, fennel seeds, black pepper, mace, and bay leaves. Garam masala is the flavor clincher in thousands of Indian recipes; it is usually added in fractional amounts right at the end of the cooking process or even after the pot comes off the stove. It springs all flavors loose and as a bonus brings tears to your eyes and a raga to your heart.

2 bay leaves

1 tablespoon coriander seeds

2 teaspoons white cumin seeds

2 tablespoons cardamom seeds

2 teaspoons whole cloves

2 inches stick cinnamon

2 teaspoons freshly ground black pepper

2 teaspoons chili powder or cayenne pepper

½ teaspoon grated or powdered nutmeg

1. Preheat the oven to 400°F.

2. Combine the bay leaves, coriander seeds, cumin seeds, cardamom seeds, cloves, and cinnamon stick in a small bowl. Spread on a baking sheet. Roast in the oven for 20 minutes.

3. In a spice or coffee grinder, grind the mixture to a fine powder. Remove to a bowl.

4. Mix in the black pepper, chili powder, and nutmeg.

5. Store in an airtight jar. The mixture will keep for several months, but is best used fresh in the first 2 weeks.

Makes about 6 tablespoons, enough for every Indian dish in this book and then some

Variation: Omit the chili powder and black pepper for a lighter, more aromatic garam masala.

Steve's Annual Dal 🏠

Every year like clockwork, our friend Steve shows up at the campsite with this dish. Every year we clean him out; it's that good. We have no idea if he knows how to cook anything else, but who's complaining?

2 cups dried lentils or split peas (Steve's not particular)

5 cups chicken or vegetable stock (pages 26 and 27)

2 teaspoons turmeric

Salt

2 cups finely chopped onion

2 cloves garlic, minced

½ teaspoon ground cumin

½ teaspoon coarsely ground black pepper

¼ teaspoon hot chili pepper flakes

2 tablespoons ghee (page 100)

1 cup coconut milk

4–6 Sierra cups water, to rehydrate

at home

1. Combine the lentils, stock, turmeric, and salt in a large pot. Simmer till the lentils are soft, about 25 minutes. Drain, reserving the liquid.

2. Fry the onion, garlic, cumin, pepper, and chili pepper flakes in the ghee in a skillet over medium heat till the onion turns golden (Steve's way of saying "brown"), 5 to 7 minutes. Stir constantly to incorporate all the spices and prevent burning.

3. Empty the contents of the frying pan into the lentils and reheat over low to medium heat, about 3 minutes. When hot, pour in the coconut milk.

If the lentils are too dry or thick, add some of the liquid that you set aside.

4. Spread on lined trays and dehydrate 12 to 15 hours, till the consistency of dried pebbles.

at camp

5. Rehydrate with the water to cover. Bring to a boil and cook, stirring, till the stew is soft, 10 to 15 minutes. Write Steve a nice note telling him how much you enjoyed it. He blossoms with praise.

Variation: Substitute 1 cup chopped tomatoes for the coconut milk for a savory alternative.

Serves 4

Yellow Dal Stew

This is a hand-me-down. We've modified a recipe from The Greens Cookbook *(Bantam Books, 1987) by Deborah Madison, founding chef of the famous Green's Restaurant in San Francisco, which she modified from an Indian cookbook. Third-hand is lucky.*

1 cup yellow split peas (at your local market or, for the Indian variety, *chana dal*, at the Middle Eastern or Indian shop)

2 serrano chiles (red or green), chopped (seeded if you want a milder fire in the gut); (see Handling Hot Chiles for precautions, page 37)

4 cloves garlic, peeled and chopped fine

2 tablespoons fresh ginger, peeled and chopped fine

½ teaspoon turmeric

4 tablespoons ghee (see page 100) or clarified butter (see page 99)

1 teaspoon brown mustard seeds

1 teaspoon cumin seeds

1 medium onion, sliced thin

4 tomatoes, chopped in large pieces

2 Japanese or Chinese eggplants, sliced in 1- or 2-inch pieces

½ cauliflower, broken into small florets

2 carrots, chopped into large dice

2 zucchini, sliced in large chunks

2 tablespoons fresh chopped cilantro

3–4 Sierra cups water, to rehydrate

Salt

Canajoharie, N.Y.
The Rocky Walls of the Canajoharie

at home

1. Wash the split peas and soak in cold water while you're preparing the other ingredients.

2. Drain the split peas, spoon into a large pot along with the serranos, garlic, ginger, and turmeric, and cover with the water. Bring to a boil, lower the heat to a simmer, and cook till very soft, about 40 minutes. It's okay if the split peas have disintegrated before your wondering eyes.

3. When cooled down but still warm, place in a blender or food processor and purée to a smooth paste. Pour into a bowl and, if necessary, add enough water to make up 3 to 4 cups.

4. You've got the veggies and chopped and sliced, right? And the spices ready to go, right? Good. Cook the ghee in a large frying pan over medium-high heat till it's hot, about 2 minutes. Spoon in the mustard seeds. As they begin to pop, about 5 seconds, quickly stir in the cumin seeds, then the onions. Sauté

a minute or two — it's okay if the onion begins to brown — then stir in the tomatoes and eggplant. After 2 minutes or so, just long enough to coat and blend the ingredients, add the cauliflower and carrots. Mix well.

5. Add the puréed split peas and the salt into the veggie mixture. Stir everything together and cook slowly over medium heat till the veggies are soft, 20 to 25 minutes. Ten minutes from home, add the zucchini. Remove from the heat, sprinkle the cilantro over all, and mix.

6. Spread on lined dehydrator trays and dry 10 to 12 hours, till the texture of your favorite desert floor.

at camp

7. Rehydrate with the water to cover. Bring to a boil and cook, stirring, till the stew is soft, 10 to 15 minutes. Add more salt to taste, if desired.

Serves 4

LENTILS AND DAL

Call us slow. We've been eating lentils, split peas, and dried beans for years but never knew until we began this book that together they're known as pulses. There are endless varieties, and in one Indian cookbook, we counted 11 just for starters. Dal refers to the split variety. Let's take each other's pulses, shall we?

Mung Beans & Red Lentils with Onions

Dried split mung beans are called moong dal. *Pair them with red lentils* (masoor dal) *and lots of Indian spices and onion, and you've got a simple, fragrant dish that can be made at home or at the campsite. The mung beans and red lentils are available at Indian markets or natural food stores, and sometimes supermarkets.*

½ pound dried split mung beans, or yellow split peas

½ pound red lentils

½ teaspoon turmeric

Salt

4 tablespoons ghee (see page 100)

Pinch asafetida (optional; see Indian Spices: What and Where?, page 57)

1 teaspoon cumin seeds

3 dried red chiles (red serranos or cayennes; see Handling Hot Chiles for precautions, page 37)

1 onion, sliced very thin

3–4 Sierra cups water, to rehydrate

at home

1. Wash and drain the dried mung beans and lentils, place in a large pot, cover with water, and add the turmeric. Bring to a boil, then lower the heat to a simmer. Partially cover and cook till tender, 30 to 40 minutes, stirring occasionally. Season with the salt to taste.

2. Meanwhile, melt the ghee over medium-high heat in a skillet; when hot, add, in order, the asafetida (if using), cumin seeds, and chiles. As soon as the chiles darken in color, just a few seconds, stir in the onion slices and sauté over medium heat, stirring till well coated and brown, about 5 minutes.

3. When the beans and lentils are done cooking, remove from the heat. Scrape the entire contents of the onion-chile skillet, including the melted ghee, into the beans and lentils pot (no need to drain); mix well, cover, and let stand away from the heat for 5 minutes.

4. Spread on lined trays and dehydrate 10 to 12 hours, till the consistency of the floor of the Gobi Desert — dark, dry, and pebbly.

at camp

5. To rehydrate, add the water to cover, bring to a boil, and cook down till the beans and lentils are tender, 10 to 15 minutes.

Note: To make this dish at the campsite, follow the same directions as above, remembering that it's hard to keep a pot of liquid simmering. Check the beans and lentils often to prevent overcooking.

Serves 3–4

[Chapter 3]

Noodles & Dumplings

There may be a people in the world who don't eat noodles, but we've never heard of them. Here's how it all must have started. A farmer took his grain to the mill. Out came flour. He got caught in the rain on the way home. The flour got wet. Trying to dry it in his hands, he began to roll, pull, and stretch the mass. Not much happened until, in his frustration, he tossed the strands into some boiling water, went to wash up, came back, forked the stuff out of the pot and, presto! Noodles and dumplings were born — in Europe, in Asia, in Africa, high in the Andes and down in the lowlands. And if you don't believe this, go make up your own tale. We'll buy it.

Asian Soup Noodles 🏠🔥

We started out calling these "Chinese soup noodles" (tang mian), then "Vietnamese soup noodles" (phô), then "Name a Country of Your Choice" noodles. Any of the following will work just fine: Chinese egg noodles, or wheat noodles, thick or thin; Chinese, Vietnamese, and Southeast Asian rice noodles; rice flake noodles; rice sticks or vermicelli; or bean starch vermicelli. Thinner noodles "eat" better than thicker ones in soups. You get to cook noodles in different ways. Boil some noodles, notably egg or wheat varieties; soak some in hot water, such as rice sticks or rice vermicelli; still others, just toss in the pot with no preparation, such as mung bean vermicelli. You can find a useful Asian noodle "thesaurus" with illustrations online (see Resources, page 224).

2 baby bok choy

1 small Napa cabbage

2 bunches scallions

2 carrots

1 package (2.1 ounces) dried tofu

Chicken or vegetable broth (see pages 26 and 27; homemade bouillon cubes work fine [see page 28]; so does plain water)

1 package (12–16 ounces) Chinese wheat noodles

1 spoon low-sodium soy sauce

½ spoon sesame oil or hot pepper oil (optional)

Salt and ground black pepper

at home

1. Cut the bok choy in large shreds and the Napa cabbage in large chunks. Roughly cut the scallions. Slice the carrots into ½-inch rounds and parboil in a small pot for 3 minutes.

2. Dehydrate all veggies on lined trays, 5 to 10 hours, till the texture is that of dried leaves, with carrot checkers.

at camp

3. Prepare the tofu according to the directions on the package. Cut into large squares and reserve.

4. Prepare the broth in a large pot. If using bouillon cubes, add 5 or 6 to the boiling water. If using plain water, don't fret; the veggies will enrich the water as they rehydrate. Bring the broth to a boil.

5. Ladle the dehydrated veggies into the broth and return to a boil. Add the noodles, soy sauce, and oil, if using, and season with the salt and pepper to taste. When the noodles are soft, about 5 minutes depending on thickness, remove the pot from the heat and ladle in the tofu squares.

6. Serve this dish in Sierra cups with lots of the broth.

Serves 3–4

Variations

• Add dried bean sprouts to the veggie mix.

• We don't make beef broth bouillon cubes, but you can, and if you do, use them as a base rather than chicken or vegetable stock.

• Add dehydrated chicken stew. The chicken will take longer to rehydrate than any of the other ingredients, so begin with that. In this case, you won't need any bouillon cubes, as the stew will give the broth flavor.

The Pasta Universe

Go to your local market and count the kinds of pasta available. We did. Ours is no fine-foods-gourmet-specialties place, just your average workaday supermarket. Here's what we found.

Acini di pepe	Fettuccine	Penne rigate
Angel hair	Fusilli	Perciatelli
Capellini	Lasagne	Rigatoni
Ditalini	Linguine	Rotini
Elbows	Orecchiette	Spaghetti
Farfalle	Orzo	Stortini
Farfalline	Penne	Ziti

Point made. "Pasta" is a generic term. For that matter, "macaroni" is too. So live a little. Take something different into the wilderness. Match it with one of our — or your own — sauces (pages 84–89).

Chinese Cold Noodles *(Liang Mian)* 🏠🔥

It gets so hot in parts of China that three of its cities are known as the "three furnaces of China." (We'll tell you which cities they are after you've tried this recipe.) Your options in the summer months there are to complain, sweat, and eat well. The Chinese have developed these into a fine art, though we assume you don't need any lessons in complaining or sweating. So let's concentrate on eating well in the high heat. Enter Liang Mian.

The key here is a sesame-soy marinade, and since you don't want to pack a container of marinade into the back-country, we've devised two ways to do end runs around the weight problem. (Of course, if you're car camping or canoeing you can haul along a barrel of the marinade and bathe in it for all we care.) The ingredients are the same; the methods, slightly different.

marinade

- 4 tablespoons sesame oil
- 4 tablespoons low-sodium soy sauce
- 1 tablespoon Chinese chili oil (such as Yank Sing Spiced Chili Oil)
- 1 tablespoon rice wine vinegar
- 2 cloves garlic, chopped fine
- 1 piece of fresh ginger, 1 inch long, chopped fine
- ½ tablespoon sugar
- Salt

noodles

- 3 Chinese or Japanese eggplants (small Italian eggplants work well, too)
- 10–12 Chinese snow peas, trimmed
- 1 carrot, sliced into thin "sticks" about 3 inches long
- 1 package (14 ounces) Chinese egg noodles (or any other very thin noodle)
- 1–2 Sierra cups water, to rehydrate
- 8–10 Sierra cups water, for boiling the noodles
- Small amount of cooking oil for greasing trays, if using Method 2

Method 1

at home

1. To make the marinade, whisk the sesame oil, soy sauce, chili oil, and vinegar in a bowl. Add the garlic, ginger, sugar, and salt (sparingly; the soy sauce is already salty). Mix well and set aside.

2. Preheat the oven to 400°F.

3. Poke the eggplants in several places with a fork. Roast on a baking sheet in the oven till soft to the touch, about 20 minutes. Remove.

4. When cool enough to handle, slice the eggplants lengthwise and remove the innards by using your fingers or a table knife. Give the eggplant entrails (there's no other word for them) a chop or two with a knife, then place them in the marinade. Set aside.

5. You can skip this step if you're short on time, but parboiling will enhance the flavor. In a small pot, parboil first the snow peas, no more than 30 seconds, then the carrot sticks, no more than 3 minutes. Drain, then run under cold water to stop the cooking.

6. Dehydrate the snow peas and carrots 45 minutes to 1 hour, till hard.

7. Spread the marinade-soaked eggplant on lined trays and dehydrate for 10 to 12 hours. Double bag in airtight bags. (The eggplant will be crisp but the marinade still clinging to it will not; hence, the need to double bag. This will be heavier than the usual dehydrated veggies, but well worth it.)

8. Don't forget to pack the noodles!

at camp

9. Rehydrate the eggplant in lightly boiling water to cover, stirring gently to prevent sticking. When the eggplant is soft and the sauce that results is thickened, about 10 minutes, remove from the heat.

10. Rehydrate the snow peas and carrots by pouring boiling water over them just to cover and letting them sit, covered, till soft. This will take only 1 to 2 minutes. Drain and set aside.

11. Boil the noodles in a large pot till soft, 3 to 5 minutes. These noodles cook fast, so be careful not to overcook them. Drain and set aside to cool. (If by the time you're ready to apply the eggplant and marinade the noodles have become stuck together, give them a quick bath in a pot of cold water. Use your hands to "wash" them gently. They'll unstick, and you can then remove them and apply the eggplant marinade directly.)

12. Stir the eggplant and marinade into the noodles, making sure the noodles are thoroughly coated and the eggplant is fully incorporated.

13. Scatter the snow peas and carrots over the noodles; mix well and serve. Slurp away with your chopsticks or forks, and quickly, or you won't get anything to eat. These things move fast.

(Method 2 on next page)

Method 2

In this version, you'll make the marinade at the campsite.

at home

1. Follow steps 2–7 in Method 1, except for the instruction to place the roasted eggplant in the marinade. Also, because you'll be dehydrating the eggplant without marinade, lightly oil the trays.

2. In separate airtight bags, store the equivalent of 4 tablespoons of soy sauce granules or powder (see Resources, page 224), the garlic, ginger, sugar, and salt.

3. Pour the sesame oil, vinegar, and chili oil into a small plastic bottle — an aspirin or pill container with a tight-fitting lid works well. (Sesame and chili oil are much heavier than other oils, so it's fine to take less than the recommended amount here. Two tablespoons of sesame oil and ½ tablespoon chili oil will achieve close to the same effect.)

4. Don't forget to pack the noodles!

at camp

5. Rehydrate the eggplant in water to cover. Bring to a slow boil, stirring occasionally. When it is soft, 5 to 7 minutes, set aside to cool. When cool, pull the strands apart and set aside in a covered Sierra cup.

6. Follow steps 10 and 11 in Method 1.

7. To make the marinade, rehydrate the soy sauce according to the package directions, and add the sesame oil-vinegar-chili oil mixture. Mix the soy sauce mixture with the garlic, ginger, sugar, salt, and rehydrated eggplant. When fully mixed, pour over the noodles and mix well. (For best results and fun, use your hands.)

8. Garnish with the snow peas and carrots. Mix into the noodles with chopsticks or forks and slurp away.

Note: And now for the promised Chinese furnaces. They are, running east to west up the Yangzi River: Nanjing, Wuhan, and Chongqing (which you used to know as "Chungking").

Serves 4

The Spice Rack

Rick can't leave home without enough cayenne pepper to bring tears to the eyes of the stoniest book critic. Hal's relationship with cumin can't be discussed in a family cookbook. Rick's daughter Nicole wouldn't think of sipping her hot chocolate unless it was sprinkled with cinnamon. In the old days, we tried bringing a gazillion small sandwich bags of spices to accommodate everyone's individual tastes. It was a disaster. With constant use, the lightweight bags opened and tore, invariably pouring their contents into a congealed mass of baking powder, oregano, and somebody's misplaced crumbled Viagra. Luckily, modern medicine came to our aid. You can't go into a drugstore without passing a large display of pillboxes, each with at least seven individual containers. Each daily pill container is just right for the dollops of cinnamon, pepper, paprika, and other life-enhancing items you need. Just be sure to wrap the whole shebang tightly in adhesive tape to prevent the little tops from opening in your pack.

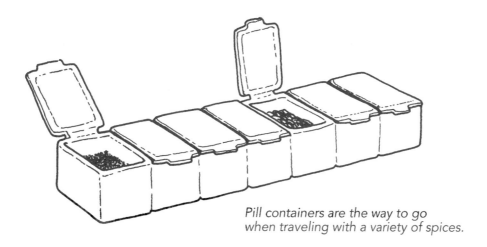

Pill containers are the way to go when traveling with a variety of spices.

Chinese Stir-Fried Noodles (Chao Mian) 🏠 🔥

When Hal first encountered Buwei Yang Chao, the cookbook writer, she was standing in the doorway of her house smoking a cigar and holding a bottle of brandy. She was the one who pointed out that when we say "chow mein," we're speaking English. It refers to those dry, crunchy noodle-things we all grew up on, thinking we were eating Chinese. Uh-unh. Real stir-fried noodles neither look nor taste like chow mein. So for something entirely different, let's do chao mian. (Try saying "chow myen.")

These noodles are not deep-fried, but wet noodles on a hot pan still need plenty of lubricating. Unless you have a nonstick and very large pan, make 'em in small servings and repeat to feed the entire crowd.

3 baby bok choy or 1 medium-sized bok choy

1 small Napa cabbage

2 bunches scallions

2 carrots

2 cloves garlic, chopped fine

6–8 Sierra cups water, to boil the noodles

1 package Chinese wheat or egg noodles (roughly 12 ounces)

2–3 Sierra cups water, to rehydrate

5 spoons vegetable or peanut oil

1 spoon low-sodium soy sauce (optional)

½ spoon sesame oil (optional)

at home

1. Cut the bok choy in large shreds and the Napa cabbage in large chunks. Roughly cut the scallions. Slice the carrots into ½-inch rounds and in a small saucepan, parboil 3 minutes.

2. Dehydrate on lined trays, 5 to 10 hours, till flaky, or, in the case of the carrots, hard like little orange checkers.

at camp

3. Rehydrate the veggies in warm water till soft, 2 to 3 minutes; 5 minutes for carrots (you may wish to rehydrate these separately). Wring or press dry and set aside with the chopped garlic.

4. Bring the water to a boil in a large pot. If the pot is large enough, place all the noodles in the boiling water. If not, do this in two steps. When soft, in 5 to 7 minutes, remove the noodles from the water and immerse in a pot of cold water (to stop the cooking and prevent the noodles from sticking together.) Remove and keep in another pot or on a plate.

5. In a frying pan, heat 2 spoons of the oil. Divide the noodles into four clumps. Fry two of the clumps on one side till just brown. Turn them over and do the same. The idea here is to brown the outside but keep the inside noodles soft. Transfer to a plate and fry the other two portions in two more spoons of the oil. Transfer these to a plate as well.

6. Add the remaining spoon of oil to the pan and fry up the veggies quickly, about 2 minutes. Some people think you have to have soy sauce in your meal to make it Chinese. T'aint true, but if you like it and have some handy, you can add a spoon as the veggies are frying.

7. Place the veggies on top of the noodles and serve. If you want to add a touch more flavor, dribble ½ spoon sesame oil over the veggies and noodles before eating.

8. Say five times fast, "Chao mian not chow mein."

Serves 4

Japanese Cold Noodles *(Zaru Soba)* 🏠 🔥

What we're trying to say in this book is, "Break out." The world doesn't end at the spaghetti factory. Live a little. Try something different. And in the heat of a summer noon, head for the deep shade and a lunch of cold Japanese noodles. Soba are Japanese buckwheat noodles, and zaru soba means "noodles in a basket" — those pretty lacquered boxes lined with slatted bamboo or rush mats, the traditional way in which this dish is served. Unless you're the most refined Japanophile ever to hit a mountain trail, you're not going to have the basket in this dish, but you can still have your soba. Or, if you prefer, the wheat noodle equivalent, udon. You can find soba and udon in many supermarkets these days, or in health food or Asian food shops.

1 bunch scallions, chopped

1 small 3- to 4-inch piece of daikon, grated and dehydrated (optional)

1 tablespoon instant dashi granules (called *dashi-no-moto* or *hon-dashi*)

2 tablespoons low-sodium soy sauce (½ cup worth reconstituted powdered or granulated soy sauce works fine)

2 tablespoons sweet cooking sake *(mirin)*

½ spoon sugar

1 sheet toasted Japanese seaweed *(nori)*

2–4 teaspoons powdered wasabi, or to taste

½–¾ pound packaged soba

8–10 Sierra cups water (5–6 for boiling, 4 for the *dashi*, and a tiny amount for reconstituting the wasabi)

6–8 Sierra cups cold water

at home

1. Dehydrate the scallions and daikon (if using), about 1 hour. Seal in an airtight bag. Pack separately the dashi granules, soy sauce, cooking sake, sugar, seaweed (take enough along for Sushi, page 124, and Japanese Tea and Rice, page 126), and wasabi (also enough for the sushi and tea-and-rice). If not using an entire package of noodles, put the amount you want in a large resealable bag and seal.

at camp

2. To make the noodles, boil the 5 to 6 Sierra cups water in your biggest pot. Add the noodles and boil till just soft, 5 to 7 minutes. Drain, then plunge the noodles into Sierra cups of the cold water till they are room temperature; this may take several changes of cold water. Set aside.

3. To make the dashi dipping sauce, place the 4 Sierra cups of water in a pot, bring to a boil, add the dashi granules, and immediately remove from the fire. Add the soy sauce, sake, and sugar.

4. Hold a sheet of seaweed very briefly over the flame to "roast" it. Cut it in slivers (the scissors on a Swiss Army knife are just the ticket here), or just crumble it onto a plate. Sprinkle over the cooled noodles just before eating.

5. To make the wasabi, add a tiny amount of water to a spoon of wasabi powder. Stir till a paste forms.

6. Pour the dipping sauce into Sierra cups. Add wasabi to the sauce to taste and mix well. Add the dried scallions and daikon. Using your chopsticks — you brought them instead of forks, didn't you? — lift some noodles into the dipping sauce and eat. When you are finished, say politely to the cook, "Gochiso-sama deshita," which is sort of the equivalent of "Ta, mate."

Serves 4

Japanese Ingredients

The *dashi* in the ingredients list is the all-purpose Japanese soup stock. Unless you're carrying a great slab of dried fillet of bonito and a whopping amount of dried giant kelp amidships in your canoe, you're going to rely on the instant variety, which just about everybody in Japan does these days, too. It's great, and because a little goes a very long way, you can stock up for the next few eons practically for pocket change. You'll find it in some supermarkets, in Asian food shops, and through the Internet. Just search using the term "dashi-no-moto," and plenty of vendors will appear. The *mirin* in the ingredients is a sweet cooking sake that can also be found in a growing number of supermarkets, in Asian food shops, and obtained through the Internet, as can *nori*, toasted Japanese seaweed. (See Resources, pages 224–25, for Internet vendors.) Daikon, Japanese white radish, and powdered wasabi, Japanese horseradish, are now available in most supermarkets.

Japanese Wheat Noodles (Udon) 🏠 🔥

Like your noodles hot rather than cold? This recipe uses the same dipping sauce as in the Japanese Cold Noodles recipe (page 72). The shichimi *in the ingredients is a mixture of seven dried spices: red pepper flakes, brown pepper pods, dried mandarin orange peel, black hemp seeds or white poppy seeds, seaweed bits, and white sesame seeds. It's sold under one of several names:* shichimi, shichimi togarashi, *or just* togarashi, *and comes in degrees of spiciness, including mild, medium, and hot. If it's not in your local market, search the Internet under "shichimi," "seven-spice mixture," or "Japanese spices."*

1 bunch scallions, chopped

1 small 3- to 4-inch piece of daikon, grated (optional)

14 Sierra cups water (4 for making the dipping sauce, 10 for boiling the noodles)

1 spoon instant dashi granules

2 spoons low-sodium soy sauce

2 spoons sweet cooking sake (*mirin*)

½ spoon sugar

½–¾ pound packaged udon

6–8 Sierra cups cold water

1 packet (3 ounces) seven-spice mixture (*shichimi*)

at home

1. Dehydrate the scallions and daikon (if using) for about 1 hour, till reduced to a flaky, weightless handful of green nothingness.

at camp

2. To make the dashi dipping sauce, place 4 Sierra cups of water in a pot, bring to a boil, add the dashi granules, and immediately remove from the fire. Add the soy sauce, cooking sake, and sugar.

3. To make the noodles, boil 10 Sierra cups water in a large pot and cook according to the directions on the package.

4. If you have the time, follow the Japanese custom of rinsing the cooked noodles in cold water to get rid of the starch, then set them back in boiling water just long enough to heat them up.

5. Provide a common pot for the dipping sauce, or pour it into individual Sierra cups. Sprinkle the dehydrated scallions and daikon into the dipping sauce. Sprinkle the seven-spice mixture over the noodles, dip, and eat.

Serves 4

Variation: Make a thick broth. While the dipping sauce is heating up, mix 1 spoon of cornstarch (or *kuzu*, a natural thickening agent from a Japanese vine plant) with 1 spoon of warm water, and add to the dipping sauce as it's cooking. Stir to thicken. Pour over the udon noodles and sprinkle on the dehydrated scallions and seven-spice mix. This is known as *ankake udon.*

Rick's Quick Pad Thai Sauce 🏠

If store-bought satay sauce seems a little greasy, that's because it is probably made with peanut butter. Here is a quick version you can make on your own, with a lot more personality and a lot less oil.

½ cup unsalted roasted peanuts

½ cup coconut milk

2 tablespoons sugar

1 teaspoon garlic, chopped

1 teaspoon onion, chopped

1 teaspoon garam masala (see page 58)

1 teaspoon hot pepper oil

1 teaspoon low-sodium soy sauce

1 teaspoon tamarind sauce

1. Place the peanuts in a dry blender or food processor. Blend to a coarse powder. Pour the powder into a small mixing bowl.

2. Blend together the coconut milk, sugar, garlic, onion, garam masala, hot pepper oil, soy sauce, and tamarind sauce in another small bowl till smooth.

3. Pour the coconut milk mixture into the peanut powder. Stir with a spoon till mixed thoroughly. Store in the fridge for up to 3 weeks in a small plastic bottle or container with a tight-fitting lid. Don't forget to take it with you! We usually use it within the first 3 to 5 days of our trip.

Makes about ½ cup, enough for 2 servings of Vegetarian Pad Thai (see page 76)

ABURAGE

You'll find *aburage* — fried bean curd — in plastic bags in the refrigerated section of Asian markets. We've had great success using it on backpacking trips, even though it tends to spoil fairly quickly. Use it on the first or second day of camping. Pack the plastic container in a resealable plastic bag.

One great use for aburage is making fox noodles. Simmer a small cake of aburage in dashi dipping sauce (see facing page) as it's cooking, then use it to top cooked Japanese Wheat Noodles (see facing page).

Another use for aburage is to slit open one end and stuff it with cooked sushi rice. Tie up the little "bag" with a piece of string or a strip of dried gourd (*kampyo*), which our friend Ed always brings along as an emergency shoelace. Pop the entire thing in dashi dipping sauce and heat it up. These are called "golden purses."

Vegetarian Pad Thai (Thai Rice Noodles) 🏠 🔥

Rice noodles are the chameleons of the noodle world, absorbing whatever flavorings they contact. In pad thai, the noodles bask in a sauce that is sweet, sour, and tangy. As you start to dig in, you'll find that the noodles are hot, the bean sprouts are cold, and the chopped peanuts are crunchy, giving the dish a variety of textures as well as flavors.

There are as many secret pad thai sauces as there are street vendors in Thailand. We mix up the sauce in advance and bring it along in a small liquid container. Nonvegetarians might want to use fish sauce instead of soy. Desperate campers have been known to use peanut butter, lemonade mix, ketchup, and soy packets (from the local mall), and black pepper. But you didn't hear that from us.

1 pound sliced onion

1 pound sliced tomato

½ pound sliced mushrooms

6 Sierra cups water, for boiling, rehydrating, and soaking

8 ounces pad thai rice noodles

4–6 heaping spoons (2 eggs' worth) powdered eggs (reconstituted according to package instructions)

1 spoon vegetable oil

2 cloves garlic, chopped

3 spoons Rick's Quick Pad Thai Sauce (see box on page 75)

¼ pound mung bean sprouts

¼ Sierra cup chopped peanuts

at home

1. Spread the sliced onions, tomatoes, and mushrooms on drying trays and dehydrate until crisp-hard, 6 to 10 hours.

at camp

2. Boil 4 Sierra cups of the water in a large pot. Place the dried vegetables in a second pot or Sierra cup. Pour 1 Sierra cup of the boiling water over the veggies to rehydrate them. Remove the veggies after about 5 minutes (once they are soft) and drain.

3. Place the rice noodles in a third pot. Add enough of the remaining boiling water to cover the rice noodles, about 2 cups. Soak the noodles for exactly 4 minutes. Drain the noodles and cover them with 2 Sierra cups cold water.

4. Heat the vegetable oil in a pan and scramble the eggs. Place them on a plate. Add the garlic and the veggies to the pan and sauté for about 1 minute, till heated through. Remove the pan from the heat.

5. Use your hand to scoop up the cold noodles and set them into the pan on top of the veggies. Pour the sauce on top of the noodles and gently mix. Gently move the pan back over the heat to warm the whole mixture. Be careful: If the pan gets too hot, the noodles will congeal.

6. Once the mixture is warm, about 2 minutes, remove the pan from the heat, add the eggs, sprouts, and chopped peanuts, stir, and serve.

Serves 2

Lydia's Instant Dumplings 🔥

To learn how our friend Lydia Itoi overcame the Great Dumpling Fiasco largely by ignoring our advice and refusing to take no for an answer, see "Lydia's Chicken Stew" (page 44). If you'd rather skip heartwarming tales for stomach-warming fare, keep on reading.

The dry ingredients for the dumplings can be combined in an airtight bag before leaving home.

¾ cup flour

4 teaspoons powdered egg whites

1 tablespoon dried herbs de Provence

1 teaspoon baking powder

¾ teaspoon salt

½ teaspoon paprika

　Dash cayenne pepper

1 tablespoon oil or clarified butter (see page 99)

4–6 Sierra cups water, if not using a stew

1. In a small pot or pot lid, mix the powdered egg whites, herbs de Provence, baking powder, salt, paprika, cayenne, oil, and enough dribbles of water to form a thick paste with the consistency of biscuit dough. Drop by spoonfuls into boiling soup or stew (see chapter 2) or the water.

2. Cover tightly and cook 12 to 15 minutes without lifting the lid. When done, the dumplings should be fluffy, with no trace of raw-flour taste.

Serves 4 adults (makes 8–10 small dumplings)

DUMPLINGS

Campers are always on the lookout for that great outdoor oxymoron, lightweight rib-sticking food. Dumplings does it. (Do it?) Grammar aside, they meet all the criteria and answer all the questions, including, "Why didn't somebody tell me about this sooner?"

Matzo Balls 🔥

Rick's grandmother once said of backpacking, "You look up, you see a tree; you look down, you see a rock. So, what's new?" Hal's grandmother regarded the wilderness as an overcrowded boardwalk. Wherever they are now, they must at least be mollified that Those Nice Boys are eating well and not starving overnight outside in the cold. So, Grannies, this recipe's for you.

The matzo meal, salt, parsley, pepper, and nutmeg can be combined in an airtight bag before leaving home. Don't worry if the parsley dries out.

1 Sierra cup boiling water

1 Sierra cup matzo meal

1 tablespoon chopped parsley

1 teaspoon salt

Dash freshly ground black pepper

Dash ground nutmeg

2 spoons oil or clarified butter

1 egg or equivalent powdered egg mix

1. Combine the boiling water, matzo meal, parsley, salt, pepper, and nutmeg in a large pot. Stir till the water is absorbed.

2. Add the oil (our apologies to purists who insist on rendered chicken fat) and the egg. Mix well.

3. If time permits, chill for 1 hour to make the mixture easier to form into balls. To chill, set the covered pot in cold mountain water, deep shade, or your cooler if car camping.

4. For best results, wet your hands in cold water. Shape the mixture into small balls. Drop no more than four or five of the balls into boiling water, then (try to) reduce the heat to a simmer and cook, covered, till the balls rise to the surface, about 10 minutes. (They will swell as they simmer, so don't crowd the pot.) Repeat to cook any remaining matzo balls. You can eat them plain or add them to a hot soup or stew as they come out of the pot.

Serves 4–6 (Makes up to 18 small matzo balls)

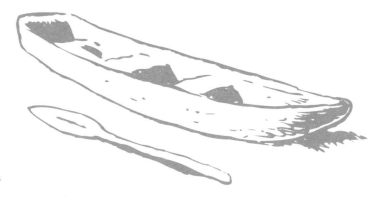

Chinese Boiled Dumplings (Jiaozi) 🔥

(Depending on what you decide to fill these dumplings with, you may have to make preparations at home, too.)

Traditionally, these dumplings are eaten with a mix of soy sauce, vinegar, and, if you're so inclined, a dab of hot sauce. One of the salsa recipes (pages 91–94) would be a perfect substitute. Hal prefers his with chocolate icing, but he eats everything with chocolate icing and is not to be followed in this appalling practice. Enjoy.

1 Sierra cup flour, plus more for dusting your fingers

½ Sierra cup water, for making the dough

Pinch salt

Filling (see Chinese Steamed Dumplings, page 80, and Other Dumpling Fillings, page 81)

6–8 Sierra cups water, for boiling

1½ Sierra cups cold water, for cooling the boiling water

1. Mix the flour, ½ Sierra cup water, and salt together to make a moist but firm dough. Knead it till the dough is smooth and pliable, 5 to 10 minutes.

2. Dust your fingers with flour. Pull off a small amount of dough and form it into a ball that fits nicely in your palm. Press the ball down into your palm with your thumb and begin to work it into a thin circle somewhat larger than your palm. This is the dumpling wrapper. Set the wrapper on a floured plate. Repeat till all the wrappers are formed.

3. Using a spoon or chopsticks, take a small amount of the filling and set in the center of the wrapper. Spread the filling evenly toward each edge of the circle of dough, but not all the way to it. Fold one half of the circle of dough over the filling till it meets the edges of the other half. Using your fingers, crimp the edges together so that they resemble the edge on a piecrust. Set aside and repeat till all the dumplings are filled and sealed.

Crimped edges of a boiled dumpling wrapper

4. To cook, bring the 6 to 8 Sierra cups water to a boil and, if possible, reduce to a simmer. Place the dumplings in the water. Allow the water to return to a boil. Pour in ½ Sierra cup of cold water. Return to a boil again. Repeat this twice more. The dumplings are done.

Serves 2–3 (Makes 4–6 dumplings)

Chinese Steamed Dumplings *(Baozi)* 🔥

At some point or other, you've probably had those barbecued pork dumplings in the local dim sum joint. Those kinds of dumplings aren't boiled, they're steamed. And once you get the hang of using our improvised campsite steamer (pages 220–221) and making the dumpling dough (see Lydia's Instant Dumplings, page 77), you're in business. All you need is the filling, rehydrated from your veggie and fruit stash and possibly from the trout you've just caught.

filling

- 2 leeks, cut into ¼-inch rounds, white part only
- 1 cup sliced mushrooms
- 1 packed cup spinach leaves, washed
- 1 small or medium onion, sliced in ¼-inch rounds
- ½ spoon low-sodium soy sauce
- Few drops sesame oil (optional)
- Salt and ground black pepper

dough

- ¾ cup flour, plus more for dusting the plate
- 4 teaspoons powdered egg whites
- 1 tablespoon oil or clarified butter (see page 99)
- 1 teaspoon baking powder
- ¾ teaspoon salt

rehydrating

- 4–6 Sierra cups water

at home

1. Dehydrate the leeks, mushrooms, spinach, and onions for 10 to 12 hours, till crumbly and desiccated.

at camp

2. Rehydrate the dried veggies by pouring the boiling water over them, allowing to stand 15 to 20 minutes. Press dry and chop fine.

3. Add the soy sauce, sesame oil (if using), and salt and pepper to taste to the veggies. Mix well.

4. Lightly flour a plate. Prepare the dumpling wrappers by mixing the dough ingredients and enough dribbles of the rehydrating water to make up to eight disks of dough. Set the wrappers on the plate.

5. Fill the disks one at a time. To do this, take a tiny amount of filling in your fingers, chopsticks, or spoon; place it in the middle of the disk; and close the dumpling around itself, pinching the top (see illustrations, facing page). These are miniature dumplings, so you won't need much filling per dumpling.

6. Steam the dumplings till done, 10 to 15 minutes. Test for doneness by tasting one. If sticky or floury, it ain't done.

Serves 2–4

Dumpling dough with filling in middle

First fold

Second fold

Finished dumpling

Other Dumpling Fillings

- Poached trout combined with some of the veggies

- A mix of poached trout and shiitake mushrooms

- A mix of rehydrated dried Chinese lilies (ask for "golden needles," *jinzhen cai*, in the local oriental food shop or order on the Internet; rehydrate these separately and change the water till it runs clear to rinse out the bitter taste); shiitake mushrooms; Chinese wood ears, *mu'er*, those black fungus shards you find in lots of Chinese stir-fried dishes; and Chinese vermicelli noodles, made from bean starch. Thanks to Tobie Meyer-Fong for this vegetarian delight.

- Curries: Mustard and Cumin Veggies, page 54; Lamb with Spinach, page 56; Spinach and Onion (page 53).

- Stewed fruits (see Fruit Cobbler, pages 200–1), for sweet dumplings

- Cranberry-Cherry Sauce (page 90), Apple Butter (pages 104–5), or Marmalade (page 102).

Hands On: Cleanliness? Godliness?

The English distinguish between dirt and earth. Dirt is what's inside, earth is what's outside. So every time you look at your hands while cooking in the wilderness, just remember, that's earth, not dirt on them, and that's okay. You won't perish from this earth or infect the entire west flank of the Great Smoky Mountains. And unless you pack along a mighty large vacuum cleaner with a very long cord, you'll find all that earth is quite hard to get rid of. Our advice is just to kick back and enjoy it.

People who use camp stoves may come back from their vacations looking a bit cleaner and tidier than those who cook by campfire. But those of us who love cooking over an open fire invariably return to civilization looking like chimney sweeps straight out of Dickens. Ash, pot black, and charred wood add a lovely layer of grime to hands and, inevitably, to ears, nose, cheeks, and brows as you swat at a miscreant mosquito or wipe away the tears of joy after making that perfect quiche or persimmon bread. Our smudged and blackened shirts and pants routinely defy all known brands of laundry detergent after we return home, and thus serve to remind us year-round of the rewards of a camping trip well spent.

What about handling food? Well, it's going to take on a patina of its own. Bread and pastry dough may look like the darkening cloud on the horizon, but once baked will take on the hues of the sunset or rainbow or the golden glow in your heart. So fuggedaboutit. It's all right if you find a few stray pine needles in your pumpkin pancakes. Don't worry about that small piece of bark in your polenta. If you see it and pick it off your plate, you probably have better eyesight than Rick and Hal put together. If you don't see it and then notice something extra chewy in your soufflé, consider it a portion of all-important fiber in your diet. However you slice it, if you cook outdoors, the outdoors will invariably end up in your cooking. Don't fret. We're on a vacation here.

Go flip that pizza.

[Chapter 4]

Sauces & Schmeers

You don't need to know this, but why not? Before the invention of the icebox, sauces were meant to kill tastes (of rotting foods), not enhance them. We both own fridges, however, so trust us, we're talking enhancement here. Your pastas shall not be deprived. If they are, we've done something wrong. And if you stop to argue that salsa isn't a sauce, you'll be wasting your breath and a good meal.

What about schmeers? Schmeer (from the German for, you should pardon the expression, "grease" or "bribe") is just another word for something good to spread on or over other foods. It's a lovely all-inclusive word, so we use it to cover chutneys, butters, marmalades, yogurts, glazes, and frostings. 'Nuf said?

PASTA SAUCES

How many pasta sauces warm the heart? Let us tell you. You can find whole books — multi-volume tomes, for crying out loud — just on pasta sauces. So, as you're now committed to trying the zillion or so different pastas and macaronis (see The Pasta Universe, page 65), you're also ready for more than Mama Malatesta's Marinara Sauce or whatever it's called in your local market. Sure, the commercial brands work. They dry and re-hy well. But would you want Luciano Pavarotti and the entire La Scala chorus to show up at your campsite with that? Right. So here's a starter set. After that, mail us your own inventions.

Fastest Sauce in the West

This is just the ticket for someone who really, really wants to get out of the kitchen. We'll time it as we go along. Result? Your basic tomato sauce, the real soldier in the trenches.

- 4 cloves garlic, chopped fine or crushed through a garlic press
- ½ medium onion, roughly chopped
- 2 tablespoons olive oil
- 1 medium can (14 ounces) plum tomatoes plus juice
- 1½ cups whole pitted black olives
- 3–4 tablespoons capers, drained
   Salt and freshly ground black pepper
   Chopped parsley
- 2 Sierra cups water, to rehydrate

at home

1. Peel and crush the garlic; let's say it takes you 90 seconds. Chop the onion, for another 60 seconds. That's 2½ minutes.

2. Heat the olive oil in a large frying pan or heavy-bottomed saucepan, 10 seconds.

3. Sauté the garlic and onion until the onion is just translucent, about 2 minutes. So far, 40 seconds.

4. Stir in the tomatoes and juice from the can, the olives, capers, and salt and pepper to taste, 10 seconds.

5. Cook, stirring and breaking up the tomatoes with a wooden spoon, for 5 minutes. Remove from the heat.

6. Stir in the parsley, 5 seconds. Finito! Nine minutes 55 seconds.

7. Lightly spray lined dehydrator trays with nonstick oil. Spoon the sauce onto the trays. Dry 10 to 12 hours, until the consistency of leather.

at camp

8. Rehydrate with the water to cover. Heat until soft, about 5 minutes. Adjust the seasonings.

Makes 1½ cups, enough for 2 people

Slowest Sauce in the West 🏠

In the old days, GIMs (Great Italian Mothers), like GJMs (Great Jewish Mothers) with their stewing hens, let the pasta sauce simmer for hours. By adding enough liquid when needed, they could keep the pot on the stove for days. So here's a long, slow visit to the past. If we had our druthers, we wouldn't give you precise measurements, just "enough chopped onions to make you weep" or "why stint on the tomatoes?" but our editors are looking over our shoulders as we write.

The ground beef may be omitted from this dish without adjusting the other ingredients.

3–4 tablespoons olive oil

2½ cups chopped onions (if they add up to 3, no one will notice)

3 cloves chopped garlic

1½ pounds ground beef (optional)

6 cups canned tomatoes plus juice (or 8 cups fresh, chopped)

3 tablespoons tomato paste

1 cup water or beef or vegetable stock (see page 27), plus extra to keep from sticking

1 cup dry red wine

1 bay leaf

2 teaspoons dried hot pepper flakes (optional)

Salt and freshly ground black pepper

4 tablespoons chopped Italian parsley

3 Sierra cups water, to rehydrate

at home

1. Heat the oil in a large, heavy-bottomed pot or Dutch oven. Sauté the onions and garlic until just soft but not browned, about 5 minutes.

2. Add the beef (if using) and cook, stirring, till no longer pink, about 10 minutes.

3. Crush the tomatoes roughly with a wooden spoon. Add them, the tomato paste, water, wine, bay leaf, pepper flakes (if using), and salt and pepper to taste to the beef mixture. Bring to a boil, immediately reduce the heat to a slow simmer, and cook, covered, for at least 1 hour and as long as 3 or 4 hours — whatever suits your fancy and sense of taste. Stir occasionally, making sure the sauce doesn't stick to the bottom of the pot or burn. Add water, stock, or wine as necessary. As the sauce simmers, it will thicken.

4. Thirty minutes before the cooking is finished, add the parsley.

5. Lightly oil the dehydrator trays. Spoon the sauce onto the trays and dry 10 to 15 hours, till the consistency of lumpy leather.

at camp

6. Rehydrate by adding the water to cover. Stir over low heat until soft and thickened, about 10 minutes.

Makes 4 cups, enough for 2–4 people

Look Ma, No-Oil Tomato Sauce 🏠

Remember Alice's Restaurant up in Stockbridge, Massachusetts, and the Moosewood Café in Ithaca, New York? This one's cut from their mold — gutsy, hippie, fresh-faced, and improvisatory — with a grateful nod to the great Mollie Katzen and her Vegetable Heaven *(Hyperion, 2000). Don't limit this sauce to pastas. Toss it on your scrambled eggs, line our pizza dough with it (pages 202–3), or pour it in your pocket and eat it on the switchbacks up to that 12,000-foot pass. (They're your pockets, not ours.)*

2 cups sun-dried tomatoes (NOT the ones packed in oil!)

1½ cups boiling water

¾ cup tightly packed fresh basil

¾ cup fresh Italian parsley, tightly packed (the standard American parsley is not as good here)

4 cloves garlic, peeled and roughly chopped

Salt

1–2 Sierra cups cold water, to rehydrate

at home

1. Place the sun-dried tomatoes in a large bowl. Pour the boiling water over the tomatoes and let them soak for 1 hour or more, till soft.

2. Using a blender on a low setting, chop the basil and parsley. Occasionally, turn the blender off and use a rubber spatula or a narrow wooden spoon to carefully nudge the uncut leaves into the blender's blades.

3. Add the tomatoes, the water they were soaking in, the garlic, and salt to taste to the basil and parsley in the blender jar. Purée until a smooth pesto-like paste results, 3 to 4 minutes.

4. Lightly oil the dehydrator trays. Spread the mixture onto the trays and dry for 8 to 10 hours, till the consistency of leather.

at camp

5. Rehydrate with just enough warm water to reconstitute the paste, about 15 minutes, without cooking. Stir occasionally to help the process along.

Makes more than 2 cups, enough for 2 people

Roasted Eggplant & Almond Sauce 🏠🔥

Say Savonarola's going to burn you at the stake unless you can come up with a reason for you and him to sit down and have a little something to eat. This is the life-saving formula. We can't prove it of course, but this sauce appears to have been the cause of the Renaissance.

3 Italian, Japanese, or Chinese eggplants (for a combined weight of 1 to 1½ pounds)

Handful almonds or walnuts

1½ cups Fastest Sauce in the West (see page 84)

Salt and freshly ground black pepper

1–2 Sierra cups boiling water, to rehydrate

2 eggs or equivalent powdered egg mix

Olive oil (optional)

at home

1. Preheat the oven to 400°F.

2. Poke the eggplants in several places with a fork. Roast them on a baking tray till very soft, 20 to 25 minutes. Test for softness by removing the tray from the oven and poking the eggplants with your finger. Remove from the heat.

3. Meanwhile, grind the nuts to a powder in a coffee grinder, or chop finely.

4. When the eggplant is cool enough to handle, scrape the insides into a bowl. Add the ground nuts, tomato sauce, and salt and pepper to taste. Mix.

5. Dehydrate on lined, lightly oiled trays for 10 to 15 hours, till thoroughly dry to the touch.

at camp

6. Rehydrate with the water to cover. Steep till soft and thick. If this requires more water, add it in small increments to retain thickness.

7. Meanwhile, boil the eggs the equivalent of 4 to 5 minutes at sea level (see chart, page 219). You're going to use the yolks (not the whites), and you want 'em barely hard.

8. Mash the egg yolks and add to the sauce, stirring them in well. If you're using powdered egg mix, which is conveniently all yolk and no white, add in the equivalent spoons.

9. If desired, drizzle a little bit of olive oil into the sauce before serving.

Makes 2+ cups, enough for 2–3 people

EGG WARNING

Eating eggs that are not completely cooked poses the possibility of salmonella food poisoning. The risk is greater for pregnant women, the elderly and very young, and people with impaired immune systems. If you are concerned about salmonella, you can use powdered egg mix or pasteurized eggs.

The Friday Night "Oh Man! I Forgot the Sauce" Sauce ⬢

It's Friday night. You're going to be at the campsite tomorrow evening, and pasta's the dinner of choice. Everything's packed. But…oh man, no sauce. Nothing's been dehydrated, cans are too heavy, and fresh tomatoes midway down your pack will transform this entire outing into a Cannery Row experience. The market's closing in half an hour. Get going, will you? (This is among our very favorite sauces. If you love it too, call us; if you hate it, call our publisher.)

The key to this sauce is sun-dried tomatoes. Because you don't have time to dry anything, you'll be carrying a fresh onion and fresh parsley. That's the only added weight — you were bringing garlic, cheese, oil, and salt and pepper anyway, right? — and you can afford it for the first night.

1 package (4 ounces) sun-dried tomatoes (not those packed in oil)

2–3 Sierra cups hot water

1 onion

2 cloves garlic

2 spoons olive or vegetable oil

Salt and ground black pepper

½ bunch fresh parsley, chopped

½ bottle (4 ounces) of capers, drained and sealed in an airtight bag

½ Sierra cup grated Parmesan

1. Soak the sun-dried tomatoes in the hot water in a medium-sized pot until soft, about 20 minutes. (If it's getting dark and cold, so will the water; thus, add hot water to the pot as needed.)

2. Chop the onion and garlic into rough pieces — remember, it will be a bit more challenging than usual with just your camping knife.

3. Heat the oil in a pan. Sauté the onion and garlic till the onion becomes translucent, about 3 minutes.

4. Stir the softened tomatoes with half their liquid into the onions and garlic.

Add the salt and pepper to taste. Continue cooking until the mixture becomes saucelike, 5 to 7 minutes.

5. In the last 2 minutes of cooking, add the parsley and capers.

6. Spoon over your pizza or pasta of choice and sprinkle with the Parmesan.

Makes 2 cups, enough for 2–3 people

White Sauce

The term white sauce usually brings to mind a stuffy maître d' with a thick French accent. It's not likely to conjure up an image of two scruffy campers in raggedy jeans who might well fail to meet the dress code at the local Dippin' Doughnuts shop. Yet such associations can be deceiving. For it turns out that this most sophisticated of sauces (also known as béchamel or cream sauce) is simple to make and uses only the most basic ingredients — butter, flour, milk, and the water you just finished using to poach fish or rehydrate vegetables (otherwise known as "stock").

2 spoons clarified butter, see page 99; (oil will also work)

2 spoons flour

1 spoon nonfat powdered milk

1 cup vegetable stock (see page 27) or poaching liquid (water will do in a pinch)

Salt and ground black pepper

1. Melt the clarified butter in a small pot. Add the flour. Stir over very low heat for about 1 minute, to get rid of the flour taste. Do not allow the mixture to burn. Remove from the heat.

2. Add the powdered milk and mix thoroughly. Slowly add the stock, stirring continuously, until the sauce is smooth. (A little more flour and a little less stock will yield a thicker sauce.) Season with the salt and pepper to taste.

Makes about 1 cup, enough for 1 soufflé (see page157)

Improv Theater: Cranberry–Cherry Sauce

We didn't set out to make this dish. Here's what happened. Our favorite Thanksgiving cranberry sauce is a cranberry chutney that beats the stuffing out of all other cranberry sauces ever invented. The recipe comes from an old newspaper clipping now barely legible for all the glop spilled on it over the years. We thought we'd try to make it at home and dehydrate it for the wilderness. We didn't expect to shoot a wild turkey, just to fress on this as a snack or as a complement to a grilled trout. Didn't work. The honey in the original never dried out (what were we thinking?). We left the mixture on the dehydrator for 2 days, then borrowed a paint scraper to peel the gunk off the tray. Back to the drawing board. Never underestimate the drawing board. Here's what we came up with, and we defy you or anybody else to try camping hereafter without making this best of all possible sweet sauces.

1 medium to large orange

6 fresh, ripe apricots

1 handful dried cranberries (commercial)

1 handful dried sour cherries (commercial)

2 large, tart apples

2–3 Sierra cups water to cover

¼ Sierra cup sugar

2 pinches cardamom (optional)

at home

1. Cut the orange into small rough bits, peel and all. Place on an unoiled dehydrator tray and dry for 10 to 15 hours, till leather-hard.

2. Halve the apricots and cut the apples into ¼-inch slices. Lightly oil the dehydrator trays and dry 10 to 15 hours, till stiff and hard.

at camp

3. Combine the dried oranges, apricots, cranberries, cherries, and apples in a large pot. Cover with the water and bring to a boil. As the mixture begins to thicken, in about 10 minutes, add the sugar and cardamom (if using). Continue to cook until the mixture has a jamlike consistency. Remove from the heat and let cool. Voilà, ambrosia! (So Escoffier never said that. Sue us.)

Serves 4

Salsa Ranchera Diana 🏠

Diana Kennedy, the great North American expert on Mexican cuisines, inspired this one.

2 large tomatoes

2 serrano or jalapeño chiles

1 clove garlic, peeled and roughly chopped

1 tablespoon vegetable oil

1 small onion, roughly chopped

Salt

¼–½ Sierra cup cold water, to rehydrate

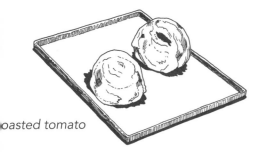

roasted tomato

at home

1. Roast the tomatoes by setting them under a broiler flame — not too close: use the middle oven shelf — and searing for about 20 minutes, turning frequently. The tomato skins should bubble and wrinkle. Don't worry if they emerge with blackened spots. No need to peel, seed, or chop them. Remove from the oven and place in a blender.

2. Toast the chiles in a small, hot iron fry pan till they are seared on all sides and softened, about 5 minutes. Slice the chiles into small bits and add to the blender, along with the garlic. Blend at the lowest speed for just a few seconds; you don't want the result to be too smooth.

3. Heat the oil in a large frying pan. Sauté the onion till translucent and just soft, about 3 minutes. Add the contents of the blender and the salt to taste. Simmer until the sauce begins to thicken, about 5 minutes.

4. Spread on a lined, lightly oiled dehydrator tray (or use a fruit-roll insert). Dehydrate till the salsa is dry to the touch, 7 to 10 hours.

at camp

5. Rehydrate by adding the cold water. Let sit for about 20 minutes, then stir and eat.

Makes 1 cup

SALSA SURVIVAL

Hal's got his huevos rancheros, his quesadillas, and his baked or poached trout; Rick's got his chocolate chip cookies. So we need salsa, right? *Si.* There are as many salsas as there are nations, regions, traditions, and chiles in the southern hemisphere. And they all dry well and rehydrate easily. Commercial salsas can be terrific, so if you don't want to mess with broiled tomatoes and toasted chiles and peeled tomatillos and life-giving garlic and cilantro, open a jar of your favorite, red or green, and spread it on a lined tray. Ten to 15 hours later, you'll have a fine dried salsa. Rehydrate with a little water and call in the mariachis. But for the do-it-yourself crowd, here are a couple of our favorites.

A NOTE ON CHILES

- There are scores of varieties of chiles, fresh and dried. You can find every measure of hotness imaginable on the Internet, including the world-famous Scoville unit, which of course you know like the back of your hand. No? Well it's there on the Web (see Resources, page 224), rank-ordering the heat content for you.
- The heat's in the seeds and veins. Remove them for a milder flavor.
- Warning: These babies burn. Handle with care, even with rubber gloves. Keep hands away from eyes. Wash hands thoroughly after use.
- Dehydrating can blanch out spices, so don't be afraid to use full-strength chiles if you like the heat.

Salsa Verde 🏠

To a non-Spanish-speaking opera lover, this is going to sound like a tribute to Giuseppe Verdi. We don't know if old Joe Green liked salsa, but this one would have made him a convert.

10–15 small tomatillos (Mexican green tomatoes) or 2 cups of canned tomatillos

4–6 cups water

3 serrano chiles (see Handling Hot Chiles for precautions, page 37)

½ onion, chopped (not too fine)

2 cloves garlic, peeled and chopped (not too fine)

2 pinches sugar

Salt

2–3 tablespoons vegetable oil

¼–½ Sierra cup cold water, to rehydrate

at home

1. Peel the tomatillos (if you are using fresh ones) and place in a medium-sized saucepan. Add the 4 to 6 cups of water and bring to a boil. Simmer until just soft, about 7 minutes. Don't worry if they break open. If you're using canned tomatillos, just drain and place in a blender.

2. Toast the chiles in a hot iron frying pan, turning often, about 5 minutes. Remove from the heat and, when cooled, slice into three or four small pieces. Place in a blender or food processor with the tomatillos. Add the onions, garlic, sugar, and salt to taste. Blend until mixed well, about 30 seconds.

3. Heat the oil in a medium-sized pot and add the contents of the blender or food processor. Stir until the mixture begins to thicken, 4 to 5 minutes.

4. Spread on a lined dehydrator tray and dry for 7 to 10 hours, till dry and almost mealy to the touch.

at camp

5. To rehydrate, add just enough of the cold water to dampen thoroughly.

Makes 1 cup; serves 2–3 adults or 1 Rick

PREPARING CASCABELS

You can prepare cascabels in one of three ways, all great:

1. Toast the cascabels in a very hot iron frying pan, turning frequently, 3 to 5 minutes, till they begin to darken and give off a fine aroma. Remove from the heat. When cool, cut open the cascabels and discard the stem and seeds. Chop the skins into small, rough pieces. This method produces the hardest cascabels.

2. Pour boiling water over the dried cascabels. Place a small dish on top to keep them from floating and soak for about 15 minutes, till soft. Or, simmer for about 10 minutes, till soft. Cut open and discard the stems and seeds. Chop the chiles into rough pieces.

3. Follow option 1 above and then soak the chopped skins in boiling water for 10 to 15 minutes till soft.

Rattler Salsa (Salsa Cascabel)

Cascabel is Spanish for "rattle." These mahogany-colored dried chiles, about twice the size of big black cherries, sound like the world's tiniest maracas when shaken. And because they're only mildly hot, they make a great smoky salsa that won't take the roof off your mouth.

8–10 cascabel chiles (see Handling Hot Chiles for precautions, page 37)

3 large tomatoes

4 cloves garlic, roughly chopped

Salt

¼–½ Sierra cup hot water, to rehydrate

at home

1. Preheat the broiler.

2. Prepare the cascabels using one of the methods in the Preparing Cascabels box, at left.

3. Broil the tomatoes on the middle shelf of oven, turning frequently, until the skins wrinkle and bubble and just begin to blacken, about 10 minutes.

4. Place the cascabels, tomatoes, garlic, and salt to taste in a blender. Blend at low speed to make a rough blend, 30 seconds to 1 minute only. If the sauce is too thick, add a little water.

5. Spread onto a lined and oiled dehydrator tray (or use a fruit-roll insert). Dehydrate for 10 to 12 hours, till dry and leathery to the touch.

at camp

6. Rehydrate by adding the hot water barely to cover. If you use too much water so that the salsa feels thin and liquidy, don't worry; just reheat till the salsa begins to thicken, about 2 minutes. Let cool.

Makes 1 cup

Mixed—Fruit Chutney 🔥

We've never eaten a banana chutney, but just about anything goes here.

- 2 large handfuls dried fruit (we use a combination of apple, peach, apricot, and mango) (see Dehydrated Fruit, page 9, for instructions)
- 3 cloves garlic, mashed
- 2 spoons sugar
  Slice of fresh ginger (optional)
- 1 pinch–½ spoon cayenne pepper, depending on tolerance and stomach lining
- 2 spoons vinegar (preferably white wine vinegar)
- 2–3 Sierra cups water, to cover

1. Place the fruit, garlic, sugar, ginger (if using), cayenne pepper to taste, and vinegar in a large pot. Cover with the water, bring to a boil, and reduce the mixture to a jamlike consistency, stirring frequently, 10 to 15 minutes. Remove from the heat.

2. Cool thoroughly. The chutney will thicken more as it cools.

Note: Rick takes the instruction "cayenne pepper to taste" literally, and we have never been able to get close to his chutneys. This makes him happy.

Serves 4 rational adults or, depending on the cayenne content, 1 Greenspan

CHUTNEYS

There seem to be as many chutneys as there are Indian dialects, and they're all meant to complement just about every Indian meal ever dreamed up. Some are spicy hot, some sweet, and many combine heat with sweet. If you're going to eat curries at camp, you'll want to make chutneys, too. As long as you've got dried fruits and some sugar, garlic, and vinegar, you're in business.

Rick's Fire-in-the-Belly Automotive-Body-Shop Chutney 🏠

It was a slow morning in the body shop when Rick discovered some shredded coconut and red chiles among the tire irons and paint spray cans. Don't ask. Anyway, the results were stupendous, and the next time you see one of those Forest Service fire advisories, know that it may be a reference to this chutney. Hal has never been able to swallow more than a pinch without draining the entire Mono Creek watershed, which means it's just about perfect.

2 heaping tablespoons shredded unsweetened coconut

6 slices fresh ginger, ¼ inch thick

3 fresh red chiles (see Handling Hot Chiles for precautions, page 37)

2 cloves garlic

Salt

½–1½ teaspoons lemon juice, plus more to rehydrate, if necessary

at home

1. Toast the coconut in an iron pan over medium-high heat till just browned, 3 to 4 minutes. Place the coconut, ginger, chiles, garlic, and salt to taste in a blender or food processor. Add the lemon juice and blend into a paste-like consistency. The traditional Indian way to do this is with a mortar and pestle; if you've got a big one, go to it.

2. Spread on a lined dehydrator tray and dry for 5 to 7 hours, till crumbly.

at camp

3. Rehydrate by adding a tiny bit of the lemon juice in ¼-spoon increments or less, just enough to reconstitute to a thickish paste. Water will also work. Stir with a spoon.

Serves 3–4

Variation: To make at the campsite, use dried chiles and the bottom of a Sierra cup to crush all the ingredients as best you can.

Cilantro Chutney 🏠

If you're canoeing or car camping, bring the fresh ingredients with you and proceed with Method 2. If you're backpacking, you'll have to prepare at home, dry, and rehydrate according to Method 1.

Indian families use this chutney like we do mustard — that is, a little goes a long way. Use as a complement to all curries and veggie dishes. (Note: campsite measures appear in parentheses.)

½ teaspoon cumin seeds (⅓ spoon ground cumin)

1 bunch cilantro leaves, chopped fine

1 fresh green chile, or less, chopped fine (see Handling Hot Chiles, page 37, for precautions)

1 or 2 cloves garlic, chopped fine

½ teaspoon salt (⅓ spoon)

Freshly ground black pepper

½–1½ teaspoons (⅓ to 1 spoon) lemon juice, plus more to rehydrate, if necessary

¼–½ Sierra cups water, to rehydrate (if necessary)

Method 1

at home

1. To roast the cumin seeds, place them in a nonoiled iron pan and heat, shaking the pan till they've slightly darkened in color, 4 to 5 minutes.

2. Grind the cumin seeds to a fine powder in a coffee grinder.

3. Blend the cumin powder, cilantro, chile, garlic, salt, pepper to taste, and lemon juice in a blender or food processor till a smooth paste results. Alternatively, use a mortar and pestle.

4. Spread on a lined dehydrator tray and dry 5 to 7 hours, until crumbly.

at camp

5. Rehydrate with a tiny bit of the water or lemon juice, working in ¼-spoon increments till you have reconstituted a thickish pastelike texture. Use a spoon to mix while adding the liquid. (No heating required.)

• •

Method 2

Using the bottom of a Sierra cup, blend the ground cumin, cilantro, chile, garlic, salt, pepper to taste, and lemon juice till a smooth paste results.

Note: This and Rick's Chutney (see page 96) will almost certainly protect you from vampires. As for your tent mates, that's another issue. Let us know how you deal with it.

Makes ½ cup, enough to burn a hole in your socks

Mango–Mustard Chutney 🏠

Remember Chacko, the Oxford Marxist who goes home to southern India to run Mammachi's chutney business into the ground in Arundhati Roy's glorious The God of Small Things? *Well, this chutney almost ran Hal into the ground. He misread "½ chile" as "2 chiles" and practically burned his lips off ignoring all our handle-with-care rules (see Handling Hot Chiles, page 37). Still, he loved the result and lived to hear Rick murmur, "Not bad for a craven coward." That's high praise.*

2 semiripe mangoes, peeled and cut into small chunks (pits discarded)

2 red chiles, seeded and chopped very fine (or 1 for a milder chutney) (see Handling Hot Chiles for precautions, page 37)

½ small red onion, chopped fine

¼ cup orange juice (fresh or frozen)

Juice of about ¼ lime (2 teaspoons)

2 teaspoons rice wine vinegar

1 teaspoon mustard

Large pinch salt

2 tablespoons finely chopped cilantro

2 tablespoons finely chopped fresh mint

1–2 Sierra cups water, to rehydrate

at home

1. Place the mangoes, chiles, onion, and orange juice in a small saucepan. Cover and cook over medium heat, stirring occasionally till the mangoes are soft, about 10 minutes. Remove from the heat.

2. Add the lime juice, vinegar, mustard, and salt. Mix thoroughly and set aside. When the mixture is slightly cooled, add the cilantro and mint, mixing well.

3. Spread on a lined dehydrator tray and dry for 10 to 15 hours, till the texture of leather.

at camp

4. Rehydrate in the water to cover to achieve a soft, jamlike consistency. Eat either warm or cold.

Serves 4

VARIATION

This chutney can also be made entirely at camp, using dehydrated mangoes and onions and dried mint and cilantro. As you probably won't be carrying orange juice while backpacking, substitute the liquid in which you rehydrated the mangoes. You've got dried mustard in your spice "rack" (see our pill box recommendation, page 69) and lime or lemon juice in a small plastic bottle for the fish and other needs. Once the mangoes and onions have been rehydrated and are soft, proceed as above.

Clarified Butter 🏠

Clarified butter — butter minus the milk solids — won't spoil in the back-country. It cooks at a higher heat than regular butter and thus won't burn over your campfire. It's easy to make and will last in your fridge almost as long as that wedding cake you stuck in the freezer 14 years ago.

½ pound unsalted butter

1. In a heavy-bottomed saucepan, melt the butter very slowly over low heat. Increase the heat very slightly and simmer 10 to 20 minutes, till white foam begins to spread over the surface. (That's butterfat, and it's gotta go. The 10-minute range has to do with varying water contents in different butters.) Skim the foam off with a spoon or a tea strainer (see illustration). Don't worry if you can't get all of it. Remove from the heat.

2. When cool, pour off the remaining liquid carefully into a small bowl or cup, leaving the white milk solids on the bottom of the pan. Alternatively, you can pour the clear butter through cheesecloth, which will separate the milk solids from the clarified butter. It will last up to 4 months in the fridge and 2 to 3 weeks (or more) on the trail.

Makes about ¾ cup

Skimming the butterfat off the top of the melted butter

Ghee

Ghee is Indian clarified butter. It's what you get if you keep on cooking the butter until it becomes a burnished brown. You can use it for all cooking purposes. It adds a fine nutty flavor to foods. You can buy it ready-made in Indian food stores. Like clarified butter, ghee doesn't need to be refrigerated, making it perfect for backpacking and other forms of summer madness.

½ pound unsalted butter

1. In a heavy-bottomed saucepan, melt the butter very slowly over low heat. Increase the heat very slightly and let it simmer 10 to 20 minutes. (The 10-minute range has to do with varying water contents in different butters.) Skim the foam off the top with a spoon or tea strainer. Watch the white solids at the bottom carefully; when they turn golden in color, take the pan off the heat.

2. Strain the butter through a couple of layers of cheesecloth. Discard the solids. Store the remaining liquid in a small jar in the fridge for up to 4 months. Will keep 2 to 3 weeks (or more) on the trail.

Makes about ¾ cup

Variation: To make flavored ghee, follow the instructions above and add any of the following as you begin to melt the butter: ¼ teaspoon cumin, ¼ teaspoon powdered ginger, ¼ to ½ teaspoon ground pepper, ¼ teaspoon cardamom.

Yogurt Masala

Smear on trout and bake. Smear on just about anything and bake.

1 cup nonfat plain yogurt

1 tablespoon garam masala (see page 58)

½–¾ cup water, to rehydrate

at home

1. Mix the yogurt and garam masala thoroughly.

2. Spread on a lined dehydrating tray and dry 5 to 7 hours, till brittle.

at camp

3. Rehydrate with a minimum amount of the water over low heat, stirring to bring back to a sauce.

Makes ½–1 Sierra cup

Yogurt-Mango-Curry Spread

This spread is hot and sweet. Works wonders on baked trout (page 145), in polenta (page 128), and with almost all our Indian dishes. We have been known to go off to a quiet corner of the campsite and eat this plain.

½ large ripe mango

½ cup yogurt (we use nonfat)

1 teaspoon curry powder or garam masala (see page 58)

½ Sierra cup water (approximately), to rehydrate

at home

1. Mix the mango, yogurt, and curry powder in a blender. Pour on a fruit-roll-lined or otherwise lined dehydrator tray. Dry until the mixture is the consistency of a fruit roll, 7 to 10 hours.

at camp

2. To rehydrate, break up the "roll" into small pieces, place in a pot lid, and barely top with the water. Heat gently, stirring until the mixture becomes smooth and begins to thicken, about 5 minutes. Add more water in very small amounts as needed. Your aim here is a thick sauce, and it will thicken as it cools.

Makes 1 cup

A YOGURT BUST

Cookbook writers never tell you about their failures. Wrong move. Nobody's *that* good. So here's one. Raitas are those cooling Indian yogurt dishes spiced with things like cardamom and mustard seeds and mint, and mixed with cucumbers or eggplant or spinach or whatever. We thought: Perfect, especially as some yogurt dishes, like those above, de- and rehydrate so nicely. Nope. We made a beautiful cucumber raita and an exquisite roasted eggplant raita. No curdling. Dried well, but rehydrated grainy and a bilious beige. Cooled and thickened. And failed every taste test known to humankind. Tried all sorts of yogurt — nonfat, low-fat, regular; Romanian, Russian, Mongolian, Oregonian. Fuggedaboutit. Got answers? Let us know.

SUGAR

Many years ago, Rick and Hal found themselves high in the Marble Mountains with a sugar jones. So they decided to make a day of it: Ate nothing but desserts. They went back to fruit and veggies the next day, but it was fun while it lasted. And so, for the sugar-deprived among you, we offer the following in remembrance of things past.

Marmalade

We used to think that dehydrating citrus fruits was a losing proposition: all pulp and pits, no juice. Actually, the dried fruit is a good nosh and a great addition to fruit compotes. It's all in the skin, sharp and tangy to the taste.

2 oranges, peeled and roughly chopped

¼ lemon, peeled and roughly chopped

2 spoons sugar, or more to taste

2–3 Sierra cups water, to rehydrate

at home

1. Scatter the chopped oranges and lemon on a dehydrator tray and dry 7 to 10 hours, till hard and dry.

at camp

2. Place the orange and lemon in a medium-sized pot. Cover with the water and boil down until the fruit begins to soften, about 20 minutes. (You can save fuel and time if you let the fruit soak in warm or cold water for about 1 hour.)

3. Add the sugar. Cook until the mixture is reduced to a jamlike consistency. If the fruit remains hard, add more water and reduce again. Taste for sweetness. Remove from the heat. Allow to cool thoroughly while you're baking the buttermilk scones (see page 176).

Serves 3–4

Applesauce 🏠

Ten minutes after Prometheus gave us fire, someone figured out how to boil water. Five minutes later? Applesauce. If we could decipher the last remaining Neanderthal graffiti, they'd probably read, "If they give you apples, make apple-sauce." For all three of you who are not paleoanthropologists, here's our own graffiti on the subject.

6 apples (Granny Smith, Braeburn, Golden Delicious, Cortland, and Mutsu are our favorites)

1½ cups water

½–¾ cups sugar

¼ teaspoon cinnamon

Freshly squeezed lemon juice (optional)

2–4 cups water, to rehydrate

at home

1. Core the apples and slice any which way (no need to peel), then place them in a medium-sized, heavy-bottomed pot. Add the water. Bring to a boil, then lower the heat to a slow simmer. Stir occasionally to prevent sticking and burning.

2. When the apples start to get soft, about 5 minutes, add ½ cup of the sugar. Stir and add the cinnamon.

3. As the apples cook down, take a spoonful, let cool, and taste for sweetness. If necessary, add more sugar. If the consistency seems too thick, add more water.

4. If the apples need a flavor pick-me-up, add a few squeezes of lemon juice just as you take the pot off the stove, 15 to 20 minutes. The result should be a thick sauce with some of the apple bits still visible. (If you're after a sauce so smooth you could leave your teeth at home, don't even bother coring the apples. Just cut 'em up and follow the directions above. When the applesauce is fully cooked and cool enough to handle, run it through a food mill — not a food processor — and you can baby yourself to death.)

5. When cool, spread on lined, lightly oiled trays (or use a fruit-roll insert) and dehydrate 12 to 20 hours, till the texture of fruit leather. For best results, flip the fruit over about halfway through the drying process. The result will be an applesauce fruit leather, which you can eat as-is or rehydrate at camp.

at camp

6. To rehydrate, add the water to cover and boil down, stirring until reconstituted, 7 to 10 minutes. Eat warm or cold.

Note: If this works right, we're going to get mail complaining that we left out This (brown sugar, cloves, you name it) and That (butter, apple cider, whatever). We like our stripped-down model, just the way Prometheus's gray-haired mom liked it.

Serves 4

Apple Butter

If you're of a certain age, you remember with grim clarity tubs of commercial apple butter spread on industrial white bread at summer camp. Bad rap. Homemade apple butter, spread on good country bread or pancakes, or just noshed straight from the jar, will change your mind and erase memories that have kept you at the therapist too many years. Think apples and winter spices — cinnamon, allspice, cloves, ginger — stirred and thickened to perfection. You may have to beat the children off in the morning rush to judgment.

We're going to make enough here for home consumption as well as on the trail, but quantities in these things really depend on what you have at hand. Just a few apples? Make a micro-amount. An orchard load? Can the stuff. Apple butter is really just applesauce that keeps going and going and going, like that annoying rabbit.

5 pounds apples (any variety), quartered and roughly chopped — seeds, core, skin and all

2 cups water or apple cider or a combination

1 cup packed brown sugar if using tart apples (½ cup if using sweet)

1 teaspoon ground cinnamon

¼ teaspoon ground allspice

¼ teaspoon ground cloves

¼ teaspoon powdered ginger

Juice of about ¼ lemon (1–2 teaspoons; optional)

3–4 Sierra cups water, to rehydrate

at home

1. Toss the apples and water in a heavy-bottomed pot and simmer until softened and thickened, 15 to 20 minutes. (At this point, if you were making applesauce, you'd stop cooking and add sugar and a little cinnamon. But we press on, literally.)

2. Run the apples through a food mill or press through a sieve to get rid of seeds, core bits, and skin. (You now have unsweetened applesauce — the kind you would feed a baby.)

3. Pour the sauce back in the pot over low heat. Add ½ cup of the brown sugar. Add the cinnamon, allspice, cloves, ginger, and lemon juice (if using), stirring constantly.

4. Reduce the liquid content till a thick sauce results, 10 to 15 minutes. When the apple butter no longer runs or easily flows off the spoon, it's done. You are not going to harm it if you keep going, as long as you continue to stir to prevent burning.

5. Cool slightly, then spread over two lined, lightly oiled dehydrator trays. Dry for 15 to 24 hours, till the texture of fruit leather. Turn over once (2 to 3 hours from the end) for best results. You'll end up with two fruit-roll shaped discs, which you can eat directly in that format if you like.

at camp

6. Rehydrate with the water barely to cover. Simmer, stirring till thickened, 5 to 10 minutes. Let cool. Use as a bread spread (say that fast five times!) or in an apple-sauce cake (page 185) or on pancakes (pages 150–53) and crêpes (pages 154–55). Rick brushes his teeth with it, but that's another story.

Serves 4

Pineapple Glaze 🏠🔥

While Rick is almost fanatical about visiting the local farmers' market whenever fresh fruits are in season, he has occasionally been known to sneak in the back door of the local dented-can emporium. A while later, he stealthily emerges with a cart loaded to the brim with cheap cans of sliced pineapple. His dehydrator is already warmed up at home.

1 can (20 ounces) pineapple chunks

or

½ whole fresh pineapple, cut into large chunks

1 Sierra cup boiling water

¼ Sierra cup sugar

1 spoon cornstarch (optional)

2 spoons cold water

¼ spoon brandy or vanilla

at home

1. Place the pineapple on lightly oiled dehydrator trays and dry 10 to 15 hours, till stiff and hard.

at camp

2. Pour the sugar into the boiling water and stir until dissolved. Add the pineapple and let soak for about 20 minutes.

3. In a Sierra cup, dissolve the cornstarch (if using) in the cold water. Add to the pineapple mixture and heat slowly, stirring constantly, until the glaze is thick and bubbly, 3 to 5 minutes. Remove from the heat.

4. Add the brandy. When the glaze is cool enough that it no longer burns your tongue, it is ready to spread. If you're in a hurry, you can speed the cooling process by floating the pot in a larger pot of cool water.

Note: Cornstarch merely quickens the thickening process. If you want your glaze to be free of cornstarch, add the sugar to the fruit, then water to cover. Boil, stirring, until thickened, 10 to 15 minutes. It works, we promise.

Serves 4 (or frosts a small cake)

Chocolate Frosting 🔥

If you intuit even a little of our wilderness cooking attitude, you'll understand why this has become an essential in our kit. Leave the global positioning system at home if necessary, or Zadie Smith's latest novel, or even the children, for heaven's sake — whatever it takes to make room and weight for the ingredients here. The backcountry's no place to be stranded without chocolate frosting for the cake.

4 squares semisweet baking chocolate or equivalent sweet chocolate (up to 6 squares if you have them to spare)

2–3 spoons water

1 spoon clarified butter (see page 99)

1 spoon brandy (optional)

2–3 Sierra cups cold water, to help thicken

1. Melt the chocolate in a pot lid by following the instructions in Melting Chocolate for Cakes (page 186) and using the 2 to 3 spoons of water.

2. When the chocolate is almost completely melted, about 4 minutes, add the clarified butter. Stir constantly.

3. When the butter and chocolate are fully melted, add the brandy, if using.

4. As the frosting cools down, it will begin to thicken. To speed the process, float the pot lid in the 2 to 3 Sierra cups of cold water from the lake or stream.

But keep your eyes open: The mixture may harden to the point where it can't be spread. If that happens, put it over heat briefly to soften.

5. When the frosting is thick but soft, spread it on cooled cake. It will harden as it cools further.

Frosts one Campsite Cake (see page 184) or The Most Dangerous Cake in the Wilderness (see page 187)

(Alternatively, you can eat the frosting before it ever reaches the cake. If you eat it all yourself, your partners will enjoy watching you infarct on the spot.)

White Chocolate Icing

First of all, let's get this straight: White chocolate isn't real chocolate. It lacks the key ingredient, chocolate liquor (which isn't a liquor), and hence fails the authenticity test. Doesn't even taste much like what we think of as chocolate. Second of all, we've never met anybody in the outback who's carrying the stuff, so this recipe is for ET types only — "ET" as in "Extreme Tinkerer."

White chocolate melts fast, like milk chocolate, and it requires no or very little water to turn it into a soft mass. Likewise, it requires very little butter to transform into an icing.

- 4 spoon-sized chunks of white chocolate
- 1 spoon water, if necessary
- ½ spoon clarified butter (see page 99)
- ¼ spoon brandy
- ½ spoon flour

1. Melt the white chocolate in a pot lid, following the instructions in Melting Chocolate for Cakes (page 186). If the chocolate begins to burn, add the water.

2. Stir in the clarified butter and brandy. Don't be distressed if the melted chocolate and clarified butter don't emulsify well. Add the flour. Stir till smooth. Remove from the heat.

3. As the icing cools down, it will begin to thicken. To speed the process, float the pot lid in some cold water from the lake or stream. But keep your eyes open: The mixture may harden to the point where it can't be spread. If that happens, put it over heat briefly to soften.

4. When the icing is thick but soft, spread on a cooled cake. Allow to cool further and thicken more. The result is a sweet, buttery frosting.

Frosts one small cake; especially suited to Carrot Cake (see page 190) and Brownies (see page 183)

Variation: For a hard, fine icing, omit the butter and flour entirely, melt the chunks of white chocolate, and spread on the cake when cool.

Ginger Frosting

Unfrosted carrot cake can be grounds for arrest in certain parts of the country. But since carrot cakes typically get a cream cheese frosting, and the Department of Defense is still working on dehydrating cream cheese, we had to turn elsewhere. It wasn't easy to create a white frosting with ingredients from a typical camping kitchen, since confectioner's sugar isn't something we usually pack along. This frosting filled the bill — it's made entirely with ingredients that have numerous other uses. Although its consistency is a little creamier than most, our carrot cake with this ginger frosting rated a "wow" from both of Rick's kids on their first bite.

1 spoon cornstarch

4 spoons water

1 spoon powdered nonfat milk

½ Sierra cup sugar

2 spoons clarified butter (see page 99)

½ spoon powdered ginger

2–3 Sierra cups water, for boiling

1. Mix the cornstarch with 1 spoon of the water in a Sierra cup and blend till creamy. Add the powdered milk and continue mixing till smooth. Add the remaining 3 spoons of water 1 spoon at a time, stirring to keep the mixture smooth.

2. In a small pot, cream the sugar, butter, and ginger together.

3. Heat about ½ inch of the water in the bottom of a large pot or pan until the water boils. Remove the pan from the heat, and place the Sierra cup with the cornstarch mixture in the hot water. Stir the mixture constantly as it warms up, to keep it smooth.

4. Once the cornstarch mixture is warm, pour it into the sugar mixture. Stir until the frosting has a soft, even consistency. Let it cool. Pour the frosting onto the top of the cake and smooth it down the sides with the back of a spoon. Dig in.

Frosts 1 small cake; especially suited to Carrot Cake (see page 190)

Chocolate Pudding 🔥

It's hard to keep a secret for 400 years. Oh sure, Shakespearean scholars may have speculated on the origin of the witches in Macbeth. But the rest of us were totally snookered into believing that witches hung around in the forest stirring pots and muttering "double, double, toil and trouble." Fat chance.

Once Harry Potter hit the best-seller list, the truth was out. Witches, we now know, live in neat row houses in London. So who were those scruffy characters with the grimy hands hunched over that bubbling pot in the forest? Obviously, they were backpackers cooking their evening pudding. Here is their recipe.

3 spoons sugar

3 spoons powdered nonfat milk

¼ spoon salt

1 spoon cornstarch

1 Sierra cup water

1 ounce (1 square) semisweet chocolate

1 spoon clarified butter (see page 99)

1. Combine no more than 2 spoons of the water, the chocolate, and the clarified butter in a small pot. Melt slowly over low heat, stirring till totally blended and soft, about 3 minutes. Remove from the heat.

2. Mix the sugar, powdered milk, salt, and cornstarch together in a small pot or lid. Slowly pour in the remaining water, stirring out the lumps as best you can. Pour the sugar mixture into the melted chocolate and stir well.

3. Now comes the fun part. Stir constantly as you heat the pudding over low heat until it just begins to bubble. If it gets too hot, it will burn and boil over. Keep it just barely bubbling, as you stir the pudding for about 5 minutes. Mumble incantations if you must. This is the origin of Shakespeare's line, "Fire burn, and cauldron bubble."

4. Remove the pudding from the heat and pour into two Sierra cups to cool. The cooling can be hastened if you float the cups in cold water. And if you find yourself cackling uncontrollably as you eat it, you'll know why.

Serves 2

SNOW CONES

On a balmy beach in Hawaii, they call it "shaved ice." On the Santa Cruz Boardwalk, it's an "icey." On a sunny afternoon at 8,000 feet in the Sierras, we call it a snow cone. Hiking is hard work, and there's nothing so refreshing at the top of a mountain pass as a cold cupful of snow flavored with your favorite sweetener. If the snow is gone, not to worry. Flavorings like these can easily be used in other things. Here are some of our favorite flavorings, along with alternate food uses for each.

- Maple syrup (or powdered maple syrup): pancakes

- Powdered, sweetened (Thai) coconut milk: curries

- Lemon/lime juice and sugar: tabbouleh

- Cinnamon and sugar: cookies, cakes

- Brandy and sugar: frosting

- Powdered hot chocolate and instant coffee: hot mocha

[Chapter 5]

Grains

"Four Crowned" Gage Mountain, Adirondack Mts. N.Y.

Here's a test. Quick, name six grains. No hesitating, no, "wait, wait, don't tell me!" After wheat, rice, corn, and oats, you're stuck, right? Okay, barley's fine, and so is rye. And sorghum and millet, though we've never cooked with them. Did somebody mutter triticale? Spelt? Emmer and einkorn? We had to look them up and wouldn't know 'em if we tripped over them. But keep going, win bonus points. At the end of this chapter, after the Italian risottos and Indian basmatis and Japanese sushi and Chinese fried rice; after the pilafs and polentas (cornmeal to you, bub), we offer you bulgur — how else to make your tabbouleh? — and quinoa, and couscous and falafel (don't quibble, we know garbanzos are beans not grains). It's about time the campsite became inter-nationalized, and we've set out here to do just that. Bon appétit. Go-enryo naku.

Risotto

"Enter stage left, Guelphs and Ghibellines, fighting." How well you remember those classic stage directions. If, that is, you weren't sleeping in drama class. We don't know who these guys were, except they came from Italy and were constantly at each other's throats. We like to think they were fighting over something important, like whether Venetians or the Milanese produced the best risotto. Even pacifists might take sides on this issue.

Entire books have been written on risotto. We, ourselves, in an earlier incarnation (*The Camper's Companion*, Avalon Travel Publishing, 1996) devoted five pages to risotto. All you really need, however, is a basic recipe and a good imagination. We'll supply the first, you the second. Here are a few basic facts about risotto.

- The plural is risotti (but we say "risottos").
- The rice used is called arborio rice, a short-grained variety that sucks up and retains liquid like a sumo wrestler on a lunch break. The kernels are short and fat, sort of the Waka-no-yama of rice grains. (Sumo fans will know who we mean.)

- Arborio rice can be used in a pinch to make sushi, but don't ever tell a sushi maven we said so.
- Northern Italians really do argue over texture (creamy or sticky), color (saffron or not), and the kinds of seafoods and cheeses and vegetables and mushrooms that make risottos great.
- Instant boxed rice never tasted like this.
- Risotto is labor-intensive work and flavor-intensive eating.
- Risotto is one of the best single-pot meals in the entire annals of wilderness cuisine.

Variations

By following the ratios of stock-to-rice and ingredients-to-risotto in these recipes, you can make an infinite variety of risotti, a spelling we had to use at least once in these pages. So, for a quick refresher course: 1 cup risotto to 4 to 5 cups stock, 2 to 3 cups chopped or sliced ingredients to each 1 (uncooked) cup risotto.

- Cheeses: Gorgonzola, Taleggio, fontina, blue
- Roasted eggplant and sautéed snow peas (It's a nice color combination. Don't worry if some of the eggplant skin comes along for the ride. Adds to the palette and taste.)
- Sun-dried tomatoes and lots of basil (Use a cup or more of wine as a portion of the broth.)
- Pesto, Parmesan cheese, and pine nuts
- Leeks and Italian parsley
- Sautéed oyster mushrooms and portobello mushrooms with roasted garlic
- Chicken, watercress, and pitted kalamata olives
- Poached trout (Add it at the campsite to any home-prepared risotto.)

Risotto: The Starter Set 🏠

Risotto takes lots of stirring and patient addition of stock to the rice, so let's assume you want more than a bunch of rice and cheese for all your effort. Let's add some of the good stuff right at the start.

1 package (½ ounce) dried porcini mushrooms (or 1 cup dried shiitake mushrooms)

1–2 cups boiling water, to cover

4–5 cups chicken or vegetable stock (canned or homemade; see pages 26 and 27)

3 tablespoons butter

1 tablespoon olive oil

¾ cup finely minced onion

1½ cups arborio rice

½ cup dry white wine or Marsala (or stock)

½ cup grated Parmesan

2 tablespoons chopped fresh Italian parsley

4–6 Sierra cups water, to rehydrate

at home

1. Place the mushrooms in a medium-sized bowl and pour the boiling water over them. Let soak. When the mushrooms are soft, about 30 minutes, strain the soaking liquid into a large pot. Add the stock. Chop the soaked mushrooms and set aside.

2. Bring the stock-and-mushroom liquid to a slow simmer.

3. Get out the heaviest-bottomed pot in your kitchen — for example, an enameled Dutch oven — and a big wooden spoon. Heat 2 tablespoons of the butter and the olive oil and sauté the onion till it just begins to turn translucent, 1 to 2 minutes at most. Using the wooden spoon, stir in the rice till all the grains are coated with the butter and oil, about 2 minutes.

4. Add the wine and stir till completely absorbed by the rice, 2 to 3 minutes or as long as it takes (risotto recipes require more of a "watch-and-see" attitude than other recipes). Add the chopped mushrooms; mix well.

5. Then, and this is the important part, begin to add the simmering stock *slooowly*, ½ cup at a time. After each addition, stir and wait till the liquid is just about completely absorbed before adding the next ½ cup. Stir frequently, because the rice has a tendency to stick to the bottom of the pot. This is going to take patience, 15 to 20 minutes' worth. Reserve ¼ cup of the stock till the very end. The aim is to have the rice tender but firm. Taste test to get it right, then add the remaining ¼ cup of stock and remove from the heat. Add the remaining tablespoon of the butter, the Parmesan, and the parsley. Mix well.

6. Spread on lined trays and dehydrate 10 to 12 hours, till dry and mealy.

at camp

7. To rehydrate, add the water to cover. Bring to a boil and stir till the rice is soft, 10 to 15 minutes. Brava!

Serves 4

What-Looks-Good-at-the-Market Risotto 🏠

It didn't take Enrico Fermi to figure out that if you put fresh seasonal produce in, you'll get fresh seasonal risotto out. Go for color combinations and great taste.

10 snow peas, trimmed

5 tablespoons olive oil

½ green bell pepper, chopped fine

½ orange or yellow bell pepper, chopped fine

2 ripe Italian tomatoes, peeled, seeded, and diced (see Note)

4–5 cups chicken or vegetable stock (see pages 26 and 27)

1 onion, chopped fine

2 shallots, chopped fine

1 cup arborio rice

½ cup dry white wine (optional)

Salt and freshly ground black pepper

½ cup Asiago or Parmesan, grated

1 tablespoon butter or olive oil

2 tablespoons chopped Italian parsley

4–6 Sierra cups water, to rehydrate

at home

1. Parboil the snow peas for no more than 30 seconds. Drain and reserve.

2. Heat 2 tablespoons of the olive oil in a large frying pan. Sauté the peppers until just soft, about 4 minutes. Add the tomatoes and cook till soft, about 3 minutes. Set aside.

3. In a large pot, cook the stock over medium heat. As the stock is coming to a simmer, in about 10 minutes, heat the remaining 3 tablespoons olive oil in a large, heavy-bottomed pot and sauté the onion and shallots until just translucent, 2 minutes at the most. Add the rice to the onion mixture and coat thoroughly, 1 more minute. Add the wine (if using); stir until the liquid is absorbed.

4. Begin to add the stock (now simmering) in ½-cup increments (reserving ¼ cup), stirring and waiting till most is absorbed, about 18 minutes.

5. Add the snow peas, peppers, tomatoes, salt and pepper to taste, Asiago, and butter, stirring quite vigorously to incorporate into the risotto. Stir in the parsley till well combined.

6. Spread on lined trays and dehydrate 10 to 12 hours, till dry to the touch.

at camp

7. To rehydrate, add the water to cover. Bring to a boil and stir till the rice is soft, 10 to 15 minutes.

Serves 4

𝒩ote: **To peel tomatoes,** set them in a bowl, pour boiling water over to cover, and let them sit for 5 minutes. Remove with a slotted spoon and, when cool enough to handle, prick with a fork or knife and peel. The skin should pull away easily.

To seed tomatoes, slice them open and squeeze out the seeds or extract them by running your finger under them.

Deep Pockets Risotto 🏠

Okay, so you don't own a 12-meter yacht, but you've had your eyes on a quarter pound of prosciutto ever since you paid off your credit card debt. Go for it.

½ pound chanterelle mushrooms, roughly chopped (there goes the college fund for the kids)

5 tablespoons unsalted butter

2 tablespoons olive oil

½–1 cup finely chopped prosciutto (hock the kids)

2 plum tomatoes, peeled, seeded, chopped (see Note, facing page)

½ cup finely chopped onion

1½ cups arborio rice

1 cup dry white wine (no cooking sherry here please)

4 cups chicken or vegetable stock (see pages 26 and 27)

¼ cup grated Parmesan (grate it yourself)

2 tablespoons chopped Italian parsley

4–6 Sierra cups water, to rehydrate

at home

1. Sauté the mushrooms in 2 tablespoons of the butter and 1 tablespoon of the oil till soft, about 4 minutes. Add the prosciutto and brown quickly, 2 minutes. Add the tomatoes and cook till soft, 3 minutes. Remove from the heat.

2. Get out the heaviest-bottomed pot in your kitchen and a big wooden spoon. Heat 2 tablespoons of the butter and 1 tablespoon olive oil and sauté the onion till it just begins to turn translucent, 1 to 2 minutes at most. Using the wooden spoon, stir in the rice till all the grains are coated with the butter and oil, about 2 minutes.

3. Add the wine and stir till completely absorbed by the rice, 2 to 3 minutes or as long as it takes (risotto recipes require a "watch-and-see" attitude).

4. Then, and this is the important part, begin to add the simmering stock *slooowly*, ½ cup at a time. After each addition, stir and wait till the liquid is just about completely absorbed before adding the next ½ cup. Stir frequently, because the rice has a tendency to stick to the bottom of the pot. This is going to take patience, 15 to 20 minutes' worth. Reserve ¼ cup of the stock till the very end. The aim is to have the rice tender but firm. Taste test to get it right, then add the remaining ¼ cup of stock and remove from the heat.

5. Add the mushroom mixture and stir to incorporate. Add the remaining 1 tablespoon butter, Parmesan, and parsley. Mix well.

6. Spread on lined trays and dehydrate 10 to 12 hours, till dry and mealy.

at camp

7. To rehydrate, add the water to cover. Bring to a boil and stir till the rice is soft, 10 to 15 minutes. Brava!

Serves 4

ROASTING VEGGIES

- To roast bell peppers, place on a baking tray in a 400°F oven. As they blacken on one side, turn them over and continue until their surfaces are mostly blackened and their skin crinkled, 15 to 20 minutes. Remove and place in a deep bowl. Cover with a plate and let stand about 15 minutes. When cool enough to handle, peel away the skin. They're roasted and ready.

- To roast fennel bulb, leeks, onions, squash, and zucchini, brush with olive oil before placing in a 400°F oven. Turn once. They're done when soft, 10 to 15 minutes.

- To roast garlic, peel the individual cloves, brush with olive oil, place in an oven-safe bowl, cover tightly with aluminum foil, and roast at 400°F until soft, 15 to 20 minutes. Shake the bowl several times during the roasting. This rotates the garlic and keeps it coated with oil. To make garlic paste, roast the whole head of garlic, unpeeled and unoiled, till soft. Remove and when cool, squeeze the garlic head until the paste is extruded. Garlic paste can be used in all recipes calling for garlic. The soft texture of the paste incorporates easily and the roasted flavor it imparts is supreme. One teaspoon equals about 2 cloves of garlic.

- To roast Chinese, Japanese, or Italian eggplants, prick with a fork in several places, set on baking trays in a 400°F oven and roast, turning on occasion, till finger-soft, 20 to 25 minutes. Remove and, when cool, slice crosswise for rough-cut rounds or lengthwise to remove the pulp from the skin.

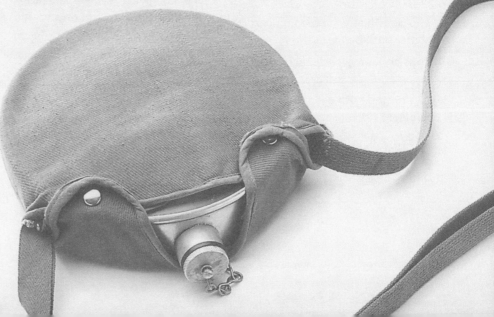

Spinach & Roasted Peppers Risotto

This risotto is simple, beautiful, and, as the good people at Berlitz would no doubt put it, delizioso.

1 bunch spinach

4–5 cups chicken or vegetable stock (see pages 26 and 27)

4 tablespoons butter

1 tablespoon olive oil

½ large onion, diced fine

1 cup arborio rice

1 large red bell pepper, roasted and cut into thin strips (see Roasting Veggies, facing page)

½ cup grated Parmesan

Salt and freshly ground black pepper

4–6 Sierra cups water, to rehydrate

at home

1. Stem and wash the spinach, but do not dry. Place the wet leaves in a large pot and cook quickly over high heat till just wilted, about 3 minutes. Spoon into a blender or food processor and purée till smooth, adding some of the water released during braising if the spinach is too dry to make a purée. Set aside.

2. Bring the stock to a simmer in a large pot over medium-high heat. Meanwhile, heat 3 tablespoons of the butter and the oil in a large, heavy-bottomed pot and sauté the onion till just softened, about 1 minute. Add the rice and stir to coat. In ½-cup increments, pour the simmering stock into the rice mixture, stirring and allowing the rice to absorb most of the liquid before adding the next ½ cup. Continue till the rice is tender but firm, 15 to 20 minutes, adding a final ¼ to ½ cup just before removing from the heat.

3. Stir in the puréed spinach, roasted peppers, Parmesan, remaining 1 tablespoon butter, and salt and pepper to taste. The result will look like Christmas in July, although dehydrating and rehydrating tend to leach the color from these great dishes.

4. Spread on lined trays and dehydrate 10 to 12 hours, till pebbly in texture.

at camp

5. To rehydrate, add the water to cover. Bring to a boil and stir till the rice is soft, 10 to 15 minutes.

Serves 4

Basmati Rice & Split-Pea Pilaf 🏠🔥 or 🔥

The rice-and-beans of Latin American cooking become rice-and-peas (khichri) *in Indian cooking. Simple, nutritious, and delicious. You can dehydrate the cilantro at home and prepare the rest at the campsite (Method 1) or prepare everything at home, dehydrate, and rehydrate at the campsite (Method 2). In the ingredients list, we'll give you campsite measurements followed by home-preparation measurements in parentheses.*

1 bunch cilantro

⅓–½ Sierra cup (½ cup) yellow split peas (supermarket variety or *chana dal* from an Indian store)

6 Sierra cups water, to cover

1½ Sierra cups (1¾ cups) basmati rice

3 spoons (3 tablespoons) ghee or clarified butter (page 99)

¼ spoon (½ teaspoon) cumin seeds

¼ spoon (½ teaspoon) garam masala (page 58), plus ½ spoon to mix if rehydrating

Salt

2 Sierra cups (2 cups) water or chicken stock (see page 26; if camping, from a bouillon cube, page 28)

4–6 Sierra cups water, to rehydrate (if necessary)

Method 1

at home

1. Cut the long stems from the cilantro. Spread on dehydrator trays and dry 1 to 2 hours, till it crumbles in your hand. You need 4 tablespoons.

Note: If you want to use commercially dried cilantro, you can skip this step altogether and make the dish entirely at camp.

at camp

2. Soak the split peas in about 2 Sierra cups of the water to cover for 3 hours if you're going fishing, less if you haven't got the time. (No less than 1 hour, though.) Drain.

3. Soak the rice in about 4 cups of the water to cover for 1 hour, less if you're hungry. (No less than 15 minutes, though.) Drain.

4. Melt the ghee in a frying pan and, when hot, stir in the cumin seeds, the split peas, and the rice till well coated, about 3 minutes.

5. Stir in the garam masala, dried cilantro, and salt to taste. Continue stirring for 2 to 3 minutes.

6. Transfer everything to your biggest pot. Add the 2 Sierra cups water, bring to a boil, cover, and cook on the lowest heat you can manage on your campfire or camp stove, 20 to 25 minutes, till the liquid is fully absorbed and the rice and split peas are soft. Remove from the heat and let the pot sit, without peeking, about 10 minutes. Fluff with a fork or stir gently with a spoon before serving.

Method 2

at home

1. Follow steps 2 and 3 in Method 1.

2. In a large, heavy-bottomed pot, melt the ghee and, when hot, stir in the cumin seeds, split peas, and rice till well coated, about 3 minutes. Stir in the garam masala, salt, and fresh cilantro. Continue stirring, 2 to 3 minutes.

3. Add the water, bring to a boil, and cook on low heat for 25 minutes, till the liquid is fully absorbed and the rice and split peas are soft. Remove from the heat and let the pot sit, without peeking, about 10 minutes.

4. Spread on lined trays and dehydrate 10 to 12 hours, till grainy-dry.

at camp

5. Rehydrate with the water to cover. Bring to a boil, reduce heat, and slowly cook down to bring back the flavors. Mix in another ½ spoon garam masala just before removing from the fire. Let the pilaf sit for 10 to 15 minutes.

Serves 2–3

Pilafs

Pilafs are to the Middle East and India what risottos are to Italy: the aromatic triumph of rice seasoned just right. Actually, pilafs — called pilau or pillau or pullao in India — can be made with other grains too, such as bulgur, wild rice (not really a rice), barley, or couscous, but we'll stick mostly to rice here. Long-grained rice. In particular, basmati rice, which translates from Hindi as the "queen of fragrance." Basmati is now available in lots of supermarkets and certainly in natural food stores.

Like risottos, pilafs begin by coating or browning the rice in oil before carrying on. But then they part company: Risottos are meant to absorb liquid slowly, whereas pilafs are meant to steep submersed in liquid. There are two methods of preparing the basmati rice for a pilaf, one involving baking as well as boiling (the baking + stovetop method), the other staying on the stovetop (the stovetop method). We'll give you directions for both and let you make the call. In the baking + stovetop method, slow baking makes perfectly fluffy rice. There is no need to measure the cooking water precisely. In the stovetop method, there is less fuss, less mess, and fewer pans. This method, however, requires properly calibrated measurements of rice to water.

Note: You can use brown rice in all of these recipes, but keep in mind that it takes much longer to cook.

North African Pilaf or

The key to all these pilafs is to let them sit and absorb all the flavors after they've been cooked. Pilaf can be eaten cold or warm, so don't worry if it loses heat while steeping. We've provided a method for baking at camp (Method 1) and a method for baking at home (Method 2). Use the ingredients given in parentheses if you choose to bake at home.

1 carrot, diced

1 small onion, chopped

1 peel from a dehydrated orange slice (minced zest from 1 medium-sized orange)

2 spoons chopped dehydrated chives (1½ tablespoons finely chopped fresh chives)

⅓ Sierra cup (⅓ cup) whole almonds (or other nuts of choice)

2 Sierra cups boiling water for blanching the almonds

2 spoons (2 tablespoons) olive oil (or clarified butter; see page 99)

¼ spoon (½ teaspoon) cinnamon

1 Sierra cup (1 cup) basmati rice

½ Sierra cup (⅓ cup) raisins (or dried cranberries or sour cherries)

¼ spoon (¼ teaspoon) cayenne pepper

3 Sierra cups (3 cups) chicken stock (see page 26; if camping, from bouillon cube, page 28) or water

2–3 Sierra cups water, to rehydrate, if necessary

Method 1

at home

1. Blanch the carrot pieces by immersing in boiling water for 3 to 4 minutes.

2. Spread the onions, blanched carrots, and orange slice on unlined trays, the chives on a lined tray. The chives will dry to a crisp in less than an hour. The other ingredients are done when dry and firm to the touch, 10 to 12 hours. When done, remove the peel and discard the remaining orange.

at camp

3. Blanch the almonds by placing in a Sierra cup and pouring the boiling water over them. Let them sit 5 minutes, or until the skins begin to crinkle. (Remember that at high altitudes, the water will boil at a lower temperature than at sea level, hence it will cool down faster, so you may have to drain the cup and add fresh boiling water.) Drain and peel, if desired, after blanching.

4. Heat the oil in a frying pan. Sauté the almonds till slightly browned, 3 to 4 minutes. Stir in the dehydrated onion, dehydrated carrot, cinnamon, and rice. Continue stirring until the rice is coated, about 1 minute.

5. Transfer the almond mixture and the raisins, cayenne, and orange to a large pot. Pour in the stock, bring to a boil, and reduce the heat to low (or as low as you can get). Let cook till the liquid is absorbed and the rice is tender, about 30 minutes. Another way to do this is to "bake" the pilaf. That is, set the covered pot on a cleared space and surround by warm (but not hot) coals and tend the pilaf as you would a slow baking cake or bread. (If the coals are too hot, they're going to burn the rice to the sides of the pot.)

6. When the rice is done, take the pot off the fire or coals, gently stir in the dehydrated chives, and fluff the rice with a fork.

. . . .

Method 2

at home

1. Preheat the oven to 350°F.

2. Blanch the almonds by pouring boiling water over them in a pot or cup and allowing to sit for 5 minutes, till the skins begin to crinkle. Drain and peel.

3. Heat the oil in a frying pan. Sauté the blanched almonds till slightly browned, 3 to 4 minutes. Stir in the onion, carrot, cinnamon, and rice.

Continue stirring until the rice is coated, about 1 minute.

4. Oil a long, shallow baking dish or casserole.

5. Transfer the rice mixture to a large pot. Pour in the stock, raisins, cayenne, and orange zest and bring to a boil. Remove from the heat and spread the rice mixture over the baking dish.

6. Bake, uncovered, till the rice is tender, about 45 minutes.

7. Spread on lined trays and dehydrate 10 to 12 hours, till grainy-dry.

at camp

8. To rehydrate, add the water just to cover, bring to a boil, and cook down slowly till the rice is soft and the liquid is gone, about 10 minutes. The aim is a fluffy, not soggy, rice. Gently stir in the chives.

Serves 2–3

Gone Fishin' Pilaf

This recipe uses bulgur rather than basmati rice. It can sit happily for hours in water expanding and doing what bulgur does when no one's around to pry. When you return empty-handed from glorious hours of snoozing by the lake in the sun, the fish having swiped your bait on the first cast, lunch or dinner will practically be ready.

2 Sierra cups boiling water

1 Sierra cup bulgur

Small handful of mixed raisins and commercially dried cranberries (currants or sour raisins are also acceptable)

½ Sierra cup pine nuts (or chopped blanched almonds)

2 spoons dried dill

4 spoons commercially dehydrated onion flakes

5–6 large pinches salt

3–4 pinches ground black pepper

Drizzle of olive oil (or canola oil)

Good squirt of lemon or lime juice

1. Get yer fishing gear together. Put on yer shades. Don't forget your visor and water bottle.

2. Fire up the stove or camp fire and set the water to boil in your medium-sized pot.

3. Measure out the bulgur and place in a separate large pot. (Bulgur expands as it's soaking, so make sure you use your biggest pot.)

4. When the water comes to a boil, pour it over the bulgur, close the lid tightly, and go fishin'. Don't forget to put the fire out first.

5. When you get back to camp, take off the lid (on the pot, not on your head — that's why we told you to wear the visor), fluff the bulgur with a fork, and add the remaining ingredients. Mix well but gently. And there ain't no more to tell. Eat.

Serves 3–4

PILAF VARIATIONS

- Add bits of dehydrated stewed chicken (pages 44–45) to the pot right at the start.

- Add poached, baked, or pan-fried trout just as you take the pot off the stove.

- Soak three or four strands of saffron in a few spoons of warm water, then add to the cooking liquid.

- Add a large piece of any of the dehydrated vegetable purées on pages 14–19 to the rice as it's cooking.

- For a sweet pilaf, add dried strawberries, pineapple, mango, or crystallized ginger to the pot, along with a spoon of sugar.

Orange Coconut Pilaf 🏠🔥 or 🔥

If you were making this at home, you'd use lots of lime juice and lime zest, but we're out here on Bald Mountain over-looking Hal's bald head, and we've got dehydrated oranges, OK? Great and interesting tastes here.

- 3 spoons clarified butter (see page 99) or cooking oil
- 3 chiles (red or green, fresh or dried), chopped (see Handling Hot Chiles for precautions, page 37)
- 3 cloves garlic, chopped
  Large handful dehydrated onions, torn into bits (see Dehydrated Veggies, page 10)
- 1 spoon peeled and chopped fresh ginger (optional)
- 1 Sierra cup basmati rice
- 4–5 Sierra cups water, to cover
- 3 slices Candied Orange (see page 12)
- 1 dehydrated kiwifruit, broken into small pieces (optional) (see Dehydrated Fruit, page 9)
  Salt
- ½–1 Sierra cup shredded unsweet-ened coconut
  Large squirt lemon or lime juice (optional)

at home

1. If using fresh chopped chiles, spread them on a lined tray and dehydrate till crumbly, 2 to 6 hours. Otherwise, skip this step and proceed with the following instructions.

at camp

2. Heat the clarified butter in a frying pan. Sauté the chiles, garlic, onions, and ginger (if using) for about 3 minutes to set the flavors and color the onions and garlic.

3. Stir in the basmati rice, coating the grains with the oil mixture.

4. Transfer to a big pot. Cover with the water. Add the candied orange, kiwifruit (if using), and salt to taste; bring to a boil. Cover and cook very slowly till the water is absorbed and the rice is tender, 15 to 20 minutes.

5. Meanwhile, toast the coconut in an unoiled frying pan, stirring till just beginning to brown, about 2 minutes.

6. When the rice is done, open the pot. Using a fork, fluff in the coconut and lemon juice (if using). Cover the pot and set aside for 15 to 20 minutes to let the flavors steep. If you want to eat it warm, set the pot in the ashes to heat up again. Otherwise, eat as is.

Serves 2–3

Sushi Rolls *(Nori-maki)*

Why not? We're testing the imagination, aren't we? We could probably prove that some famous tracker on the way up Mount Fuji in the 18th century insisted on stopping and making some sushi rolls. But we're not doing research here; we're feeding your fancy. So, with a little short-grained rice, vinegar, seaweed, veggies, and Japanese horseradish, you can do your John Belushi imitation and get away with it. Nobody'll hear you except your mates, and they already know you're not to be trusted near an open mike.

4 onions, sliced in ¼-inch rounds

2 red bell peppers, halved and cut lengthwise in ¼-inch slices

2 small zucchini, cut lengthwise in ½-inch slices

1 Japanese eggplant, cut lengthwise in ½-inch slices

4–5 Sierra cups water, 1¾ to cook the rice, 2–3 to rehydrate the veggies, plus a small amount to rehydrate the wasabi powder and moisten your hands, if necessary

1 Sierra cup short-grained rice

1 piece giant kelp *(konbu)*, ½ inch long (optional)

1 spoon sugar

½ spoon salt

2 spoons rice vinegar, plus more to moisten your hands

2 sheets toasted Japanese seaweed *(nori)*

Sushi rolling mat (a flexible, bamboo-slatted square mat called a *maki-su*, obtainable in Asian food shops; see Resources, page 224, for Internet source)

½–1 spoon wasabi powder (Japanese horseradish)

¼ Sierra cup low-sodium soy sauce

at home

1. Dehydrate the onions, peppers, zucchini, and eggplant by spreading on lightly oiled trays and dehydrating till reduced in size and chew-hard in texture, 10 to 15 hours. This will yield about 1 cup dried veggies.

at camp

2. Put the 1¾ cups water in a pot, the rice in the water, and the kelp (if using) on the rice. Bring to a boil. Remove the kelp and discard. (Even Rick's pit bull, Buddy, wouldn't touch the stuff, and he eats the bark off trees.)

3. Cover the pot and cook the rice until the water disappears and the rice feels soft, 10 to 15 minutes. Remove the rice from the pot and cool it as fast as possible. We suggest placing the rice in another pot and placing that in some cold water.

4. While the rice cools, dissolve the sugar and salt in the vinegar in a warm Sierra cup. Using a spoon, fold the solution into the rice. Mix gently.

5. Toast the seaweed over the fire just enough to crinkle it a bit, no more than a few seconds.

6. To rehydrate the veggies, cover with the 2 to 3 Sierra cups water, bring to a boil, remove from the heat, cover, and set aside for 20 minutes. Drain and squeeze dry. If it's a sunny day, spread on a plate to dry further.

7. You're ready to roll. Place the seaweed on the rolling mat. Moisten your hands with the vinegar if you have enough to spare (if not use water). Spoon half of the rice onto the seaweed and press to cover three quarters of it, starting at the end nearest you. It should be about a ¼ inch thick, but relax; no one's measuring. Place half of the rehydrated veggies across the rice about one-third of the way down the seaweed from the end nearest you. With your thumbs under the mat at your end and your fingers holding the filling in place, lift the mat over the filling, roll back and forth gently, open the end of the mat, and extend it further over the remaining

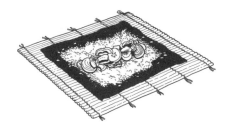

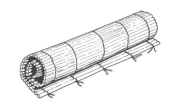

Rolling the sushi

rice. Roll back and forth again, then carefully unroll the mat. There it is, a veggie *maki*.

8. Repeat to make the second roll.

9. Cut the rolls into bite-sized rounds. This is the hardest part, since no camping knife is going to come close to the razor-sharp sushi knives used by the pros. No matter, saw away. Lay the cut pieces on their sides and take the required photo.

Cutting the sushi roll

10. Mix the wasabi powder in a tiny amount of the water in a Sierra cup, just enough to make a paste. Put the soy sauce in another Sierra cup and add the wasabi to taste. Dip the pieces in the soy mixture and eat. *Oishii, yo!*

Serves 2

Japanese Tea & Rice (Ochazuke)

Every culture has its comfort foods, and this is one of Japan's favorites. It's so simple that it defies description. But we'll try. All you need is hot green tea and hot rice. And since you already have the short-grained rice, Japanese horseradish (wasabi), and seaweed (nori) for the sushi (without which no self-respecting backpacker would be caught), you're in business.

VARIATIONS

- Add bits of poached or pan-fried trout to the rice.
- Add shredded dehydrated onion.
- Look for dried packaged toppings in the local Asian market.

½–1 spoon wasabi powder

Small amount of water to mix with the wasabi powder

1 sheet Japanese seaweed (*nori*)

2 Sierra cups cooked short-grain rice

2 cups hot Japanese green tea (It's fine to make them with tea bags.)

1. Mix the wasabi powder with a small bit of water in a Sierra cup to make a paste.

2. Toast the seaweed by passing it quickly over a flame, then shred it.

3. Place the rice in two Sierra cups. In each, add wasabi to taste, half the shredded seaweed, and a bare Sierra cup of tea. Mix (with chopsticks of course) and eat.

Note: To serve more (or fewer) than two people, adjust the recipe according to the ratio of 1 cup of rice per person, ½ sheet of seaweed per person, and 1 cup of tea per person.

Serves 2

Chinese Fried Rice 🏠🔥

Rick's family is hopelessly addicted to Chinese take-out. After 3 or 4 days of camping, withdrawal invariably begins. This dish brings everyone back down to earth.

3 tomatoes

2 onions

1 cup chopped fresh shiitakes or dried white shiitakes

½ Sierra cup rice

1½ Sierra cups water

2 cloves garlic

2 spoons cooking oil

1 spoon low-sodium soy sauce

Dash ground ginger

Dash dry mustard

Dash ground black pepper

at home

1. Slice the tomatoes and onions into ¼-inch rounds. Chop the mushrooms into rough chunks. Lightly oil dehydrator trays and dry 10 to 15 hours, till hard and desiccated.

at camp

2. Pour the rice and 1 Sierra cup of the water into a pot. Bring to a boil and simmer about 20 minutes, till the liquid is almost gone and the rice is fluffy.

3. Meanwhile, chop or break the dried vegetables into small pieces. Bring the remaining ½ Sierra cup water to a boil. Rehydrate the veggies in the boiling water, about 5 minutes. Drain and set aside.

4. Chop the garlic.

5. Heat the oil in a large pan. Add the garlic, rice, and vegetables. Fry, stirring, till the rice is coated with the oil and the veggies are thoroughly mixed in, about 5 minutes.

6. Stir in the soy and spices thoroughly. This dish is best when served in a white cardboard "take-out" box, accompanied by several fortune cookies. But if you didn't have room in your pack, Sierra cups will work just fine. You can always create your own fortune.

Serves 2

About Polenta

While Marco Polo was schlepping across Asia trying to hide cold Chinese noodles in his cloak, his smarter younger brother stayed home and invented polenta (Italian cornmeal), grew fat and sleek on the profits, and saved the Polo family from the ridicule heaped on big bro for claiming, yuk yuk, that he had discovered pasta. What we've discovered is that polenta is one of the most versatile backpacking foods around. It can be boiled, fried, baked, or roasted, eaten sweet for breakfast or savory for dinner. And the beauty of it is that a little goes a very long way: A cup prepared right would feed the entire College of Cardinals. Two bishops and a pawn will do fine with less. Watch.

Most markets now carry polenta, and in many health food stores you can buy it in bulk. If you can't find it, substitute American cornmeal. The difference is in the milling. Ours is milled fine; polenta is milled coarse. Cooking times will be just about the same. If anything, American cornmeal may get done a bit faster. The ratios of meal to water may vary, but the basic recipes here ought to get you home free. We start out with two basic recipes and then show you how to do riffs using either.

Basic Polenta ◉

You want basic? Have we got a bargain for you. This recipe is bared to the bone. Get this right and all others will follow as the night follows the day (or conversely).

3 Sierra cups water

½ cup polenta (measured at home and carried in a resealable bag)

1 spoon clarified butter (see page 99)

¼ spoon salt

1. Bring the water to a slow boil in a large pot. Add the polenta gradually and stir constantly, till thick but not dry, about 15 minutes. Remove the polenta from the heat.

2. Stir in the clarified butter and salt.

Serves 3 (or, with side dishes, 4)

Basic Creamy Polenta 🔥

By using milk or milk powder, you'll have a really creamy polenta, which makes sense given its name here, doesn't it?

2 Sierra cups milk (or reconstituted milk powder: 4 spoons of powder to 2 Sierra cups water)

1 spoon clarified butter (see page 99), plus more to finish, if necessary

1 spoon sugar (optional), plus more to finish, if necessary

¼ spoon salt, plus more to finish, if necessary

½ cup polenta (measured at home and carried in a resealable bag)

1. Combine the milk, 1 spoon clarified butter, 1 spoon sugar (if using), and ¼ spoon salt in a large pot. Bring just to a simmering boil. If the milk begins to boil over, it's too hot.

2. Stir in the polenta in a slow stream. Try to keep the mixture at a low simmer, which you can achieve by constant stirring. The mixture will begin to thicken like a hot cereal.

3. When the mixture is thick but not dry, about 10 minutes, take it off the heat. It's ready to eat as-is or to cool in preparation for other dishes.

4. If you eat it immediately, try adding another spoon of clarified butter and more sugar or salt to taste.

Serves 3 (or, with side dishes, 4)

POLENTA FIXIN'S

Add sautéed onions and garlic, mushrooms, rehydrated tomatoes, or any of the tomato sauces on pages 84–86 to a polenta fresh off the fire — delicious.

VARIATIONS

- **Yogurt Masala Polenta.** Add 2 spoons of reconstituted yogurt masala (page 100) to the first layer of polenta, either under or over the cheese. Believe us, the West-meets-East tastes here are as good as they are surprising.

- **Lasagna Polenta.** Layer the polenta as you would lasagna, with cheeses, tomato sauce, and a mix of Italian spices (oregano, basil, and tarragon), ending with a layer of cheese.

- **Herbed Polenta.** Sauté a large handful of dehydrated onions in oil, season with tarragon, and mix directly into the Basic Polenta while just off the fire. Then spread on a plate to cool, about 30 minutes. When completely cool and thick, cut into triangles, place in the frying pan, and bake.

- **Herbed Cheese Polenta.** Make Herbed Polenta (above) and sprinkle finely crumbled cheese over the individual triangles.

Baked Polenta

You've all heard of Variations on a Theme by Paganini, right? Well, here are some variations on a theme we like to tell people are by his grandma, Pappagena. They begin with the simplest and progress until you've used up all your culinary, not to mention musical, ingenuity.

Basic Polenta 1 or 2
(see pages 128 and 129)

Cooking oil

1 Sierra cup sliced and/or chopped cheeses (Swiss, mozzarella, Gruyère, Parmesan, fontina, or whatever's in your pack)

Ground black pepper

1. Spread the thickened polenta about 1 inch thick on a plate. Allow to cool. Oil a frying pan.

2. Using your hands, layer the fry pan with half the polenta.

3. Sprinkle on about ¾ Sierra cup of the cheese and the pepper to taste.

4. Spread the final layer of polenta. Top with the remaining cheese and pepper to taste.

5. Bake as you would pizza (see pages 217–19), about 15 minutes, till the edges begin to brown.

Note: If using a medium-sized camping pot instead of a frying pan, you'll need to make three layers instead of two. Divide the polenta, cheese, and pepper accordingly. Bake as you would bread (see pages 217–19), about 15 minutes, till the edges begin to brown.

Serves 3

Fried Polenta

A great substitute for morning pancakes. And after years of campsite pancakes, you're ready for a little variation in your life. Live a little? Live a lot!

1 small handful commercially dried cranberries

1 small handful crushed walnuts or other nuts

1 spoon maple syrup (or more to taste)

Basic Polenta 1 or 2 (see pages 128–129)

Cooking oil or clarified butter (see page 99) for frying

Strawberry jam (or any other fruit jam) or maple syrup for topping

1. Immediately stir the cranberries, walnuts, and maple syrup into the prepared polenta. Mix well.

2. Spread the polenta mix on a plate till completely cool and thick, about 2 hours. If eating for breakfast, the cooling can be done the night before if you can store your food safely away from bears and smaller fressers. If you can't safely store it, the cold morning air will speed up the process, and you'll be ready to cook in 30 minutes.

3. Cut the polenta into squares. Heat the oil in a fry pan and and fry the polenta till lightly browned on both sides, about 2 minutes each. Don't be alarmed if the polenta softens in the process. It's supposed to.

4. Eat with the strawberry jam or maple syrup.

Serves 3

Coconut–Kiwi Quinoa 🏠🔥

Creating a recipe based solely on the value of its title as an alliteration may not be the norm, but we've based recipes on far less. Quinoa (pronounced "keen-wa") is a seed native to the Andes, but it cooks like a grain. It's available at natural food stores and on the Internet (see Resources, page 224).

8–10 fresh kiwifruits (or equivalent apricots, raisins, whatever you have)

½ Sierra cup quinoa

Several Sierra cups cold water, for rinsing the quinoa

1 Sierra cup boiling water

2 spoons Thai coconut cream powder, available at some Asian markets and on the Internet (see Resources, page 224)

2 spoons sugar

¼ Sierra cup chopped walnuts

¼ spoon lemon juice

at home

1. To dehydrate ripe kiwis, cut them in half and scoop the innards out with a spoon. Place them on an oiled rack and dry about 24 hours, till hard. Discard the rinds.

at camp

2. Place the quinoa in a medium-sized pot and rinse two or three times with the cold water. Drain, then pour in about ¾ of the Sierra cup of boiling water. Simmer the quinoa and water at a low boil for about 10 minutes as if you were cooking rice, till the water is absorbed and the quinoa is soft. (The beauty of quinoa is that it takes just half the time to cook as ordinary rice.) Stir every 2 to 3 minutes.

3. Meanwhile, mix the coconut powder and sugar into the remaining ¼ cup boiling water. Stir it up, but don't worry if it's a little lumpy. Break the dried kiwi into small pieces, ¼ to ½ inch long. Add the kiwi to the coconut-sugar mixture.

4. After the quinoa has simmered for about 10 minutes, add the kiwi mixture. Simmer another 10 minutes, till the liquid has been absorbed and the kiwi is rehydrated. Remove from the heat.

5. Stir in the walnuts and lemon juice and serve.

Serves 2

Falafel 🏠 🔥

Falafel could be the original "fast food" patty, predating your local burger barn by thousands of years. And while biblical scholars were astounded to find a delicious falafel recipe among the Dead Sea Scrolls, Hal and Rick weren't surprised at all. Here it is.

1 cup dried (or one 15-ounce can) garbanzo beans

One or all of the following four vegetables, to make ½ cup dried vegetables (dehydrating instructions provided below):

2 onions (less if using in combination)

2 bunches scallions, chopped (less if using in combination)

2 red bell peppers (less if using in combination)

½ pound mushrooms (less if using in combination)

¼ teaspoon ground cumin

¼ teaspoon salt

¼ teaspoon freshly ground black pepper

1 Sierra cup boiling water

2 spoons flour

3 spoons cooking oil

at home

1. Soak the dried beans overnight in water to cover. Drain. Cover with water again in a saucepan, bring to a boil, then reduce to a simmer for 20 minutes, till done but not mushy. Drain again. Spread on a lined tray and dehydrate 5 to 7 hours, till pebble-hard. For canned beans, just drain and dehydrate.

2. Spread the vegetables on trays and dehydrate 7 to 10 hours, till sandpaper dry and hard.

3. Chop the beans and vegetables in a blender till the consistency of a coarse wheat flour. Supposedly this can also be done in a food processor. But we couldn't swear to it, because until recently, the closest thing to a food processor in either of our houses was Sugar, Rick's "eat anything" Samoyed.

4. Place the mixture, cumin, salt, and pepper, in a resealable bag and shake.

at camp

5. Pour the mixture into a pot. Pour the boiling water over the mixture and stir as it cools down. Once the mixture is cool enough to touch, stir in the flour.

6. Heat 2 spoons of the oil in a frying pan. Drop a hearty spoonful of the falafel mixture into the pan and pat it down by using a spatula. It should be about the size of a dollar pancake. Your pan should hold about six falafel cakes. When they get browned on one side, about 3 minutes, flip them over. Add another spoon of oil before cooking the next batch.

Note: Traditionally, falafels are served with tabbouleh and hummus in pita bread. (See recipe on page 134 if you would like to do this.)

Makes 12 dollar-pancake-sized falafels; serves 3–4

Tabbouleh & Hummus in Pita Bread ◉

Here's a culinary conundrum. Your first day in the wild, you plan to camp in a no-fire zone. But during the rest of the trip, campfires will be allowed. Your problem? If you can just come up with a dinner that doesn't involve cooking, you can leave the stove and the fuel at home. Have we got a deal for you.

1 box of tabbouleh mix, typically including ¾ cup bulgur wheat and a spice packet

or

¾ cup fine bulgur wheat plus ¼ cup chopped and dehydrated parsley (one bunch), scallions (one bunch), and 3 tomatoes

2 spoons olive oil

1 spoon lemon juice

1½ Sierra cups water, plus 2 spoons more, if necessary

Pinch of salt

½ cup dried hummus mix

4 pita breads (in a resealable bag)

¼ pound bean sprouts

1. Store-bought tabbouleh mixes include a packet of dehydrated parsley and spices. If you prefer, you can combine the dehydrated parsley, scallions, and tomatoes with the bulgur wheat to create your own mix. (This, of course, must be done at home.) The mix will look like a bag of tiny green and red flakes.

2. About 2 hours before you reach camp (as you're taking a break beside a bubbling brook, perhaps), combine the tabbouleh mix, 1 spoon of the olive oil, and lemon juice in a resealable bag. Add 1 Sierra cup of the water. Seal the bag securely and place it inside an upright pot in your pack. (If you reach your campsite with a couple of hours to spare before dinner, simply place all the ingredients into a pot with a top, and set it out in the sun. If the sun's behind a cloud, leave in your pack.

3. After 1 hour, check the mixture and stir, shake, or mush around. If there is no liquid left, add a little more water (about 2 spoons). After 1 more hour, the tabbouleh should be done. It shouldn't be crunchy, and it should be fluffy and dry. If it isn't quite dry, drain the remaining water, stir it, and leave the bag open to the air for about 20 minutes to dry it out. Season with the salt to taste.

4. To prepare the hummus, add the remaining ½ Sierra cup water and the remaining spoon of olive oil to the dry mix. Stir.

5. Carefully split the pita breads in half and spread with the hummus, tabbouleh, and sprouts.

Serves 4

Bulgur Lentil Salad with Eggplant & Walnuts

Berkeley Bill's central philosophy of cooking was simple: If a little is good, a lot must be better. When it was Bill's turn to cook beans, he would cook so much that it would invariably bring to mind the phrase, "It don't mean a hill of beans." In fact, Bill could cook more than a hill's worth. He could have filled entire Alpine ranges with pots of red beans, black beans, and lentils. When it came to leftover beans, camping with Berkeley Bill taught us to be creative.

This salad was one of our better efforts. We would make it in the evening, leave it in a resealable bag overnight, and eat it for both breakfast and lunch the following day.

½–1 Sierra cup Japanese eggplant

4–5 Sierra cups water

½ Sierra cup green lentils

½ Sierra cup bulgur wheat

3 spoons Japanese rice vinegar

2 spoons olive oil

½ spoon dried tarragon

½ Sierra cup chopped walnuts

Salt and ground black pepper

at home

1. Slice one or two Japanese eggplants into ½-inch rounds and dehydrate, about 10 to 15 hours, till hard and crisp.

at camp

2. Although the lentils, bulgur, and eggplant are all cooked with boiling water, this salad works best if you prepare each ingredient separately. Combine 2 Sierra cups water and the lentils in a medium-sized pot; simmer 10 to 15 minutes. Sample the lentils frequently, and stop cooking them when they are tender but not mushy. The cooking time will vary with the size of the lentils and the altitude at which they're cooked. Pour off the hot water and add cold water to the lentils in the pot. Once the lentils are cool, pour off as much of the water as you can.

3. Meanwhile, in another pot, simmer the bulgur in ¾ Sierra cup water, stirring frequently, about 10 minutes, till the water is completely absorbed and the bulgur is fluffy. If the water disappears before the bulgur is done (still crunchy), add a little more water and continue cooking.

4. Mix the vinegar, oil, and tarragon in a Sierra cup.

5. Break up the dehydrated eggplant into ¼-inch chunks and rehydrate with boiling water to cover, 1 to 2 Sierra cups. Once the eggplant is soft, about 10 minutes, pour off the excess water.

6. Allow everything to cool down, then mix the lentils, bulgur, and eggplant with the nuts. Add the tarragon dressing and the salt and pepper to taste. Mix well. Of course, you are free to eat this salad when warm, but it will taste even better in the morning.

Serves 3

Apricot–Mint Couscous 🏠🔥

Couscous is a Middle Eastern staple that can be found in numerous prepackaged forms in the "international foods" section at your local supermarket. The couscous cooks by absorbing hot liquids, so it can take on any number of flavors. This is a sweet and fragrant variation you aren't likely to find packed in a box. It can also be prepared at home and dehydrated in advance.

1 packed cup fresh mint

6–10 fresh apricots (or other fruit)

1½ Sierra cups water

½ vegetarian bouillon cube (optional)

½ spoon ground cumin

1 spoon olive oil (optional)

½ Sierra cup couscous

1 spoon lemon juice

at home

1. Remove the mint leaves from their stems. Spread them on a tray and dehydrate 2 to 4 hours, till the leaves crumble in your hands (or purchase dried mint at the market). Pack 2 tablespoons' worth for your trip.

2. Slice the apricots in half and spread on lightly oiled trays. Dehydrate 10 to 12 hours, till dark, flat, and hard.

at camp

3. Cut the apricots into chunks about ¼ inch across.

4. Place the water in a medium-sized pot. Add the bouillon cube (if using) to the water and bring to a boil. (No bouillon? If you have leftover vegetable stock from a previous meal, use that. No stock? Just add a pinch of salt to the water and proceed.)

5. Add the apricots, cumin, and oil (if using) to the boiling stock. Simmer 2 to 3 minutes, till the fruit is rehydrated and soft.

6. Place the dried mint in a Sierra cup and pour about ¼ Sierra cup of the boiling stock into the cup.

7. Add the couscous to the remaining stock mixture, cover, and let it stand, fluffing occasionally with a spoon to let out the steam.

8. After about 10 minutes, add the lemon juice and the mint mixture to the couscous. Wait another 5 minutes for the couscous to absorb the liquid. Once the liquid is gone and the couscous is fluffy, it is ready to eat.

Note: This dish can also be made entirely at home and dehydrated. Use 1 cup of chopped apricots or other fresh fruit. Start with just 1 cup water in a large pot. Add bouillon (if using), oil (if using), and cumin and bring to a boil. Add the couscous, cover, and remove from the heat. Stir occasionally. Once the couscous has absorbed the liquid, add the fresh fruit, fresh mint leaves, and lemon juice. Mix, fluff with a fork, and dehydrate on a lined tray for 6 to 10 hours, till dry and crumbly to the touch.

Serves 2

[Chapter 6]

Trout

Years ago in the mountains we saw an old biplane drop low over our lake. All of a sudden we noticed the lake surface come alive with thousands of pock marks. We were scared. What were they dropping on us? We found out the next day. The fishing was lousy. Nary a nibble. Finally we bagged a rainbow and inside it got our answer. That old fish was stuffed with tiny hatchlings. The plane had been seeding the lake with trout, each encased in an ice pellet.

There's nothing quite like eating fresh trout high in the mountains. While most of these recipes would likely work with other fish as well, trout is our catch of choice. And who knows? If Tom Sawyer had run away from his Aunt Polly to a high mountain lake full of foot-long Golden trout, he might never have returned.

Cleaning Trout

Find a spot far away from the lake or stream. Nothing is more disgusting than walking along a lakeshore and seeing fish guts strewn along the bank, courtesy of another group of campers. Bring a pot of rinse water with you. With the heel of your boot, dig a hole a couple of inches deep. Hold the fish in your hand, belly up, over the hole. Slice open the belly from the vent (just in front of the back fin) to the head. If you want to cut off the head, do it now. The fish will be slippery; don't drop it. And be careful with that knife.

Once the fish is open, the entrails will almost fall out on their own (into the hole you've dug). Remove the remainder with your hand or your knife. Rinse out the cavity, put the fish in a bag or pot, clean your knife and hands, pour out the dirty rinse water, and cover up the hole. To store trout, either before or after cleaning it, keep it as cool as possible, in a tent, under a tree, behind a rock, anywhere that is cool and shady. And don't forget Mark Twain's advice: However you cook your trout, the sooner you eat it, the better it will taste.

Slicing from vent to head

Removing the entrails

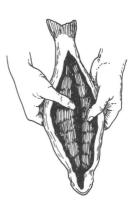

Clean, empty cavity

Pan-Fried Trout

There's something about fresh trout sizzling in a pan at a campsite that can't be equaled. The fish need almost nothing to enhance their flavor; they invariably taste delicious. One caution: Make sure the oil doesn't burn. It starts to smoke and turns black if it gets too hot.

1 spoon cooking oil

1 spoon clarified butter (see page 99)

2 trout, 8–10 inches long (they are traditionally cooked with heads left on)

Salt and ground black pepper

Dash lemon juice

1. Heat the oil and clarified butter in a frying pan. (The oil prevents the butter from burning.)

2. Brown the trout on one side, 4 to 5 minutes (less if they're small or if the fire is very hot). Flip and repeat. Don't over-cook the trout. As soon as the flesh flakes with a fork, it's done. If you aren't sure, take the fish off the fire sooner rather than later. You can always put it back, but you can't reverse overdone fish.

3. Season with the salt and pepper to taste. Turn out on plate, pour the cooking oils over the fish, and add the lemon juice. Can't be beat.

Serves 2

VARIATIONS

- **Trout Amandine**
  When the trout is done, remove the fish from the pan and add ½ Sierra cup chopped almonds (or other nuts) to the oils in the pan. Brown the nuts slowly for 2 to 3 minutes; don't burn them. Pour the toasted almonds over the trout.

- **Trout Flambé**
  Just before eating, hold ¼ Sierra cup brandy over the fire until it's warm to the touch, and light with a match. As the brandy catches fire, pour it over the trout. A soft blue flame will dance over and around the trout for up to half a minute and add another delicate flavor to the dish.

Pouring flaming brandy over trout

Trout Meunière ⬤

(Flour-Dipped, Pan-Fried Trout)

Meunière is French for "miller," as in someone who grinds grain to make flour. This is one of the classic ways of preparing fresh whole trout.

2 trout, 8–10 inches long

2 spoons flour

2 spoons mix of clarified butter (see page 99) and cooking oil

Salt and ground black pepper

½ spoon lemon or lime juice

1. Dip the trout in the flour to coat.

2. Heat the oil and butter mixture in a large pan and add the trout. Season with the salt and pepper to taste.

3. Brown the trout on one side, 4 to 5 minutes. Flip and repeat.

4. Add a dash of lemon juice.

Serves 2

VARIATIONS

- **Cornmeal Meunière**
  Coat the fish with a mixture of flour and cornmeal. Some old-timers put the flour-cornmeal mixture in a bag, drop in the fish, and shake to coat.

- **Milk-Breaded Meunière**
  Make a small cup of milk by mixing instant powdered milk and water. Dip the fish into the milk, then the flour or flour-cornmeal mixture.

- **Egg-Breaded Meunière**
  Substitute a beaten egg for the milk. To make it go farther, add water or milk. Dip the fish into the egg mixture and dredge with seasoned flour.

Grilled Trout

This is how a middle-aged Tom Sawyer would have prepared his fish, once his doctor pointed out the astronomical levels of cholesterol produced by frying fish in bacon fat. It does require a grill, which many campsites already have in place over the fire ring. Lightweight camping grills also work well.

- 1 spoon cooking oil
- 2 trout, 8–10 inches long
- 3 spoons low-sodium soy sauce
- 3 spoons rice vinegar or lemon juice

Lightweight camping grill

1. Oil the grill lightly to prevent the fish from sticking. Place the grill about 5 inches above the coals.

2. Sprinkle the fish cavity with the soy sauce and rice vinegar. Lightly coat the trout's skin as well.

3. Place on the grill. After about 5 minutes, flip the fish by using a spatula and grill another 5 minutes. If some of the skin sticks to the grill, don't worry. When the flesh flakes off easily when poked with a fork, it's ready to eat.

Serves 2

IDEAS AND VARIATIONS

- Add poached trout to a rehydrated meal, turning Barley Soup with Mushrooms (page 30) into Barley Soup with Mushrooms and Trout.

- Add poached trout to Chinese Fried Rice (page 127).

- Add poached trout to white sauce made with the trout stock (page 89). Pour the trout-in-white-sauce over spaghetti or noodles, use as a filling for crêpes (pages 154–55), or use it to make a soufflé (page 157).

- Add leftover cold poached trout to salads made with grains and beans.

- Sauté poached trout in ghee with Indian spices (see Curried Trout, facing page).

- Sprinkle poached trout with soy sauce and ginger and use as filling for Chinese Dumplings (pages 79–81).

Poached Trout

A poached fish is tender and delicious all by itself. But it can also be part of a more complicated dish. The choice is entirely yours.

2 trout, 8–10 inches long
3–4 Sierra cups water, to cover
Salt and ground black pepper
Italian herbs, such as oregano, basil, and thyme

1. Put the trout in a large frying pan and pour in enough water to barely cover. Season with salt, pepper, and Italian herbs of choice to taste.

2. Place the pan over the fire and allow the water to come to a slight boil. The fish will curl up — no problem. There's no need to turn the fish over. It's done when the skin peels off easily and the flesh has lost its translucency and comes easily off the bone. This usually takes about 10 minutes from the time the water begins to boil.

3. Remove the pan from the heat. Remove the fish from the pan, peel off the skin, and flake the flesh from the bones. Ideally, the backbone will come off in one piece, taking most of the skeleton. (Work fast. Flies love poached fish.)

4. When finished, place the fish in the tent till ready to eat and go bury the skin and bones. If you won't be using the poaching water as trout "stock" throw it out far from both your living area and the lake or stream.

Serves 2

Curried Trout

In our ongoing effort to support the noble cause of improvisation, we ask you to blindfold yourself, feel your way to the "spice rack" you intend to take camping, open all the containers or slots, dump the contents into the garbage or, if you miss the garbage can, on the floor. Take off the blindfold and proceed to your own stash of Indian spices, haul 'em out, and commit yourself to a South Asian camping trip. The basic spices are cumin, coriander, turmeric, cayenne, and garam masala (see page 58). Refill the containers with these items and get thee to a mountaintop. Catch a couple of small trout and go to work.

Eat with Spinach and Onion Curry (see page 53) and a nice chutney (see pages 95–98).

½ spoon ground coriander

½ spoon ground cumin

¼ spoon cayenne pepper

¼ spoon ground turmeric

   Salt

2 spoons cooking oil or ghee (see page 100) for frying (or a mixture of both)

2 trout, 8–10 inches long

¼ spoon garam masala (see page 58)

1. You've got two options here. Either mix the coriander, cumin, cayenne, turmeric, and salt to taste and coat the insides and outsides of the trout before frying, or sprinkle them on as you're frying the trout.

2. Heat the oil in a fry pan and add the trout. If not already spiced, spice now.

3. Sauté till the trout flakes easily, about 10 minutes, turning the fish over once halfway through the cooking process. Just before removing the trout from the pan, sprinkle the garam masala over the top.

Serves 2

Baking Trout

To bake a trout, just wrap it in aluminum foil, set it on a bed of hot coals, and cover it with another layer of coals. Bake 15 to 25 minutes, depending on the size of the trout. If you're short on coals, lay it on the coals you have and flip it over after a few minutes. There are lots of flavorful variations to this method of cooking trout. You can wrap the trout individually or lay out several in a row on a single piece of aluminum foil. Crimp the edges upward, so the juices won't drip out. If you want to open the foil wrap to check for doneness, set it up with a "flap" for that purpose. Remember that, because foil doesn't burn, you'll have to pack out the remains of the foil with your other nonorganic garbage.

Flap "down" for baking

Flap "up" to check for doneness

Baked Trout with Rosemary, Tarragon, and Garlic 🔥

Once you get the hang of it, you'll create your own favorite variations of baked trout. All you'll need is a lake or stream where the trout are biting. And don't forget the aluminum foil!

2 trout, 8–10 inches long

    Small dab of clarified butter (see page 99) or oil

1 clove garlic, sliced thin

½ spoon rosemary, or to taste

½ spoon tarragon, or to taste

    Salt and ground black pepper

1. Rub the trout cavities with the clarified butter. Season the cavities with the garlic, rosemary, tarragon, and salt and pepper to taste.

2. Wrap the fish tightly in aluminum foil and place on a bed of hot coals. Cover with more hot coals.

3. Bake until done, about 20 minutes. Once you get good at it, you'll be able to test for doneness by poking a fork through the foil while the fish are cooking. If the fork slides in and out easily, meeting little resistance, dinner is done. Otherwise, check by lifting the foil flap and seeing whether the fish flakes easily with a fork, indicating it's done. If need be, you can add more coals or cook longer.

Serves 2

- **Lemon Trout**
  Omit the clarified butter or oil from the recipe and spritz the inside of the trout with lemon (or lime) juice.

- **Asian Spicy Trout**
  Bake with soy sauce, garlic, ginger (powdered or fresh), and sesame oil. Mix the ingredients together and use 2 to 3 spoons per fish.

- **Yogurt Masala Trout**
  Stuff each fish with rehydrated Yogurt Masala (see page 100), 2 to 4 spoons per fish.

- **Mango-Curry Trout**
  Stuff each fish with rehydrated Yogurt-Mango-Curry Spread (see page 101).

- **Nutty Trout**
  Stuff each fish with a spoon of finely chopped nuts and 2 to 3 prunes soaked for an hour or so in brandy and warm water. Add a dash of sesame oil.

- **Trout over Rice**
  Lay the fish on a bed of cooked rice on the foil; stuff each fish with ½ Sierra cup of a mixture of chopped nuts and cut-up dried fruits (apricots, raisins, apples, and prunes), salt, curry powder, and lemon juice. Bake.

Trout Sashimi ◉

The first rule of trout sashimi is that the fish must be absolutely fresh. They can't sit around for a couple of hours in a pot, even cleaned. You need to eat them soon after catching. If you're fishing near a snowfield, you can pack your catch in snow for 2 to 4 hours. Be sure to clean the fish thoroughly.

There's not a lot of flesh on a trout. Some is also lost in skinning and boning. Don't expect a filling meal, but sashimi is a perfect lunch snack. It also goes well with sushi (pages 124–25).

(1) Loosening the skin from the gills

1 trout, 8–10 inches long

1 spoon wasabi powder

Small amount of water for mixing

3 spoons low-sodium soy sauce

Method 1: Trout in Pieces

1. Skin the trout and peel the flesh from the bones. To skin a fish, begin by cutting under the fins and yanking them toward the head. Then slice along the backbone from head to tail. Using your knife, loosen the skin around the gills (1). Work your fingers or the knife, or both, under the skin at the head and strip it back toward the tail (2).

2. Once the fish is skinned, cut away the flesh, beginning at the backbone and working down (3). Toward the end, fingers work better than a knife.

3. Place the raw fish in a Sierra cup.

4. To finish, mix the wasabi powder with enough water in a Sierra cup to make a paste. Stir in the soy sauce. Dip and eat straight away. Trout sashimi is worth it for the fish stories you can tell at the local sushi bar back home. *Go-enryo naku.*

(2) Stripping the skin from head to tail

Variation: As an alternative to the wasabi powder, try using hot mustard powder. This can also be used in soups and stews.

(3) Cutting away the flesh

Method 2: Whole Trout

1. Bone the fish. Spread open the cleaned fish, gutted side up. Cut gently along one side of the backbone from top to tail (1). Do the same on the other side (2). This severs the spine from the skeletal bones or ribs so that the spine can be pulled out, working from neck to tail. Now get the skeletal bones out. Starting from the tail, work your blade under the bones gently toward the neck, turn the knife around, and come back toward the tail. Starting from the neck, lift the bones away (3). This leaves a whole, flat, boned fish with the skin still on the "under" side.

2. You can now remove the flesh from the skin by working your blade under the flesh and scraping it away. Start at the tail, which you can grasp for leverage, and move up (4). You'll have the fish in one piece this way. Put flesh into a Sierra cup.

3. Finish same as Method 1, step 4.

Serves 1

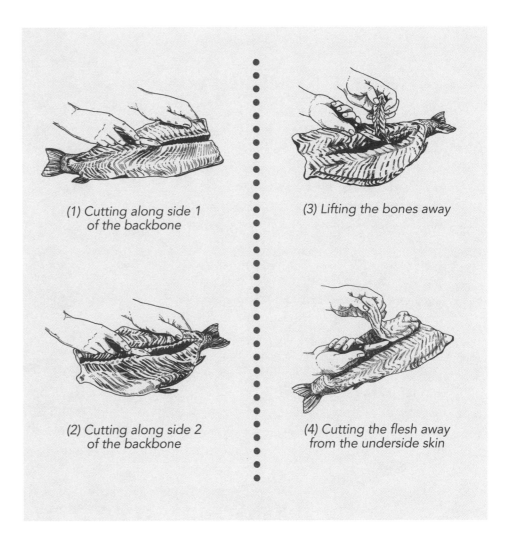

(1) Cutting along side 1 of the backbone

(3) Lifting the bones away

(2) Cutting along side 2 of the backbone

(4) Cutting the flesh away from the underside skin

TOM SAWYER'S SPECIAL SAUCE

"While Joe was slicing bacon for breakfast, Tom and Huck asked him to hold on a minute; they stepped to a promising nook in the river-bank and threw in their lines; almost immediately they had reward. Joe had not had time to get impatient before they were back again with some handsome bass, a couple of sun perch and a small catfish — provisions enough for quite a family. They fried the fish with the bacon and were astonished, for no fish had ever seemed so delicious before. They did not know that the quicker a fresh-water fish is on the fire after he is caught the better he is; and they reflected little upon what a sauce open-air sleeping, open-air exercise, bathing and a large ingredient of hunger makes, too."

— MARK TWAIN, *Tom Sawyer*
(Chapter 14, "Happy Camp
of the Freebooters")

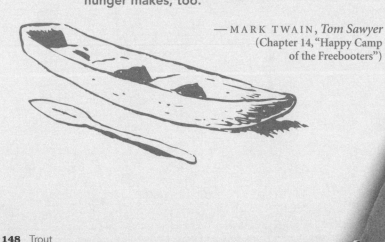

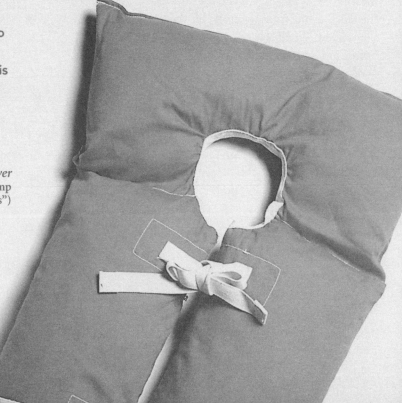

[Chapter 7]

Pancakes, Crêpes & Soufflés

Pancakes are the culinary equivalent of camping equipment. Nobody goes up a mountain or down a stream without 'em. As long as that's the case, you might as well have the best that imagination can provide. That means NO READY-MADE MIXES. Think about it — what else can you do with prepackaged pancake mix except make more pancakes? Not a good strategy if you might want to make a cake, or crêpes, or anything else that requires flour. So follow along and make your own. We'll give you a basic recipe and a couple of variations. It'll be sort of like moving from the wool blanket of yore to the high-tech lightweight fibers in your sleeping bag or parka. And if you're not wedded to maple syrup, try our sweet schmeers (pages 102–5) as toppings.

HOT CAKES AND HEAT

Whatever your preference in pancakes, you'll need to keep the pan hot, but not too hot. If the pan is too cool, the batter won't cook and your pancakes will be leathery and yellowish white, rather than fluffy and golden brown. On the other hand, too much heat will burn the butter or oil, and charbroil your pancakes.

One way to check the pan temperature is to simply make a small "test" pancake. If it isn't right, just feed it to Fido and alter the heat accordingly. Another way to test the heat is to flick a few drops of water into the hot pan. When the water just starts to "dance" over the surface, the temperature is just right.

Basic Pancakes ◉

This is the stripped-down model, as in stripped down to your wool skivvies. In fact, eat 'em in your wool skivvies. That way, you'll get more faster as the rest of the crowd is fiddling with their Velcro tabs and Capilene-treated polyester microfiber thermal bottoms.

1 Sierra cup flour

2 spoons powdered milk

¼ spoon baking powder (optional) (see Powder & Soda, facing page)

⅛ spoon salt

2 eggs or equivalent powdered egg mix

1 spoon oil or melted clarified butter (see page 99), plus more for cooking

1 Sierra cup water

1. Mix together the flour, powdered milk, baking powder (if using), salt, and powdered egg mix (if using) with a fork or spoon in a medium-sized pot.

2. Add the eggs (if using fresh), oil, and enough of the water to make a thick batter that just runs off a spoon. Don't worry if there are lumps.

3. Heat a few drops of oil or a bare ¼ spoon clarified butter — you don't need more because there's already oil in the batter — in a fry pan over medium heat. When the pan is hot, drop a spoon of batter in the middle and cook till little holes begin to appear on the surface of the batter, 2 to 3 minutes. Flip with a spatula and cook no more than 1 minute on the other side. This is the test pancake (See Hot Cakes and Heat, at left), and it may not look as golden brown as the others will. Thereafter, spoon batter to make up two or three small pancakes at a time.

4. Cook and serve, then let the eater make a batch for the eatee.

Makes 10–15 small pancakes, enough for 2 people

Buttermilk Pancakes 🔥

We've been backpacking for over half a century and have yet to see a "buttermilk sky." Hoagy Carmichael saw one in Canyon Passage and wrote the song that keeps us on the lookout. In the meantime, however, we've discovered powdered buttermilk, which works the way powdered milk does, only better. You can find it in lots of supermarkets and natural food stores. You may never go back to powdered milk pancakes again.

- 1 Sierra cup flour
- 2 spoons powdered buttermilk
- ¼ spoon baking powder
- ¼ spoon baking soda
- 2 large pinches of salt
- 2 eggs or equivalent powdered egg mix
- 1 spoon oil or clarified butter (see page 99), plus more for cooking
- 1 Sierra cup water

1. Mix together the flour, powdered buttermilk, baking powder, salt, and powdered egg mix (if using) with a fork or spoon in a medium-sized pot.

2. Add the eggs (if using fresh), oil, and enough of the water to make a thick batter that just runs off a spoon.

3. Heat a few drops of oil or a bare ¼ spoon clarified butter — you don't need more because there's already oil in the batter — in a fry pan over medium heat. When the pan is hot, drop a spoon of batter in the middle and cook till little holes begin to appear on the surface of the batter, 2 to 3 minutes. Flip with a spatula and cook no more than 1 minute on the other side. This is the test pancake (see Hot Cakes and Heat, facing page), and it may not look as golden brown as the others will. Thereafter, spoon batter to make up two or three small pancakes at a time.

4. Cook and serve, then let the eater make a batch for the eatee.

Makes 10–15 small pancakes, enough for 2 people

POWDER & SODA

Baking powder allows the pancake to rise while cooking, yielding a thicker (and, some people say, lighter) pancake. Leave it out, and the result will be thinner but faster cooking. It's a matter of taste. Rick likes the baking powder blimps, Hal likes the leavenless silver dollars. When they're camping together, first one up makes the call, though when recipes call for buttermilk, a combination of baking powder and baking soda is required. Why baking soda? It reacts quickly to leaven acid-containing ingredients like buttermilk, molasses, honey, and fruits. And it's even kosher to mix with baking powder for an extra lift. Think of the possibilities: buttermilk biscuits or pancakes with raisins and strawberries and even a banana or two. Dream on.

PUMPKIN PURÉE

To make your own purée, cut in half a small pumpkin or a medium-sized butternut or kabocha squash. (Kabocha is the round, dark-green squash with lighter green streaks and pale-orange flesh.) Scrape out the seeds, place cut side down on a baking tray, and bake in a 400°F oven until the flesh is soft, 25 to 30 minutes. When cool enough to handle, scrape out the flesh and mash with a fork or potato masher, or, for a finer purée, place in the blender.

Pumpkin Pancakes 🏠 🔥

Since pumpkins and squash are both in the gourd family, you can always find something to make pumpkin pancakes. Anyway, you can always open a can of pumpkin purée and get to work.

1 cup canned or homemade pumpkin purée (see box at left)

½ Sierra cup cold water, to rehydrate

¾ Sierra cup flour

1 heaping spoon sugar

½ spoon baking powder (¾ spoon if not using baking soda)

¼ spoon baking soda (optional) (see Powder & Soda, page 151)

2 big pinches salt

1 lightly beaten egg or equivalent powdered egg mix

2 spoons powdered buttermilk (or powdered milk)

1 Sierra cup water, for mixing

1 spoon oil or clarified butter (see page 99), plus more for cooking

1 handful pecan halves or walnut halves

2–3 spoons pure maple syrup or equivalent powdered syrup

at home

1. Spray a light coat of oil onto a lined dehydrator tray. Spread the pumpkin purée on the tray and dehydrate 24 hours, till the consistency of fruit leather. Fold in half or quarters and store in an airtight bag.

at camp

2. Rehydrate the pumpkin purée in just enough of the cold water to cover. Bring to a boil and simmer 5 to 10 minutes. If you've added too much and the pumpkin is watery, just boil away the excess, stirring till thick.

3. Combine the flour, sugar, baking powder, baking soda (if using), salt, powdered egg mix (if using), and powdered buttermilk in a pot. Add the purée and beaten egg (if using fresh).

4. Pour in enough of the water to make a smooth, thick batter. Let it sit while you prepare the nuts.

5. Toast the nuts in a small, unoiled frying pan over the fire till they're warm but not burned, 2 to 3 minutes. Add 1 to 2 spoons of the maple syrup and stir to coat the nuts. Remove from the heat and set aside in a Sierra cup or on a plate.

6. Spread a thin film of oil in a fry pan. When the pan is hot, drop in a spoon of batter. When the batter begins to show a couple of little holes, 2 to 3 minutes, flip. Cook another 30 seconds or so. This test pancake (see Hot Cakes and Heat, page 150) may not look as golden brown as the others will. Thereafter, spoon batter to make two or three pancakes at a time.

7. Serve by topping with the glazed pecans and a drizzle of maple syrup. Our trick, your treat.

Makes 10–15 medium-sized pancakes, enough for 2 adults or 1 alienated teenager

Pecan Pancakes ⬤

We use pecans, you use almonds, the people in the next campsite use walnuts, and who knows, maybe Ranger Ron himself is into filberts. It just don't matter. In fact, if you're an obsessive-compulsive, sit down and lovingly pick out all the little nut bits in your gorp stash and use them. Nuts to you.

1 Sierra cup flour

½ Sierra cup finely chopped pecans, or other nuts of your choice

2 spoons milk powder or buttermilk powder

½ spoon baking powder (¾ spoon if not using baking soda)

¼ spoon baking soda (if using buttermilk; see Powder & Soda, page 151)

½ spoon sugar

¼ spoon salt

2 eggs or equivalent powdered egg mix

1 spoon oil or clarified butter (page 99), plus more for cooking

1 Sierra cup water

1. Place the flour, pecans, milk powder, baking powder, baking soda (if using), sugar, salt, and powdered egg mix (if using) in a pot. Mix in the eggs (if using fresh), oil, and enough of the water to make a batter that is barely thin enough to run off a spoon.

2. Heat a few drops of oil or a bare ¼ spoon clarified butter in a fry pan over medium heat. When the pan is hot, drop a spoon of batter in the middle and cook till little holes begin to appear on the surface of the batter, 2 to 3 minutes. Flip with a spatula and cook no more than 1 minute on the other side. This is the test pancake (see Hot Cakes and Heat, page 150), and it may not look as golden brown as the others will. Thereafter, spoon batter to make up two or three small pancakes at a time.

Makes 10–15 small pancakes, enough for 2 people

Crêpes ⬤

Do you remember Paris? Seems like only yesterday: that little café on the Left Bank, the red-and-white checkered table-cloth, the crêpes. Well, you can have it all again. Set up camp on the left bank of your favorite creek, spread your poncho over a tree stump, and get to work on the crêpes.

½ Sierra cup flour

1 spoon milk powder

Dash of salt

1 egg, beaten (if using fresh), or equivalent powdered egg

2 spoons cooking oil or melted clarified butter (see page 99), plus more as needed to grease the pan

½ Sierra cup water, for mixing

½ Sierra cup crêpe filling (see Crêpe Fillings and Fancifications, page 155)

1. Combine the flour, milk powder, salt, and powdered egg (if using) in a pot and mix with a fork or spoon. Stir in the egg (if using fresh), 1 spoon of the oil, and enough of the water to make a thin batter, about the consistency of a smoothie.

2. Heat 1 spoon of the oil in a pan. Pour 2 to 3 spoons of the batter into the center of the pan. Tilt the pan away from you, then to the side, then toward you, so the batter spreads out in a circle as thin as you can get it. The crêpe will cook in about 1 minute and is ready to turn when the center looks almost, but not quite, dry.

3. Work a spatula underneath the crêpe to turn it, or pick it up with your fingers (very carefully) and flip it over. The second side takes less time to cook than the first, about 30 seconds. The crêpe should be pliable, so it can be wrapped around the filling. If the batter begins to stick, add a spritz or two of oil to the pan between the crêpes.

4. Hal stacks the crêpes on a plate and lets each camper fill theirs individually. Rick, on the other hand, spoons the filling onto each crêpe in the pan after he flips it, forming a line down the center. Then he flips the sides of the crêpe over the filling with the spatula, thus warming the filling as he cooks the crêpe. Both ways work well.

Makes 3–4 crêpes, enough for 2 people

Spreading the crêpe around the pan

CRÊPE FILLINGS & FANCIFICATIONS

Dinner crêpes:

- Grated (sliced) cheese
- Poached Trout (page 142)
- Rehydrated shiitake mushrooms or sun-dried tomatoes
- White Sauce (page 89)
- Any combination of the above

Dessert crêpes:

- Rehydrated fruit, fruit purée, or yogurt spread
- Sprinkle the crêpe with lemon juice, cinnamon, or sugar

Crêpe flambé:
Pour a little brandy in a Sierra cup. Hold it over the fire until it's warm to the touch. Light it with a match. As the brandy catches fire, pour it over the crêpe. Works best when served after sundown.

Quesadillas

The shelf life of a tortilla in the sealed package at the corner grocery is almost 3 weeks. As long as you keep them relatively cool and stored in a resealable bag, tortillas will easily keep 5 to 7 days on a camping trip. Quesadillas are essentially small tortilla pizzas. They are especially good for kids, since slices can be eaten with little hands (no forks or plates needed) and each quesadilla can be seasoned individually to taste: lots of salsa and cayenne pepper for dad, plain cheese quesadillas for your picky 4-year-old.

1½ pounds tomatoes

½ pound mushrooms

1–2 Sierra cups water, to rehydrate

4 spoons cooking oil

8 corn or flour tortillas

1 Sierra cup sliced cheese (such as mozzarella or Monterey Jack, or whatever is in your pack)

¼ Sierra cup dehydrated salsa (see recipes on pages 91–94)

Seasonings of choice (we suggest salt, ground black pepper, and cayenne as you dare)

at home

1. Slice the tomatoes and mushrooms ¼ to ⅜ inch thick. Dehydrate on oiled trays for 24 hours, till hard.

at camp

2. Place the tomatoes and mushrooms in a pot with the water. Bring to boil and cook, stirring, for 5 minutes till rehydrated. Drain, reserving the water, and set on a plate (to dry).

3. Rehydrate the salsa with just enough of the boiling water so that it ends up the consistency of, well, salsa.

4. Heat 1 spoon of the oil in a frying pan. Place one tortilla in the pan. Spread about ¼ Sierra cup of the cheese on the tortilla, then ¼ of the rehydrated mushrooms and tomatoes. Spoon on some of the salsa and add your favorite seasonings to taste. Top with another tortilla.

5. After about 1 minute, when the cheese has started to melt, flip the quesadilla. After another 30 seconds, when the cheese has melted completely, it is ready to slice and eat.

6. Add a little more oil before cooking the next one.

7. Cut the quesadillas into slices, like a pizza. Eat with your hands; no plates or utensils allowed.

Makes 4 quesadillas, enough for 2 people

Spinach & Cheese Soufflé 🏠🔥

This whole thing started years ago when somebody we met in the Marble Mountains said, "You guys talk a good meal, but what can you really do?" We looked at each other, and one of us blurted out, "Come back in an hour and we'll feed you a soufflé." That was real smart. We'd never made one but had read enough about egg whites and sauces to do stand-up comedy, and we were now going on stage in an hour. We tinkered, fiddled, and faked and produced the first-ever Greenspan-Kahn You-Name-It-We'll-Make-It soufflé. He never knew what hit him.

  1 cup baby spinach leaves

  ½ Sierra cup boiling water, to rehydrate the spinach

  ½ Sierra cup thick White Sauce (page 89; use the spinach stock discussed in step 2)

  ½ Sierra cup diced cheese

     Salt and ground black pepper

  2 eggs or equivalent powdered egg whites

2–3 spoons water, if necessary

  ½ spoon ghee (see page 100) or vegetable oil, for greasing the pot

     Small amount of flour, for flouring the pot

at home

1. Throw the spinach in the dehydrator. Walk the dog for an hour.

at camp

2. Rehydrate the spinach with the boiling water in a medium-sized pot for about 5 minutes. Pour the water off the spinach and use it as the vegetable stock for the white sauce.

3. Add the spinach, diced cheese, and salt and pepper to taste to the prepared white sauce.

4. Separate the eggs (if you are using real eggs) and add the yolks to the white sauce. If you are using powdered egg whites, you'll have to add 2 or 3 spoons of water to the white sauce instead. When the sauce mixture is the right consistency, it should be wet and thick, like a cake batter.

5. In a large pot, use a fork to whip the egg whites — powdered or real — until they are foamy and stiff ("stiff but not dry" is what the cookbooks say). With powdered egg whites, it ain't easy. Your partner may need to take a shift whipping the whites after your wrist gets sore. But trust us, it can be done.

6. Grease and lightly flour a small pot. Gently fold the egg whites into the sauce mixture. Pour it into the pot and bake 20 to 25 minutes, till double in bulk and slightly browned on top.

Serves 2

Variations: **Mushroom and Cheese Soufflé.** Substitute dried shiitake mushrooms for spinach. Break the mushrooms into small pieces before rehydrating.
Trout Soufflé. Substitute poached, boned and skinned trout (page 142) for the spinach and cheese. Use the poaching liquid as stock for the white sauce.

ONE POTATO, TWO POTATO...

While supermarket shelves are full of instant (powdered) mashed potato mixes, they are sorely lacking in anything that can be reconstituted into latkes. Even the products claiming to be latke mixes are full of white potato powder. Powder might be alright for potato pancakes, but we refuse to call them "latkes" unless they are made with grated potatoes. Don't despair. Go to a restaurant supply store and ask for dehydrated hash browns. For the same price as you'd pay for a single 8-ounce pack of freeze-dried hash browns at your local camping store, you'll get almost 2½ pounds of freeze-dried grated potato. If you use these for latkes, they will take longer to reconstitute (15 to 20 minutes in boiling water), but otherwise they work fine.

Latkes (Potato Pancakes)

It is well known that anyone who is away from home during the 8 days of Chanukah is required by Talmudic law to cook latkes, *Jewish potato pancakes. Traditionally,* latkes *are deep-fried in oil, but during the holiday season (or any other time of the year), hauling vast containers of cooking oil to your camp can be difficult. Instead, our recipe stretches a small quantity of cooking oil into a large stack of* latkes. *And lots of* latkes, *after all, is what Chanukah is all about!*

Serve with rehydrated applesauce (page 103).

3 medium-sized potatoes	1 egg or reconstituted powdered egg
2 medium-sized onions, chopped fine	2 spoons flour
1 bunch scallions, chopped fine	Dash salt and ground black pepper
2 Sierra cups boiling water, for rehydrating	3 spoons cooking oil

at home

1. Grate the potatoes.

2. Blanch the potatoes by dropping them into boiling water for exactly 2 minutes. Drain, and plunge the grated potatoes into a container of ice water for about 5 minutes. Pour off the ice water.

3. Lightly oil and line two dehydrator trays. Spread the grated and blanched potatoes on one and the chopped onions and scallions on the other. Dehydrate for 24 hours.

4. You can bag the potatoes and veggies together, or you can mix everything later at your campsite. If you don't want to use onions and scallions, almost any chopped vegetable will do (mushrooms or peppers, for example). When you're done, the total volume of the potatoes and chopped veggies should be about 1¼ cups (dehydrated).

at camp

5. Put the dehydrated potatoes and vegetables into a pot and pour the boiling water over them. Rehydrate for 2 minutes. Drain off the water.

6. Mix in the egg, then the flour. Season with the salt and pepper to taste.

7. Heat 2 spoons of the oil in a fry pan. Drop one heaping spoon of the latke batter into the pan. Use your spatula to spread this large dollop till 3 to 4 inches across. We fit about three latkes at a time in our fry pan. Once the bottoms are browned, 3 to 4 minutes, flip the latkes over with a spatula. Cook 2 to 3 minutes longer. Remove and set aside. Add the remaining spoon of oil to the pan before cooking the next batch.

Makes 6–8 latkes, enough for 2 hungry hikers

Corn Cakes 🏠🔥

A camping trip, whether by canoe, car, foot, or pack animal, isn't exactly intergalactic travel (though you've never met our friend Virgil, who's been there), but a new, never-made-at-a-campsite recipe still boldly goes where no man has gone before. If Captain Kirk's ever eaten a corn cake in warp drive, we haven't seen him. But he ought to.

3 red or yellow bell peppers

3 bunches fresh scallions

3 cobs fresh corn or 1 can (12 ounces)

1–2 Sierra cups boiling water, to rehydrate

2–3 spoons clarified butter (see page 99) or cooking oil

½ Sierra cup cornmeal or polenta

½ Sierra cup flour

½ spoon baking powder

¼ spoon baking soda

2 big pinches salt

2 eggs or equivalent powdered egg mix

2 spoons powdered buttermilk

at home

1. Slice the peppers ¼ to ⅜ inch thick. Slice the scallions thin.

2. Shuck the corn and cook in boiling water no longer than 3 minutes. When cool, slice off the kernels. Spread on drying trays. If using canned corn, drain and spread on drying trays.

3. Dehydrate the peppers and corn for 24 hours, till hard. Dehydrate the scallions for 1 hour, till crumbly.

at camp

4. Rehydrate the bell pepper in the boiling water to cover. Remove and squeeze dry. Reserve the water. Chop the pepper into small bits.

5. Bring the reserved water back to a boil and rehydrate the corn kernels in the water till soft. Drain, but reserve the liquid.

6. Sauté the bell pepper and corn in 1 spoon of the clarified butter, about 5 minutes. Crumble the dehydrated scallions into the pan. Set aside.

7. Mix together the corn meal, flour, baking powder, baking soda, and salt in a large pot. Add the eggs and powdered buttermilk. Mix well.

8. Pour in 1 Sierra cup of the reserved liquid; mix. If pockets are still dry, add more liquid or water, but don't — DON'T — overdo it. The aim here is not a smooth batter, but a clumpy one.

9. Lightly oil a pan and heat. Spoon the batter into the pan and fry till golden and slightly puffed, about 2 minutes on each side. Each corn cake should be about 4 inches across.

10. Top with a sweet schmeer, such as Apple Butter (page 104) or Applesauce (page 103), or a savory one, such as Rick's Chutney (page 96) or Rattler Salsa (page 94). Beam up the crew.

Serves 3–4

[Chapter 8]

Breads & Cakes

"Breakneck Hill" Hudson River.

Marie Antoinette, poor dear, lost her head over baked goods. "Let them eat cake," indeed.

What's hidden from view is that she had already proclaimed, "Let them eat bagels and baozi and challah too, and a nice nut bread for tea." Smart lady. Terrible timing. But we've got time, so let's go to work. First, however, you're going to have to overcome your fear and trembling when somebody says, "yeast." Baking yeast breads is fun. It's easy. It's satisfying. It's life-enhancing. Like Hemmingway's sun, the dough will rise. Honest, it will, and you'll live to tell about it. And then you'll move on to the baking powders and sodas and get down and dirty (we're always dirty) with the sweet stuff: enough cakes to put a lowland bakery out of business.

Baking with Yeast

Proofing yeast.
You'll want to proof the yeast before using. "Proofing" means just that: testing to see if it works. Empty a packet of yeast into a Sierra cup. Add two large pinches of sugar. (Yeast loves to nosh on sugar as it's coming out of its coma.) Then add just enough warm water to allow it to "swim," about ¼ Sierra cup. Cover with a plate, place a rock on the plate to keep the seal in a wind, and place in a warm spot, near the fire or in the sun. Check in 5 minutes. The yeast should have begun to bubble and expand. It's ready. If you start with cold water, it may take 15 to 20 minutes to proof. *Note:* Don't use hot water with yeast. Water over 115°F will kill it.

What do to in cold, cloudy weather.
Place the Sierra cup with the yeast mixture in your sleeping bag. This'll work, honest.

Dry before wet ingredients.
You've got a finite amount of flour, salt, sugar, yeast, milk powder, buttermilk, nuts, raisins, and other things that go into breads. You've got plenty of water. Begin with too much water, and you're going to use up all the dry stuff. Results? No pancakes tomorrow, no cake, no nothin'. So measure out the dry ingredients first, then add the liquid to them.

Kneading.
When dry and wet are mixed, the kneading begins. That's the best part. Dust your hands and a plate with flour. On the plate, form the dough into a ball. Then, using the heel of your hand, push the ball away from you, bring it back, and keep at it until the dough has a nice elastic feel to it. You can't over-knead, so if you like, just keep on till the pleasure wanes.

Rising.
The kneaded dough needs time for the yeast to do its work. Place the dough in an oiled and floured pot — the one you're going to bake it in — and place the pot in the sun or near the fire. If it's got to go in the sleeping bag, place the pot on a plate to

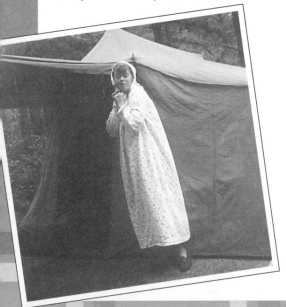

protect the bag from pot black. In warm weather, the rising can take as little as 15 minutes; in cooler, about 25 minutes. Rising is complete when the dough is soft and spongy and has doubled in bulk.

Second rising.
A second rising makes some breads lighter. It also allows you to do other things around the campsite, like snooze, fish, read, or — do we really have to tell you? To start a second rising, punch the dough. Literally. Flour your fist, and punch it into the risen dough. The dough will deflate like a May-through-September romance. Cover the pot and place it back in the warm spot. Another 15 to 25 minutes will bring it back up to speed.

Small pot or large pot?
Camping pots are notoriously inefficient conductors of heat. If you want the middle of the bread to be done, use a small pot (usually about 5 inches in diameter), except when making a circle bread, such as challah (pages 169–71), which works fine in a medium-sized pot (about 6 inches in diameter).

Salt.
Salt evens out the leavening process and helps lighten the load. That's why unsalted breads are so heavy.

Flours.
If you'd like to include whole wheat, rye, or other non-white flours, use half-white, half the other flour of your choice. The bread dough will be easier to handle and the end result lighter.

Other ingredients.
The more things you add to the dough, the harder it is to get it to rise. Use ingredients such as dried fruits, nuts, garlic, and onion in sparing amounts.

Turning the pot.
The heat in the fire ring is hotter near the burning coals than away from them. For even baking, occasionally turn the pot halfway round in its nested coals.

Testing for doneness.
To test for doneness, tap the top middle of the baked bread with the fingernail on your middle finger. If the bread sounds hollow, it's done. If not, keep on baking until it is. It will be worth the wait.

Baguette in a Pot: The Generic Loaf 🔥

Flour, yeast, salt, water. From these the French nation was built, or at least the long loaf that all characters in all French films tuck under their arms as they cycle home or to work or to war or to l'amour d'après-midi. Since your camping oven is a pot and pots are round, you may want to rename the baguette and call it La Rondelle. Or something. (We never got to third-year French.) Master this, and you've mastered the art of bread baking.

See assorted schmeers in chapter 4 for suggested spreads.

½ spoon cooking oil or clarified butter (see page 99), for greasing the pot

1 packet (¼ ounce) dried yeast

2 pinches sugar

¼ Sierra cup warm water to raise the dough

1 level Sierra cup flour, plus more for dusting the plate, the pot, and your hands

¼ spoon salt

½–1 Sierra cup water to form the dough

1. Make preparations for baking in coals or on a camping stove (see pages 217–219).

2. Spread a thin layer of oil on the bottom and sides of a small camping pot. Sprinkle with flour.

3. Sprinkle the yeast into a Sierra cup. Add the sugar and warm water, and stir with a fork or spoon. Cover and set in the sun or another warm spot until proofed (see Baking with Yeast, page 162), about 5 minutes.

4. In the meantime, mix the flour and salt together in a large pot. When the yeast is ready, mix it into the flour mixture with a fork. Gradually mix in enough of the water to form a slightly moist ball of dough.

5. Dust your hands and a plate with flour. Knead the dough (see Baking with Yeast, page 162) on the plate till the dough is pliant and elastic to the touch. If you've started with too wet a dough, you'll need to add more flour, a very little at a time. If you've started with too dry a dough, you'll have to add more water, a very little at a time.

6. Once the dough is thoroughly kneaded, place it in the oiled and floured pot, cover, and leave in a warm spot to rise till doubled in bulk. This will take 15 to 25 minutes, depending on ambient warmth, the quality of the dough, the temperature of the water used, and the calculations of the annual astrologers' convention in Ashtabula, Ohio.

7. Bake the bread as is, or punch down the dough (see Baking with Yeast, page 163) for a second rising. If you choose the latter option, place the punched-down loaf back in the warm spot and give it another 15 minutes or so, till it rises again into a soft, spongy dough.

8. Bake 15 to 20 minutes, or until the top sounds hollow when you tap it with your finger or fingernail.

9. Remove from the heat and allow to cool in the pot until it easily tips out onto a plate. Take one too many photos of the brilliant result, proclaim "Ma foi! C'est magnifique!" to whomever's in earshot, then sit down, shut up, and eat.

Makes 1 small loaf, enough for 2–4 people, depending on appetite, accompanying dishes, and piggishness

VARIATIONS

- **Buttermilk Baguette.** Add 1 spoon milk powder or buttermilk powder to the flour mixture.
- **Butter Baguette.** Add 1 spoon melted clarified butter or oil to the flour mixture.
- **Garlic Baguette.** Add 1 clove finely chopped garlic to the flour mixture.
- **Onion Baguette.** Rehydrate 2 spoons onion, squeeze dry, chop fine, and add to mix. Because the onions will be moist, adjust the amount of water that you'll add to the dough before kneading.
- **Golden Baguette.** Spread ½ spoon melted clarified butter over the top of the risen dough just before baking. This will give the crust a golden hue. At home, you'd use a pastry brush; here, you'll use the back of a spoon or your fingers to "brush" the butter on the dough.
- **Herbed Baguette.** We don't much like overly flavored herbed breads, but if that's your thing, sprinkle as much or as little as you like of your favorite herbs onto the dough and knead them in.

Whole Wheat Bread ⬤

How many kinds of flour should you take camping? As many as you like. Of course, if you're backpacking you'll need to make some weight adjustments — more of one will mean less of another. We've met flour fanatics who proudly carry white, whole wheat, rye, potato, high gluten, low gluten, high starch, low starch flours into the backcountry all packed in separately labeled, tidy airtight bags for days of mixing and matching. It's not much different from the angler who hauls in lures, flies, bubbles and bobbers, three kinds of bait, four sizes of hook, and a couple of different weights of monofilament line and leader material. So no finger-pointing or guilt-tripping permitted. Enjoy what you enjoy. We enjoy whole wheat.

½ spoon cooking oil, for greasing the pot

1 packet (¼ ounce) dried yeast

2 large pinches sugar

¼ Sierra cup warm water to raise the dough

½ Sierra cup white flour, plus 2 spoons for dusting the pot, your hands, and the kneading plate

½ Sierra cup whole wheat flour

½ spoon salt

1 spoon milk powder (optional)

1 spoon melted clarified butter (optional; see page 99)

1 Sierra cup water to form the dough

1. Make preparations for baking in coals or on a camping stove (see pages 217–19).

2. Spread a thin layer of oil on the bottom and sides of a small camping pot. Dust with flour.

3. Sprinkle the yeast into a Sierra cup. Add the sugar and the warm water, and stir with a fork or spoon. Cover and set in the sun or another warm spot until proofed (see Baking with Yeast, page 162), about 5 minutes.

4. Mix the flours, salt, and milk powder (if using) in a large pot.

5. Allow the melted clarified butter (if using) to cool slightly so that it doesn't kill the yeast. Add it and the proofed yeast to the flour mixture.

6. Pour the 1 Sierra cup water into the mixture in small amounts, stirring till the dough gets too thick to mix further with a spoon.

7. Dust a plate with flour, and spill out the dough onto the plate. Dust your hands with flour and begin to knead (see Baking with Yeast, page 162). If you need to add more water, do it in very small amounts, so that you don't over-moisten the dough. Ditto with the flour if the dough is too wet. Whole wheat flour (and other non-white flours) may tend to produce a stickier dough. Don't worry; just keep dusting your hands and kneading.

8. When you have a glossy, elastic dough, place it in the prepared pot, cover, and set in the sun or another warm place to rise. The rising will take a little longer than with a white flour loaf; it will double in bulk in about 25 minutes.

9. Punch the loaf down (see Baking with Yeast, page 163) and let it rise again, 15 minutes or so.

10. Bake 15 to 20 minutes, till a sharp rap on the top rings hollow.

11. Allow the loaf to cool in the pot till it tips out easily onto a plate.

Makes 1 small loaf, enough for 2–4 people, depending on appetite and other culinary variables

VARIATIONS

- **Buttertop Wheat Bread.** Brush the top of dough with ½ spoon melted clarified butter before baking.

- **Rye Bread.** Substitute ¼ Sierra cup rye flour for the same amount of white flour.

- **Potato Bread.** Rehydrate ½ cup grated potatoes (see Latkes, pages 158–59), wring dry, and add to the flour mixture. Omit the clarified butter and substitute buttermilk powder for the milk powder.

- **Wholly Whole Wheat Bread.** Omit the white flour entirely and use just whole wheat flour. This will require patience as you knead the dough, which will be quite sticky. We recommend using white flour for dusting your hands and the kneading plate, but even that's not necessary if you're an Orthodox whole wheatnik.

- **Peppery Garlic Wheat Bread.** Add 2 cloves peeled garlic, sliced fine, plus 2 large pinches black pepper and 2 large pinches dried parsley or rosemary. You may also substitute oil for the melted clarified butter.

Raisin Bread ◉

It is possible to backpack without raisins. It is not possible to do any other kind of camping in which weight is no issue without raisins. We'll show you some lighter substitutes below, but once this bread comes out of the pot, you may be stuck carrying raisins wherever and however you go.

Small handful raisins, soaked in water or brandy in a Sierra cup

½ spoon cooking oil or clarified butter (see page 99), to grease the pot

1 package (¼ ounce) dried yeast

1 spoon sugar, plus 2 large pinches for proofing the yeast

¼ Sierra cup warm water to raise the dough

1 level Sierra cup flour, plus 2 spoons for dusting the pot, your hands, and the kneading plate

1 spoon milk powder

½ spoon salt

1 spoon melted clarified butter (optional; see page 99)

1 Sierra cup water to form the dough

2 pinches candied orange, chopped fine (optional; see page 12)

1. Soak the raisins an hour or so before you begin to bake. This allows them to plump up. If you don't have the time, let them soak while you're getting all the ingredients together and setting up to make the bread. Drain just before adding to the dough.

2. Make preparations for baking in coals or on a camping stove (see pages 217–19).

3. Spread a thin layer of oil on the bottom and sides of a small camping pot. Dust the pot with flour.

4. Sprinkle the yeast into a Sierra cup. Add the 2 pinches sugar and warm water and stir with a fork or spoon. Cover and set in the sun or another warm spot until proofed (see Baking with Yeast, page 162), about 5 minutes.

5. Mix together the 1 spoon sugar, 1 Sierra cup flour, milk powder, and salt in a large pot. Allow the melted clarified butter (if using) to cool slightly, then stir it and the yeast into the flour mixture. Mix well.

6. Pour in the water or brandy from the soaking raisins and enough additional water in small increments till the dough is stiff and slightly moist

7. Dust a plate with flour. Spill out the dough onto the plate. Dust your hands with flour and begin to knead the dough (see Baking with Yeast, page 162).

8. Add the drained raisins and the candied orange (if using) as you are kneading the dough. Keep kneading till the dough is plastic 'n' elastic.

9. Place the dough in the prepared pot, cover, and allow to rise till doubled in bulk, about 20 minutes.

10. Punch down and allow to rise again (see Baking with Yeast, page 163), 20 minutes, till doubled in bulk.

11. Bake till the top rings hollow when tapped with your finger. Remove from the heat. When the loaf is cool enough to tip from pot, empty it onto a plate. Sell by the slice. You may get rich.

Makes 1 small loaf, enough for 2–4 people, depending on appetite, accompanying dishes, and armed felons

Variations

Berry Bread.
Substitute dried cranberries or cherries for the raisins. They're a little lighter than raisins.

Nutty Raisin Bread.
Add 2 spoons finely chopped nuts.

Buttermilk Raisin Bread.
Substitute buttermilk powder for the milk powder.

Raisin 'n' Spice Bread.
While kneading the dough, add a pinch of cinnamon or mace or nutmeg.

Braided Challah (Egg Loaf) 🔥

There are three personality types that define how this beautiful bread is eaten: the nosher, the fresser, and the chozzer. The nosher has a little bite and maybe comes back in 5 minutes so it shouldn't go to waste. The fresser's a serious nosher who hacks off a slice big enough to use as a pillow while keeping a gimlet eye on everybody else, who (s)he knows are just a pack of fressers, too. The chozzer's a pig, literally and figuratively, and you can forget about ever getting a bite. This loaf has to be braided. When it emerges, it is to ovations, hosannas, and other raucous though kvelling *noises.*

2 spoons cooking oil, plus more to grease the pot

1 packet dried yeast (¼ ounce)

2 large pinches sugar

¼ Sierra cup warm water to raise the dough

1½ Sierra cups flour, plus 2 spoons to dust the pot, your hands, and the kneading plate

½ spoon salt

2 eggs (or 2 heaping spoons powdered egg mix)

1 Sierra cup water to form the dough

Note: Braided challah is cooked in a medium-sized pot, not the small pot used in most of our bread recipes.

(continued on next page)

Braided Challah Instructions

1. Make preparations for baking in coals or on a camping stove (see pages 217–19).

2. Spread a thin layer of oil on the bottom and sides of a medium-sized camping pot. Dust with flour.

3. Sprinkle the yeast into a Sierra cup. Add the sugar and warm water, and stir with a fork or spoon. Cover and set in the sun or another warm spot until proofed (see Baking with Yeast, page 162), about 5 minutes.

4. Mix the flour, salt, and powdered eggs (if using) in a large pot. Add the proofed yeast, eggs (if using fresh), and 1 spoon of the oil; mix well.

5. Pour in just enough of the 1 Sierra cup water in small amounts to make a firm, slightly moist dough.

6. Dust a plate with flour; turn the dough out onto the plate. Dust your hands with flour and begin to knead (see Baking with Yeast, page 162). Continue kneading till the dough becomes glossy and elastic. This is easy dough to work, and the kneading is practically guaranteed to produce the result you want.

7. Let the kneaded dough rest for 5 to 10 minutes on the floured plate. If you have a clean cloth or handkerchief (even a T-shirt will do), use it to cover the dough while it's resting, to keep out dust or dirt. Then begin the braiding. Here's what to do.

8. Roll the dough into a cylinder — like a long cigar — about the length of your plate. Divide the dough into three equal parts, either by cutting it with a knife or

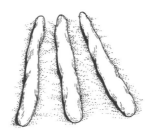

Challah strands

Braiding the challah

breaking off the pieces with your hand. Roll each part into a ball. Let them rest 3 to 4 minutes.

9. Roll out each dough section into a long strand, 12 to 14 inches. Pinch three ends together and braid the strands just as you would three hanks of hair. When finished, pinch the ends together, too. You now have a long braided bread dough. And if you were home, you might just bake it that way.

10. But you're not home. You need to fit the braid into the prepared pot. Wrap the braid into a circle that will fit into the pot, just touching the outside edge, and pinch the two ends of the braid together.

11. Carefully lift the braided circle of dough into the prepared pot. Cover and place in a sunny or other warm spot and let rise till doubled in bulk, 15 to 25 minutes.

Wrapping the challah around the inside of the pot

12. Bake 15 to 20 minutes, till the top rings hollow when tapped with your finger. Remove from the heat.

13. Allow the loaf to cool in the pot till it will easily tip out onto a plate. This is going to be the most festive bread you've ever seen in the wilderness. The egg will give the dough a golden gloss, the braid will keep its shape, and the texture and taste will make all other breads pale before it. Keep those hosannas below five decibels. There's a noise ordinance out here, you know.

Makes one small challah, enough for 2–4 people, depending on appetite and competitive urges

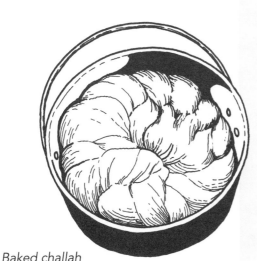

Baked challah

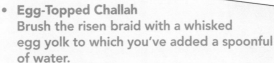

VARIATIONS

- **Potato Challah**
  Some traditional recipes call for a mashed potato. If you're packing dehydrated shredded potatoes, rehydrate a couple of spoons, press out some of the liquid, and add to the flour mixture. In fact, use the potato water instead of the plain water as needed. Make sure, however, that the potato water is cooled to lukewarm before using. You don't want to kill that yeast, right?

- **Egg-Topped Challah**
  Brush the risen braid with a whisked egg yolk to which you've added a spoonful of water.

- **Poppy Challah**
  Sprinkle the top with poppy seeds, either with or without the whisked egg yolk.

- **Saffron Challah**
  In the unlikely event that you've brought along a couple of strands of saffron, tear them into small bits and let them steep in a spoonful or two of warm water. Add both the saffron bits and steeping water to the dough before kneading. The saffron gives a lovely orange tinge to the baked bread, but doesn't change the flavor.

Backpackers' Bagels ⊚

We did not make this up. "According to legend the first bagels rolled into the world in 1683 when a Viennese baker wanted to pay tribute to Jan Sobieski, the King of Poland. King Jan had just saved the people of Austria from an onslaught of Turkish invaders. The King was a great horseman, and the baker decided to shape the yeast dough into an uneven circle resembling a stirrup (or 'beugal'). (Other German variations of the word are: 'beigel,' meaning 'ring,' and 'bugel,' meaning 'bracelet.')" Source: "History of Bagels," Bagel Boss Café, http://www.bagelboss.com/bagels.html.

Well, you're up in the Cascades, 5,383 miles from Vienna, and there's not a king or queen in sight. You're on your own.

½ spoon cooking oil or clarified butter (see page 99), for greasing the pot

1 level Sierra cup flour, plus more for dusting the pot, your hands, and 2 plates

1 packet (¼ ounce) dried yeast

2 pinches sugar

¼ Sierra cup warm water to raise the dough

¼ spoon salt

1 Sierra cup water to form dough

1 large pot boiling water for submerging the bagels

1 egg or 1 spoon powdered egg mix (optional)

Sprinkling of poppy seeds (optional)

1. Make preparations for baking in coals or on a camping stove (see pages 217–19).

2. Spread a thin layer of oil on the bottom and sides of a small pot. Dust the pot with flour.

3. Sprinkle the yeast into a Sierra cup. Add the sugar and warm water, and stir with a fork or spoon. Cover and set in the sun or another warm spot until proofed (see Baking with Yeast, page 162), about 5 minutes.

4. In the meantime, mix the 1 Sierra cup flour and the salt together in a large pot. When the yeast is ready, mix it into the flour mixture with a fork. Gradually mix in enough of the 1 Sierra cup water to form a slightly moist ball of dough.

5. Knead the dough (see Baking with Yeast, page 162) on one of the floured plates till pliant and elastic to the touch. If you've started with too wet a dough, add more flour, a very little at a time. If you've started with too dry a dough, add more water, a very little at a time.

6. Once the dough is thoroughly kneaded, place it in the oiled and floured pot, cover, and leave in a warm spot to rise until doubled in bulk. This will take 15 to 25 minutes, depending on ambient warmth, quality of the dough, and the temperature of the water you used.

7. Dust your hands with flour. Take the risen dough out of the pot and knead it gently on a floured plate, 2 to 3 minutes.

8. Tear off a small piece of the dough, about half the size of your palm. Roll it in a ball in your hands and then, on the other floured plate or between your floured hands, roll it into a cigar-shaped strand about ½ inch thick.

9. Form the cigar into a ring 2 to 2½ inches in diameter, pinch the ends together, and set on the plate.

Forming the bagel

10. Repeat till you have four or five dough rings, using about half the dough in the process. (Any more and you won't have room on the plates to let them rise.) These will be mini-bagels, necessitated by pot size.

11. Cover with a reasonably clean cloth or T-shirt. Set in the sun and let rise till doubled in bulk, about 15 minutes. (This is the second rising.)

12. While the bagels are rising, set the remaining dough in the small oiled and floured pot. Let it rise. This will be your next batch.

13. Okay, order of business: First boil, then bake. Submerge each bagel, one at a time, gently into the boiling water for 20 seconds. Flip and repeat, then remove and set on a plate.

14. Oil and lightly flour a fry pan. Place the boiled bagels in the pan. Whip the egg (if using) slightly in a Sierra cup and brush the tops of the bagels. Sprinkle with poppy seeds (if using).

15. Place a plate on top of the fry pan. Cover with foil. Bake as you would a pizza (see pages 217–18) till the bagels ring hollow when tapped, about 10 minutes. Continue till all are baked. The deli opens immediately after.

Makes 8–10 mini bagels, enough for 2–4 people, depending on appetite and altruism

Chinese Steamed Bread (Mantou) 🔥

North China is wheat, noodle, and dumpling country, and up there they eat their bread steamed, not baked. Its flavor comes from dunking. You eat it with soups (which you're permitted to slurp), stews, and stir-fried dishes. The bread is made in a small bun-shaped loaf and it's called mantou *(steamed bun). See pages 220–21 for steamer set-up.*

½ spoonful cooking oil, for greasing the pot

1 level Sierra cup flour, plus more for dusting the pot, your hands, and the kneading plate

1 packet (¼ ounce) dried yeast

2 pinches sugar

¼ Sierra cup warm water to raise the dough

¼ spoon salt

1 Sierra cup water to form the dough

2 Sierra cups boiling water for steaming

1. Spread a thin layer of oil on the bottom and sides of a small pot. Sprinkle with flour.

2. Sprinkle the yeast into a Sierra cup. Add the sugar and warm water and stir with a fork or spoon. Cover and set in the sun or another warm spot until proofed (see Baking with Yeast, page 162), about 5 minutes.

3. In the meantime, mix the 1 Sierra cup flour and the salt together in a large pot. When the yeast is ready, mix it into the flour mixture with a fork. Gradually mix in enough of the 1 Sierra cup water to form a slightly moist ball of dough.

4. Dust your hands and a plate with flour. Knead the dough (see Baking with Yeast, page 162) on the plate till pliant and elastic to the touch. If you've started with too wet a dough, add more flour, a very little at a time. If you've started with too dry a dough, add more water, a very little at a time.

5. Once the dough is thoroughly kneaded, place it in the prepared pot, cover, and leave in a warm spot to rise until doubled in bulk. This will take 15 to 25 minutes, depending on ambient warmth, quality of the dough, and the temperature of the water you used.

6. Dust your hands and the plate with flour once more. Form a small bun-shaped loaf a bit smaller than the inside of your steamer. Set the loaf on the plate, cover, and let it rise again till doubled in bulk, 10 to 15 minutes.

7. Prepare a steamer (see pages 220–21).

8. Place the loaf on the foil in the steamer and steam till done, about 12 minutes. This bread won't "tap" hollow. To test for doneness, remove from the steamer — *wear gloves!* — and cut off a small piece. It should taste springy and chewy, not wet and soggy.

9. Steamed bread will go stale quickly, so get out the dehydrated soup or stew or whip up a stir-fry and dunk away.

Makes 1 small loaf, enough for 2–3 people, depending on appetite and adventurous taste buds

Scones

Scones are biscuits with a Scottish burr. Contrary to what you may think, they were not invented by the local latte joint. They take their name from the Stone of Scone, where Scottish kings were crowned, and, appropriately, if baked too long, the scones (not the kings) become more stone than scone. Originally, scones were made of oats and were griddle cooked, and in our *Camper's Companion* (Avalon Travel Publishing, 1996), you'll find some pan-baked recipes that substitute oats for flour. Here we concentrate on "oven"-baked scones. They're almost the perfect campsite baked good: simple ingredients, easy preparation, fast "oven" time, easy eatin'.

Alternative Baking Techniques

- Slice the scone dough into eight wedge-shaped slices and place in a frying pan. Bake as you would a pizza (pages 217–19), until the tops are just golden.

- If using a camping stove, slice the dough into eight wedges and bake in a fry pan.

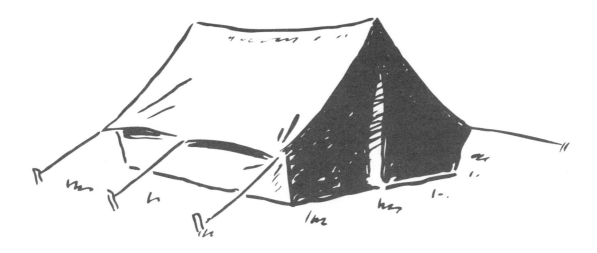

Buttermilk Scones ⬤

We haven't the slightest idea whether the Scots used buttermilk in their day, but we do in ours. If you're a Midlothian purist, go ahead and use milk instead. Nobody's going to know the difference.

1 level Sierra cup flour, plus 1 spoon more for dusting the kneading plate

1 spoon powdered buttermilk (or powdered milk)

½ spoon baking powder

½ spoon baking soda

¼ spoon salt

2 spoons clarified butter (see page 99; oil doesn't quite do it here)

¼–⅓ Sierra cup water

1. Make preparations for baking in coals or on a camping stove (see pages 217–19).

2. Using a fork, mix the 1 Sierra cup flour, powdered buttermilk, baking powder, baking soda, and salt together in a large pot.

3. Cut the clarified butter into small pieces with your trusty Swiss Army knife,

then, using your fingers — don't be finicky, camp-grimed hands won't end civilization as we know it — work it into the flour mix till it is the rough consistency of cornmeal. (This is exactly the exercise involved in making pie pastry.)

4. Add just enough of the water a little at a time to moisten the dough so that it sticks together in a malleable ball. Don't worry if it's a bit moist.

5. Sprinkle a little flour on a plate and knead the dough on the plate till it's smooth and pliant, 2 to 3 minutes. The goal is to create a disc about ½ inch thick. It will measure about 5½ inches in diameter, but we've never met anyone with a tape measure in the backcountry, and any size that fits the pot will work. Now for the baking.

6. Place the scone disc in a medium-sized pot (about 6 inches in diameter), cover, and bake for 10 to 15 minutes, till the top starts to turn golden, *no longer.*

Baked beyond that, you're going to be feeding hardtack to your family and former friends. Note that you do *not* need to prep the pan with oil and flour (the butter in the dough prevents sticking), and note further that despite our injunction about big pots when baking breads, the medium-sized pot works just fine here and the scones will be baked evenly throughout.

7. Remove the pot from the fire, and, when cool enough to handle, tip the scone onto a plate and cut into eight wedges. When cool enough to handle, serve with Marmalade (page 102), Pineapple Glaze (page 105), Apple Butter (page 104), or Cranberry-Cherry Sauce (page 90).

Makes 8 small scones, enough for 4 people (though Hal has been known to hog all eight scones, sinking like the hallowed Stone of Pig Iron shortly thereafter while trying to swim off the excess)

Raisin–Cranberry Scones 🔥

After making these, Rick decided we could score unseemly profits if we set up shop and sold 'em at the trailhead, with or without the double low-fat grande latte.

Small handful mixed raisins and commercially dried cranberries (dried apricots and pineapple also work well)

1 Sierra cup boiling water, for rehydrating, if using apricots and pineapple

1 level Sierra cup flour, plus more to dust your hands and the kneading plate

1 spoon powdered buttermilk (or powdered milk)

½ spoon sugar (more or less to taste)

¼ spoon baking powder

¼ spoon baking soda

¼ spoon salt

2 spoons clarified butter (see page 99), cut into small bits

1 Sierra cup water

1. Make preparations for baking in coals or on a camping stove (see pages 217–19).

2. If using apricots or pineapple, rehydrate by pouring the boiling water over the fruits and letting sit 5 to 10 minutes. Cut into pieces, about ¼ inch square. (The cranberries and raisins do not need to be rehydrated.)

3. Using a fork, mix well the 1 Sierra cup flour, powdered buttermilk, sugar, baking powder, baking soda, salt, and raisins and dried cranberries in a medium-sized pot. (Baking soda helps fruit-laden doughs rise better.)

4. Work the clarified butter into the dough to the consistency of small peas.

5. Add just enough of the water to moisten. Form the dough into a ball.

6. Dust your hands and a plate with flour. Knead the dough until smooth, 2 to 3 minutes. Press into a round disc about ½ inch thick.

7. Place the disc in a medium-sized pot, cover, and bake for 10 to 15 minutes, till the top begins to turn golden, *no longer*. Note that you do *not* need to prep the pan with oil and flour (the butter in the dough prevents sticking), and note further that despite our injunction about big pots when baking breads, the medium-sized pot works just fine here and the bread will be baked evenly throughout.

8. Remove from the heat, tip onto a plate as soon as it's cool enough, slice, eat, and kvell. (That is, beam with pride and enjoyment.)

Makes 8 small scones, enough for 4 people, depending on appetite and gluttony

The Biscuit That Ate Chicago

Biscuit dough and scone dough are practically interchangeable, though we like to add an egg to our biscuits. We also like the mix of baking powder and soda, though either alone will do. When baked whole, this biscuit was the most humongous thing we ever saw, hence the name. You will find it topping our cobblers (pages 200–1) and bringing importunate demands for thirds from the assembled masses.

1 level Sierra cup flour, plus more to dust your hands and a kneading plate

1 spoon powdered buttermilk (or powdered milk)

1 spoon sugar

¼ spoon baking powder

¼ spoon baking soda

¼ spoon salt

2 spoons clarified butter (see page 99)

1 lightly beaten egg or equivalent powdered egg mix

Small amount of water to moisten, if necessary

1. Make preparations to bake in coals or on a camping stove (see pages 217–19).

2. Using a fork, mix the flour, powdered buttermilk, powdered egg (if using), sugar, baking powder, baking soda, and salt in a medium-sized pot.

3. Work the butter into the dough to the consistency of small peas.

4. Stir in the egg (if using fresh) to moisten. If this doesn't make a moist ball (or if you're using powdered egg), add water.

5. Dust your hands and a plate with flour. Form the dough into a ball and knead it on the plate till smooth, 2 to 3 minutes. Press into a round disc about ½ inch thick.

6. Bake in a medium-sized pot for about 12 minutes, till the top begins to turn golden.

7. Slice into eight wedges, or leave whole if using on a cobbler.

Makes 1 giant or 8 small biscuits, enough for 2–4 people, depending on the median body size of your camping party

Polenta & Buttermilk Cornbread 🔥

You've packed in polenta to make those polenta dishes we've been talking to you about (pages 128–31) and a pocket full of buttermilk powder. Tain't nuffin' else to do but follow along.

2 spoons cooking oil, plus more to grease the pot

½ Sierra cup flour, plus more to dust the pot

½ Sierra cup polenta

2 spoons buttermilk powder

1 spoon sugar

½ spoon baking powder

½ spoon salt

¼ spoon baking soda

¼ spoon cumin

   Large pinch cayenne

1 egg or equivalent powdered egg mix

½ Sierra cup water (approximately)

1. Make preparations for baking in coals or on a camping stove (see pages 217–19).

2. Spread a thin layer of oil on the bottom and sides of a small or medium-sized pot. Dust with flour.

3. Mix the ½ Sierra cup flour, polenta, buttermilk powder, sugar, baking powder, salt, baking soda, cumin, cayenne, and powdered egg (if using) in another medium-sized pot.

4. Whisk the egg (if using fresh) and the 2 spoons of oil together in a Sierra cup. Stir into the dry ingredients.

5. Mix in just enough of the water to make a moist but not runny batter.

6. Spoon into the baking pot, cover, and bake 10 to 12 minutes, till a knife comes out clean from the center. Do *not* break into some cornball song. Just cut slices out of the pot and eat while hot, or cool for 10 minutes and remove from pot and stuff yerself.

Makes 1 small loaf, enough for 2–4 people, depending on appetite or who's closest to the pot

CORNBREAD

Craig Claiborne, the famous food writer, once said that there are "more recipes for corn bread than there are magnolia trees in the South." Well, while ol' Craig was counting magnolias, we were hanging with Huck Finn in that cave telling Jim, "Pass me along another hunk of fish and some hot cornbread." He could have called it "quick bread" and he could have been asking for hushpuppies or johnny-cakes or spoon bread or a lot of other things. It's all cornbread to us, and in these pages are a few corn-bread recipes to pass to your friends, even if you're not in a cave.

Magnolia Blossom Cornbread

All right, so the name of this bread is slightly misleading. No blossoms in the bread, just on your glowing cheeks, bearded or not, at the thought of how good this is going to be.

½ spoon cooking oil, to grease the pot

½ cup cornmeal (polenta will also do just fine)

¼ cup white flour, plus more to dust the pot

¼ cup whole wheat flour (whole wheat pastry flour is excellent too)

½ spoon baking powder

¼ spoon baking soda

¼ spoon salt

2 spoons buttermilk powder

1 spoon milk powder

1 egg or equivalent powdered egg mix

2 spoons pure maple syrup

1 spoon clarified butter (see page 99)

Small amount of water, to moisten

1. Make preparations for baking in coals or on a camping stove (see pages 217–19).

2. Spread a thin layer of oil on the bottom and sides of a small or medium-sized pot. Dust with flour.

3. Mix the cornmeal, flours, baking powder, baking soda, salt, buttermilk powder, milk powder, and powdered egg (if using) in another pot. Add the maple syrup, egg (if using fresh), clarified butter, and just enough of the water to make a moist batter that will just barely drop off a spoon.

4. Pour into the prepared pot and bake till done, about 15 minutes.

5. Allow to cool in the pot for 10 minutes. Eat from the pot or, if you've got any manners, after the bread's been removed from the pot and cut into slices.

Makes 1 small loaf, enough for 2–4 or one Ignatius J. Reilly wannabe

Corn Cornbread 🏠 🔥

We thought you'd never ask. Yes, cornbread can also contain kernels of corn. If you stop at the local farmstand for some ears of fresh corn, just cook the corn for eating, save an ear, cool it down, and cut the kernels onto a plate, reserving them for the batter. (A lot of those kernels are going to spray onto the ground as you slice them off the cob. So what? Just pick them up, put 'em back on the plate, and keep mum when the hygiene police come around.)

1 large ear of corn, cooked and kernels shaved off (about 1 cup fresh or ¼ Sierra cup dehydrated)

2 jalapeño chiles, chopped fine (with seeds for heat, without seeds for warmth) (see Handling Hot Chiles for precautions, page 37), or ½ spoon commercially crushed red peppers

2–3 Sierra cups boiling water

½ Sierra cup cornmeal (polenta will also do)

½ Sierra cup flour, plus more to dust the pot

2 spoons buttermilk powder (or milk powder)

¾ spoon baking powder

¼ spoon baking soda (very useful here with the corn kernels)

¼ spoon salt

Ground black pepper

1 egg or equivalent powdered egg mix

1 spoon oil, plus more to grease the pot

at home

1. Place the corn on a dehydrator tray and dry for 4 to 5 hours, till hard.

2. Dehydrate the chopped jalapeños 2 to 4 hours, till crisp. Alternatively, take fresh jalapeños with you. They're light and won't spoil, though they may begin to dry out, which is okay.

at camp

3. Rehydrate the corn in the boiling water. Cool and reserve the liquid.

4. Dice the jalapeños, if using fresh.

5. Mix together the corn, jalapeños, cornmeal, flour, buttermilk powder, baking powder, baking soda, salt, pepper to taste, and powdered egg (if using).

6. Add the egg (if using fresh), oil, and reserved corn liquid to make a moist batter that just runs off the spoon.

7. Spread a thin layer of oil on the bottom and sides of a small or medium-sized pot. Dust with flour. Pour the batter into the pot and bake till a knife comes out clean, about 15 minutes.

8. Cool in the pot just long enough to allow you to tip out the baked bread, about 10 minutes. Don't worry if you can't remember who sank whom, the *Monitor* or the *Merrimac*. Just enjoy good Southern fare.

Makes 1 small loaf, enough for 2–4 people

Chapati (Indian Flat Bread)

Hal and Rick are firm believers in reincarnation. We've not only camped and cooked our way through this lifetime, but through multiple previous ones as well. How else could we have accumulated so many recipes?

It was in one of our very early incarnations on the Indian subcontinent that Rick realized he had neglected to pack the yeast. Hal thought a moment and then quietly assumed his one-of-a-kind yoga stance, known as "The Schlimazel." "No problem, my wily young grasshopper," he counseled Rick. "We can make do with baking powder."

"That would be nice," admitted Rick sheepishly, "but I forgot to bring the baking powder as well." Thus was born chapati, traditional Indian flat bread.

1 Sierra cup flour, plus more for dusting

¼ spoon salt

⅓ Sierra cup warm water

1 spoon clarified butter (see page 99)

1. Mix the 1 Sierra cup flour and salt in a small pot. Add the warm water, a little at a time, till the dough forms a ball. The dough should be soft, pliable, and somewhat sticky.

2. Dust the outside of the ball with flour and knead (see Baking with Yeast, page 162) for 4 to 5 minutes, till smooth and pliable. Let it sit in a covered pot for about 20 minutes, till even more pliable.

3. Knead the dough again for a few minutes, then tear into three pieces. Form each piece into a thin pancake, 5 to 7 inches across. In a regular kitchen, this is done with a rolling pin. However, if you left your rolling pin at home,

Flattening the chapati dough with the bottom of a Sierra cup

simply flatten the ball by hand, dust it lightly with flour, and place it on a plate. Then use the bottom of a Sierra cup to press on the top of the pancake and squeeze it down. Work your way around, flattening as you go. Flip the pancake over (on the plate), dust the top with flour, and repeat. Get it as thin as you can.

4. Meanwhile, heat a pan. Chapati is cooked on a dry, hot pan. Be careful about the temperature. If the pan is too hot, the chapati will burn on the outside and be raw in the middle. If the pan isn't hot enough, the inside will be tough and dry. On your burner at home, you'd set the heat to "medium." (If water droplets just begin to bounce, it is about right.)

5. Once the chapati is as thin as you can get it, it's ready to cook. Pick it up off the plate and drop it into the pan. Keep the same side down, so the surface that touches the hot pan is as flat as the plate. Depending on the temperature of the pan, it will take between 30 seconds and 1 minute to cook the first side. If you look at the bottom, it will be whitish with brown spots. Flip it over. It will take 15 to 30 seconds on the other side.

6. When both sides have been cooked, remove from the pot. While still hot, spread the chapati with clarified butter or eat plain with any Indian curry (pages 53–57).

Makes 2 chapatis

Brownies

It's a little-known fact that brownies were first baked by John Muir just after a grizzly bear made off with his baking powder. John had planned to make a chocolate cake, but without baking powder, he was afraid his cake wouldn't rise. The rest is history.

- 4 squares semisweet chocolate
- 4 heaping spoons clarified butter (see page 99), plus more to grease the pan
- ⅔ Sierra cup sugar
- 2 eggs or equivalent powdered egg mix and reconstituted powdered egg whites
- ½ spoon brandy or vanilla
- ⅔ Sierra cup flour
- ½ Sierra cup chopped nuts (such as walnuts, cashews, or almonds; anything but peanuts)

1. Make preparations for baking in coals or on a camping stove (see pages 217–19) as you would for a pizza.

2. Melt the chocolate and clarified butter together over low heat. Pour the chocolate-butter mixture into a large pot and stir in the sugar, eggs, brandy, and flour.

3. Stir until evenly mixed. Fold in the chopped nuts.

4. Coat a fry pan with a thin layer of clarified butter.

5. Pour the mixture into the pan. Smooth it into a circular shape at an even depth all around the pan.

6. Bake for 20 to 25 minutes. The brownies are done when a knife comes out of the center clean. Allow to cool, then cut into squares. Keep an eye out for grizzlies.

Makes 8–10 brownies, enough for 4 people, unless someone is hungry as a grizzly

Campsite Cake 🔥

Some call this the white cake basic recipe. We call it the template. On it, you can inscribe your own true confections. (Whatever that means.) Anyway, listen up.

2 spoons clarified butter (see page 99)

2 spoons sugar

2 eggs or equivalent powdered egg mix

1 spoon brandy (or other flavoring; this is our vanilla substitute)

½ spoon baking powder

¼ spoon salt

¼–½ Sierra cup flour, plus more to dust the pot

¼–½ Sierra cup water, if necessary

½ spoon cooking oil, to grease the pot

1. Make preparations for baking in coals or on a camping stove (see pages 217–19).

2. "Cream" the clarified butter and sugar, like this: Put the clarified butter in a small pot or pot top, pour the sugar over the butter, and, using the back of a spoon, smush the two together till the sugar is completely incorporated into the butter. It's creamed.

3. Beat the eggs into the creamed butter. Pour in the brandy and continue beating. (If using powdered egg, just add the brandy to the creamed butter at this point; see note below for when to add the powdered egg.)

4. Stir the baking powder and salt into the thin batter.

𝒩𝑜𝑡𝑒: If using powdered eggs, add with the baking powder and salt. Pour in the water immediately afterward to create a loose, egg-rich batter *before* you add the flour.

Add the flour, 1 spoon at a time, mixing it into the batter thoroughly. Your aim is to create a batter just thick enough to run slowly off a spoon. You may need as much as half a Sierra cup, but sometimes a couple of spoons will be sufficient. If you add too much, bring in the water reserves, adding just enough to restore that ribbon-like batter.

5. Spread a thin layer of oil on the bottom and sides of a small or medium-sized pot. Dust with flour.

6. Pour the batter into the prepared pot, cover, and bake till done, 15 to 25 minutes. If a knife blade comes out clean from the center, it's done. Let cool in the pan till it spills out easily onto a plate. You may have to cut around the edges to loosen the cake before removing.

7. Eat as is or, if frosting, allow to cool thoroughly. We recommend Ginger Frosting (page 108) or Chocolate Frosting (page 106).

Makes 4 small servings

Campsite Cake Variations

- **Coconut Cake.**
Add a handful of sweetened shredded coconut to the dry ingredients. (The unsweetened coconut that you might use in Indian cooking will not do the trick, though by adding more sugar, you'll get a reasonable facsimile.)

- **Cranberry Cake.**
Soak 1 to 2 spoons dried cranberries in warm water till softened. Add them to the dry ingredients. If you have baking soda with you, add ½ spoon in addition to the baking powder called for by the recipe. This goes for all cakes that contain fruit.

- **Raisin Brandy Cake.**
Soak 2 spoons of raisins (or sour cherries) in 2 to 3 spoons brandy and add to the creamy batter. (You never know, this brandy poultice may come in useful for healing wounds, too). Don't forget the ½ spoon baking soda if you've got it.

- **Banana Cake.**
Rehydrate and mash 2 spoons bananas. Reserve the liquid. Add the mashed bananas and ½ spoon baking soda to the batter. If more liquid is required, use the reserved banana liquid.

- **Applesauce Cake.**
Rehydrate 2 spoons applesauce (see page 103). Add to the batter with a ¼ spoon cinnamon and ½ spoon baking soda. Frost with Chocolate Frosting (see page 106).

- **Light White Cake.**
Separate the eggs in the master recipe. Add the yolks as called for. Reserve the whites. After you have added the flour, whip the egg whites with a fork till they froth and begin to stiffen. Don't worry if you can't get 'em stiff. Just fold into the batter gently. This will allow the cake to rise more and make it lighter. If using powdered eggs — they don't contain whites — use two spoons of powdered egg whites in addition. Mix the powdered egg whites with water, whip with a fork till they froth and begin to stiffen, then add them to the batter.

- **White Layer Cake.**
While the cake is baking, rehydrate 1 Sierra cup strawberries, adding sugar to taste. Reduce to a smooth jam. When the cake is thoroughly cooled, slice it in half to create two layers. Spread the strawberry filling on the lower layer and cover with the top layer. Frost.

MELTING CHOCOLATE FOR CAKES

Baking chocolate contains no milk solids, unlike all those candy bars that are helping make America fat. That means two things: Candy bars will melt in your hand and are a misery to pack on a camping trip; and baking chocolate needs tending to melt for cooking purposes. (Semisweet baking chocolate and sweet baking chocolate are perfect camping substitutes for candy bars. They can be eaten as-is *and* used for cooking.)

The standard way to melt baking chocolate is to use a double boiler. But that's a lot of trouble at a campsite. Here's what we do, even it breaks the rules of every cooking school west of Passaic, New Jersey.

Place the chocolate to be melted, say 4 squares of semisweet, in a pot lid. Add just a spoonful or two of water to the chocolate. Hold over the heat (wearing a glove) and stir constantly as the chocolate begins to melt. You may have to add a little more water to prevent it from burning or sticking. But do this gradually. The goal is to have melted chocolate, not chocolate milk. It should take only 2 to 3 minutes to melt completely.

If the melted chocolate cools down before you use it, it may harden. Just repeat the melting process and bring it back to the consistency you want for icings or cake batters.

The Most Dangerous Cake in the Wilderness 🔥

Don't get caught scarfing this cake by yourself. In the first place, you'll experience a sugar rush that'll have you ricocheting around the campsite like a steel ball in a Tokyo pachinko parlor. In the second place, if your mates catch you hogging their allotted portions, you'll experience something entirely different: death at an early age. This is all chocolate all the time. There's never a year we don't choose to live dangerously.

2–3 spoons water, for melting the chocolate

2 spoons clarified butter (see page 99)

2 spoons sugar

2 eggs or equivalent powdered egg mix

1 spoon brandy (or other flavoring: this is our vanilla substitute)

½ spoon baking powder

¼ spoon salt

¼–½ Sierra cup flour, plus more to dust the pot

½ spoon cooking oil, to grease the pot

Strawberry filling (see White Layer Cake instructions under Campsite Cake Variations, page 185)

Chocolate Frosting (page 106)

1. Make preparations for baking in coals or on a camping stove (see pages 217–19).

2. Melt the chocolate (see Melting Chocolate for Cakes, page 186), stirring with the water.

3. Cream together the clarified butter and sugar in a small pot, using the back of a spoon.

4. Stir in the eggs or egg powder and brandy and mix vigorously. Pour in the melted chocolate and continue mixing.

5. Mix in the baking powder and salt, then the flour, 1 spoon at a time, till the batter runs off the spoon in a thick ribbon.

6. Spread a thin layer of oil on the bottom and sides of a small or medium-sized pot.

7. Pour the batter into the prepared pot and bake till a knife blade emerges clean from the center, 15 to 25 minutes.

8. Cool in the pot. Remove carefully, cutting around the edges if necessary, and cool thoroughly on a plate.

9. Slice into two layers and spread the strawberry filling over the bottom layer. Cover with the top layer.

10. Spread the chocolate frosting over the cake, starting at the top center. Use the back of a spoon and apply all the frosting to the top and sides. Allow the frosting to cool. Then stand out of the way, or you're gonna get hurt.

Serves 4 if you're working on democratic principles, more if you're a Communist, less if you're an armed tyrant

Persimmon "Bread"

Don't be fooled by the name. It's really a cake, as in "Can I have a third piece, pleeeze?" The original, which Hal has been making for years when the persimmons ripen in the fall, is filled with enough bourbon to warm the cockles of Jack Daniels's heart and enough sugar and eggs and butter to give Dean Ornish apoplexy, let alone heartburn. But the virtuous need not fret. Our backpacking version reduces a cup of bourbon to a camping spoon (alas!) and the other ingredients accordingly. Still, you will not want to go hiking in October without it.

The persimmons here are those beautiful, large acorn-shaped fruits that must be mush-soft before they're edible. If you try eating 'em before fully ripened — the persimmons, not you — they'll make your mouth pucker and taste as if its filled with alum. Ask for hachiya persimmons, not the fuyu variety, which you eat like an apple.

1 ripe hachiya persimmon, medium to large

1–2 Sierra cups boiling water, for rehydrating

½ Sierra cup flour, plus more for dusting the pot

¼ spoon baking soda

4 spoons sugar or more to taste

Large pinch of mace or nutmeg

Large pinch of salt

2 spoons clarified butter (see page 99), plus more for greasing the pot

2 eggs or equivalent powdered egg mix

1 spoonful bourbon (or brandy), or more to taste

Small handful commercially dried cranberries (or raisins) (optional)

Small handful walnuts (or other nuts), broken into small pieces (optional)

at home

1. Mash or blend the ripe persimmon, peel and all, till smooth.

2. Spread the persimmon mash on the fruit-roll insert of your dehydrator (or on a very lightly oiled lined tray). Dry for 12 hours, and then turn over to dry for another 5 to 7 hours. Persimmon pulp is very juicy, hence the long drying time needed to get it to crumble and fit in a small resealable bag. When it's done, it looks leathery. (If you want to use as a fruit roll, it need not be turned over, but it still must dry 17 to 24 hours.)

at camp

3. Make preparations for baking in coals or on a camping stove (see pages 217–19).

4. Rehydrate the persimmon by pouring the boiling water over it, barely to cover, and allowing to sit for 10 minutes. If you've got the time, it can sit in cold water for about 20 minutes and will reconstitute nicely. Mash it to a smooth pulp, adding small amounts of water if needed.

5. Mix the flour, baking soda, sugar, mace, salt, and powdered eggs (if using) in a pot.

6. Melt the 2 spoons clarified butter in a Sierra cup.

7. Beat the eggs lightly (if using fresh).

8. Pour the melted clarified butter, lightly beaten eggs, and bourbon into the persimmon pulp. Stir well.

9. Stir in the cranberries and walnuts (if using).

10. Gradually stir in the flour mixture till you have a smooth, thick batter. (If using whole eggs or a large persimmon, you may need to add a little more flour; if using powdered eggs, you may need to add a little more water.)

11. Grease the bottom and sides of a small pot with clarified butter. Dust with flour.

12. Bake in the prepared pot till a knife comes out clean, about 20 minutes. Surrender all valuables in exchange for a slice.

Serves 3–4

Carrot Cake

As part of our ongoing effort to prepare our readers for any eventuality, we realized that many campers would be singularly unprepared if they should need to take part in a PTA bake sale at, say, 9,000 feet. That issue can now be laid to rest. Frost with Ginger Frosting (page 108).

3 cups grated carrots (about 9 medium carrots)

⅔ Sierra cup boiling water

½ Sierra cup sugar

2 spoons clarified butter (see page 99), plus more to grease the pot

1 egg or equivalent powdered egg mix

¼ spoon vanilla or brandy

1 Sierra cup flour, plus more to dust the pot

1 spoon powdered milk

½ spoon baking powder

½ spoon ground cinnamon

Pinch of salt

at home

1. Drop the grated carrots into boiling water for exactly 4 minutes. Drain; plunge into ice water for 5 minutes. Drain again.

2. Lightly oil dehydrator trays and dry for 24 hours, till crunchy.

at camp

3. Make preparations for baking in coals or on a camping stove (see pages 217–19).

4. Pour the boiling water over the dehydrated carrots in a large pot. Let the carrots soak in the water for 5 to 10 minutes to rehydrate.

5. Meanwhile, cream the sugar with the clarified butter in a small pot. Stir in the egg and vanilla till blended.

6. Mix the flour, powdered milk, baking powder, and cinnamon in a medium-sized pot. Fold into the liquid batter.

7. Drain the rehydrated carrots and add them to the batter. The batter will be thick and sticky.

8. Grease a small pot with clarified butter. Dust with flour. Pour in the batter and bake about 30 minutes. When a knife comes out of the center clean, it's ready to eat. Now all you'll have to worry about are those pesky parent-teacher conferences.

Makes 1 small carrot cake, enough for 2–4 people, depending on how much you charge for each slice

[Chapter 9]

Pies, Quiches, Cobblers & Pizzas

Back in the sixteenth century, in the days before rock concerts or professional baseball games, pies were a prime source of entertainment in the royal court. The king's chefs would bake giant piecrusts and fill them with live turtles, birds, or even small people. When the crust was opened, the guests would be amused by the lively filling as it lumbered, flew, or hopped onto the banquet table. Remember the nursery rhyme about "four and twenty blackbirds" baked in a pie? In all likelihood they ended the evening nesting in the rafters above the royal dinner table. Pies, quiches, cobblers, and pizzas have come a long way since then. Above all, the fillings are much tastier, believe us. Even if you aren't royalty, in this chapter we'll show you how to create your own banquet at your next campsite. It will be a feast worthy of a king.

Pie Dough ◉

A piecrust is as simple as suet in theory and not much harder in practice, but for reasons we've never understood, friends take fright at the sight of a rolling pin, and we're not talking domestic disputes here. First, theory. The piecrust is a mix of flour and shortening — butter, margarine, vegetable shortening, or lard — and just enough water to hold the dough together. Plus a bit of salt and sugar. That's it. Oh, there are all kinds of warnings and alarums, imprecations and exhortations: Do This or else; Don't do That or die. Americans instruct us to handle the dough as little as possible; the French, bless 'em, tell us even to knead the dough a bit. At the campsite, you'll be doing lots of handling, enough to give Sarah Lee and Betty Crocker heart palpitations and assorted nervous disorders. Tough on you Sarah and Bett. Next, practice. Here are the ingredients for enough dough to make one piecrust and instructions on how to handle.

1 Sierra cup flour

¼ spoon salt

2 large pinches sugar

2 spoons clarified butter (see page 99), the cooler the better

5–8 spoons water

Flour, to dust the frying pan and your hands

1. Mix together the flour, salt, and sugar in a medium-sized pot.

2. The clarified butter should be reasonably hard, though this may be difficult in the heat of the day. As long as it's not melting, you're in biz. Cut the butter into small bits and toss into the flour mixture. Using your fingers, pinch the flour and butter together until you get a texture sort of like a rough cornmeal — tiny pellets of flour and butter. It's not going to be perfect, and you're not going to care one bit.

3. Add the spoons of water one at a time, mixing with a fork after each addition. The goal here is to get dough that you can press together into a ball without it either falling apart or being so wet that it feels like a snowball. (You may fall apart *and* feel like a snowball, but that's a problem for your therapist, not us.)

4. Okay. One dough ball. You have neither a fridge to cool the dough nor a rolling pin to roll it. So get to work with your hands. You'll be baking the pie in a frying pan, so that's where you begin. Scatter a light layer of flour on the frying pan, place the dough ball in the middle, dust your hands, and press down. Begin to work the dough out toward the edges of the pan with fingers, knuckles, heel of the hand — all three if necessary. This is the equivalent of rolling the dough. (Hal once used a full beer can as a roller, but he was car camping, and it's unlikely you'll be bringing in a six-pack unless you're traveling with goats, llamas, or horses.)

Pressing the dough into the pan

5. Turn the dough over several times so that it doesn't stick to the bottom of the pan, flour the down side lightly, and continue. It's going to look as if it will never be big enough to fill the pan up to its edge. But the proportions are right, honest. You're after the thinnest crust you can manage, so keep pressing and fingering away. (As you handle the dough and the blackened pan, the dough is going to resemble the Black Sands of the Gobi. Not to worry. Just remember what you read in Hands On, page 82: This ain't dirt, it's earth.)

That's about it. You've made a fine pie dough, and it's going to become a fine piecrust.

Dough for 1 piecrust

Pie Facts

- One-crust pies work better than two-crust pies if you're baking in coals. It's awfully hard to get a top crust to bake properly at camp without compromising all your environmental ethics.

- You can roll a piecrust without a rolling pin.

- Campsite pie doughs are inevitably tougher than home-rolled doughs, because they are manhandled more in the "rolling." Can't be helped. Nobody'll care.

- Fruit dumplings (see Apple Dumpling, page 196) are the nearest equivalent to a two-crust pie and don't require a pan for baking.

- An apple pie can include almost any kind of fruit you've brought along. Just keep repeating the mantra, "It's an apple pie," and no one will complain to Mom and General Motors (Chevrolet division).

- Pizza is a pie, but doesn't use a pie dough, so go on over to Rick and Hal's High Mountain Pizza Dough (pages 202–3) to find out the difference.

- Quiche is a pie but isn't sweet. It's a veggie pie. Stay right here.

- Campers baking on a camping stove can pretend they're home and bake accordingly.

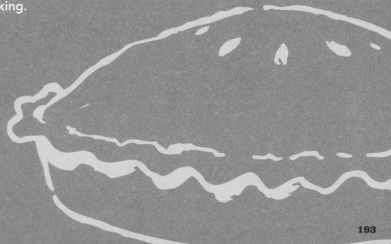

PIES AND PIECRUSTS

Every Thanksgiving Hal bakes five pies — pumpkin, apple, cranberry-pecan, olallieberry (a particularly big blackberry), and mince. Every year he hopes no one will show up and he'll have leftovers for days. Never happens. So every year he goes out in the woods and bakes a pie and hopes no one will show up. Never happens. Here's what we've learned as we've tracked him down and taken our tithe.

Berry Pie

Remember that flat of delicious mixed berries you brought home from the local farmers' market? Let's see what you can do with them on your next camping trip.

3–5 cups fresh berries (strawberries, blackberries, and/or raspberries)

1 Sierra cup boiling water, to rehydrate

2–3 spoons sugar

2 spoons flour

1 spoon brandy (or port or Kahlúa)

Dough for 1 piecrust (see pages 192–93)

Clarified butter to dot (see page 99)

at home

1. If using strawberries, slice in half. Blackberries and raspberries don't need to be sliced. Just spread on trays and dehydrate 24 hours, till hard and brittle.

at camp

2. Make preparations for baking in coals or on a camping stove (see pages 217–19) as you would for a pizza.

3. To rehydrate the berries, pour the boiling water over them in a small pot and let sit for 10 minutes. Drain.

4. Stir the sugar, flour, and brandy into the berries and let the mixture sit for 10 to 15 minutes.

5. Pour the mixture into the piecrust, dot with butter, and bake till the crust is crisp and the berries are thickened, 20 to 25 minutes.

6. If you're near a snowfield, eat with Snow Cones (page 110).

Note: Here's a time-saving tip: Make the crust for this pie while the flour and berry mixture is resting.

Serves 4

Apple Pie

We're dogmatists. We like two-crust apple pies. But we're willing to bend a little out here in the backcountry. Still, we'll give you an alternative if you're as fundamentalist as we are: Check out Apple Dumpling: The Great Alternative, on page 196.

About 6 medium-sized apples

2 Sierra cups boiling water

3 spoons sugar

½ spoon ground cinnamon

Dough for 1 piecrust (see pages 192–93)

Clarified butter to dot (see page 99)

at home

1. To dehydrate the apples, core and slice them about ⅜ inch thick. Lightly oil trays and dehydrate 24 hours, till the slices are hard.

at camp

2. Make preparations for baking in coals or on a camping stove (see pages 217–19) as you would for a pizza.

3. Rehydrate the apples by dropping into the boiling water and removing the pot from the heat. Let sit for 5 to 10 minutes, till soft. Drain.

4. Mix the rehydrated apples with the sugar and cinnamon and spread over the pie dough.

5. Dot with the butter, cover with the foil, and bake for 15 to 20 minutes, till the crust is firm and turning golden.

6. Allow to cool, or you'll burn the roof of your mouth, your tongue, and other body parts as you swoon.

Makes 1 fry-pan-sized pie, enough for 2–4 people, depending on appetite

Apple Dumpling: The Great Alternative 🏠🔥

Forget the frying pan — well, almost. You'll need it to "roll" the dough. This will be the largest apple dumpling west of the Pecos and your everlasting equivalent of a two-crust pie.

About 3 medium-sized apples

2 Sierra cups boiling water, to rehydrate

Dough for 1 piecrust (see pages 192–93)

3 spoons sugar, plus more for sprinkling over the piecrust

½ spoon ground cinnamon, plus more for sprinkling over the piecrust

Clarified butter to dot (see page 99)

1 spoon milk powder (optional)

1 spoon cold water, for reconstituting milk, if necessary

at home

1. To dehydrate the apples, core and slice about ⅜ inch thick. Lightly oil dehydrator trays and dry 24 hours, till hard.

at camp

2. Make preparations for baking in coals or on a camping stove (see pages 217–19).

3. If baking in coals, transfer the pie dough gently to a large piece of aluminum foil. Otherwise, leave in the pan.

4. To rehydrate the apples, drop them into a large pot with the boiling water and remove the pot from the heat. Let sit 5 to 10 minutes, till soft. Drain.

5. Mix the rehydrated apples with the sugar and cinnamon in the same large pot. Spread the apple mixture over one half of the dough. Dot with butter.

6. Lift the unfilled side over the top of the filling and pinch to close, as you would if making a calzone (page 208). Poke a couple of holes in the top of the dough with a fork.

7. If you'd like to add a final touch, mix the milk powder and cold water in a Sierra cup and, using the back of a spoon, "brush" a very light film of milk over the dough. Mix a bit of sugar and cinnamon and sprinkle over the milk.

8. If baking with coals, fold a flap of foil over the pie and seal the edges of the foil by crimping them together. Lift the entire package gently onto the coals. In 10 minutes, flip it over so the top can bake on the coals, 7 to 10 minutes longer. If baking with a stove, just leave in the fry pan. There's no need to flip.

9. Remove from the heat, place on a plate, and open the aluminum package (if baked in coals). Call in the troops. Apple calzone's on.

Makes 1 large dumpling, enough for 2–4 people in what you will come to know as The Great Dumpling Feeding Frenzy

Alternative Quiche/ Dumpling Dough ⬤

There's more than one way to skin a quiche or a tart, and if you're bored with the usual pie dough (page 192–93), try this instead. The egg in the dough gives it a nice golden finish when baked. Fill this dough with the quiche filling or alternative fillings on the facing page, or with the Apple Dumpling filling on page 196, and bake according to those recipe instructions.

½ spoon dry active yeast

2 pinches sugar

¼ Sierra cup warm water, plus more to moisten, if necessary

1 egg or equivalent powdered egg mix

1 Sierra cup flour, plus more for dusting the pot

¼ spoon salt

1 spoon clarified butter, softened (see page 99)

1. Make preparations to bake in coals or on a camping stove (see pages 217–19).

2. Proof the yeast (see Baking with Yeast, page 162) with the sugar and the water.

3. Stir together the egg, flour, and salt in a medium-sized pot. Add the clarified butter and proofed yeast, and more water, if necessary, to make a moist ball.

4. Knead lightly (see Baking with Yeast, page 162) on a floured plate till the dough is soft and pliable.

5. Dust a pot with flour, place the dough inside, and set in a warm place to rise until doubled in bulk, about 25 minutes. If you're not ready to bake yet, punch it down and let it rise again (see Baking with Yeast, page 163). Otherwise, line a fry pan up to its edge with the dough. If there's too much dough, crimp the edges as you would regular pie dough and discard any extra.

Dough for 1 quiche or tart

WILD QUICHE

Rick caught the first wild quiche ever recorded some years ago at an unnamed lake in the high Sierras. He tracked it over an 11,180-foot pass and through some rough moraine, down the flanks of a nasty defile to a frying pan overlooking some of the most spectacular scenery in California. This guy is relentless. The quiche never had a chance. But you do. The only thing you need aside from the ingredients is a steady hand. We'll explain this in a minute.

As the quiche bakes, the crust crisps and the filling stiffens.

ALTERNATIVE FILLINGS

- ¼ pound each wild mushrooms and leeks (dehydrated at home and rehydrated at camp) and cheese of choice

- ½ pound each zucchini and tomatoes, as well as ¼ pound red peppers (all dehydrated at home and rehydrated at camp) and cheese of choice

- **Any of the above with 2 spoons reconstituted salsa (pages 91–94)**

Chard (or Spinach) Quiche 🏠🔥

Chard and spinach dry and rehydrate well and are the perfect filling for a mountain quiche. You can tinker with the seasonings. Nutmeg, dill, saffron (if you can afford it), lemon or orange zest, and any number of cheeses can be mixed and matched.

1 bunch chard, washed, stemmed, and pulled from the central white spine

OR

1 bunch spinach, washed and stemmed

1 spoon pine nuts, lightly toasted (or finely sliced almonds or walnuts) (optional)

1⅔ Sierra cup boiling water

1 large onion, sliced into rounds

½ candied orange peel (see page 12) (optional)

2 spoons powdered milk

2 eggs or equivalent powdered egg mix plus 2 spoons powdered egg whites

Up to ⅓ Sierra cup water, to reconstitute powdered eggs, if necessary

Dough for 1 piecrust or quiche (pages 192–93 and 197)

2 spoons clarified butter, (see page 99)

2 cloves garlic, chopped fine

3 spoons finely chopped or sliced cheese (Parmesan, Monterey Jack, or whatever you've got on hand)

Nutmeg

Salt and ground black pepper

at home

1. Remove the tough veins, then dehydrate the chard (or spinach) leaves, about 1 hour, till brittle. Don't attempt to chop the leaves first. These things dry so fast that the chopped leaves would practically turn to dust. Store in an airtight bag until camping time.

at camp

2. Make preparations for baking in coals or on a camping stove (see pages 217–19) as you would for a pizza.

3. If you plan to use the toasted pine nuts, now's the time to toast them in a dry pot lid for just a few minutes till slightly golden. Remove from the lid and set aside.

4. Sauté the garlic and 1 spoon of the clarified butter in the pot lid for 3 to 4 minutes, till soft but not burned.

5. Rehydrate the chard by dropping in ⅔ Sierra cup of the boiling water to cover and removing the pot from the heat. Let it sit for just a few minutes. Drain and save the liquid. Squeeze dry and chop or pull the leaves into bits with your fingers. Set aside.

6. Tear the dehydrated onion into small bits and set aside.

7. Rehydrate 1 slice of candied orange (if using) by soaking in the remaining Sierra cup boiling water, then cut away the pulp from the peel and cut the peel into small bits. Set aside.

8. To make the quiche "pudding," reconstitute the milk powder with the rehydrating liquid you saved and mix together with the eggs in a medium-sized pot. (*Note:* If using powdered eggs and egg whites, mix together with the *dry* milk powder before adding the liquid. Of course, you'll need more of it. See ingredients for guidelines. Start with the rehydrating water.) If you run out of the rehydrating liquid, use water.

9. Add the sautéed garlic, rehydrated chard, onion bits, orange peel bits (if using), cheese, nutmeg to taste, and salt and pepper to taste. Stir until well mixed.

10. Pour over the pie dough. Sprinkle the pine nuts (if using) over the top. Dot with the remaining 1 spoon clarified butter.

11. Cover with foil or with a plate and foil and bake till both the crust is done and the filling is thickened and no longer runny, 20 to 25 minutes.

12. Slice as you would a pizza and fight bitterly over the last piece.

Serves 4

ALTERNATIVE COOKING METHOD

You can make the dough and the filling separately with this two-step method.

1. Set the dough in a pan. Prick the bottom and sides all round with a fork to prevent swelling. Bake, following the instructions in the recipe.

2. Cook the pudding mixture slowly over a fire, stirring constantly until it thickens. Pour into the baked pie shell. Cover with the toasted pine nuts.

Fruit Cobbler 🏠 🔥

We were sitting around the campsite a year or so ago mulling. And since there was no wine available to mull, we went for desserts. How could you make a cobbler — a deep-dish fruit pie with only one crust, and that on the top — without leaving most of the contents epoxied to the side of the pot? Lining the pot with the standard oil-and-flour coat wouldn't do much good, because two radically different things had to happen at the same time: The fruits had to rehydrate and be stewed, and the biscuit dough had to bake. And if the fruits were already rehydrated and stewed, baking it would permanently laminate it to the metal pot. (Ever burn stewing fruit to the bottom of your prized Creuset pot — the one you picked up in Paris when Gene Kelly was still singin' in the rain? If so, you know what we're talking about.) Enter the two-step recovery program: Stew and bake separately, then join 'em at the hip. Watch.

the fruit

4–6 cups sliced fresh fruit (preferably strawberries and apples, though any mixture will do)

1 Sierra cup water

2–3 spoons sugar

1 spoon brandy (optional)

the biscuit

1 level Sierra cup flour, plus more to dust your hands and a kneading plate

1 spoon powdered buttermilk (or powdered milk)

1 spoon sugar

¼ spoon baking powder

¼ spoon baking soda

¼ spoon salt

2 spoons clarified butter (see page 99)

1 lightly beaten egg or equivalent powdered egg mix

Small amount of water to moisten, if necessary

at home

1. Slice the strawberries in half; core and slice the apples about ⅜ inch thick. Spread on trays and dehydrate 24 hours, till hard and brittle.

at camp

2. Make preparations to bake in coals or on a camping stove (see pages 217–19).

3. To make the fruit mixture, place the fruit in a pot of the water to cover and bring to a boil. Reduce to a simmer, stir in the sugar and brandy (if using) and cook 5 to 10 minutes, till thickened to the consistency of a moist and fluid jam. Stir often to prevent sticking. It will thicken further as it cools. Set aside.

4. To make the biscuit, mix the flour, powdered buttermilk, sugar, baking powder, baking soda, salt, and powdered egg (if using) with a fork in a large pot.

5. Work the clarified butter into the dough to the consistency of small peas or cornmeal.

6. Stir in the egg (if using fresh) to moisten. If this doesn't make a moist ball (or if you're using powdered egg), add water.

7. Dust your hands and a plate with flour. Form the dough into a ball and knead it on the plate till smooth, 2 to 3 minutes. Press into a round disc about ½ inch thick.

8. Bake in a medium-sized pot for about 12 minutes, till the top is just turning golden.

9. To finish and serve, lift the biscuit in one piece onto the stewed fruit. Cobbler completed. Break the biscuit as you spoon portions into Sierra cups or onto plates. A more disciplined camper tells us that this dessert will keep overnight. We wouldn't know. It's never lasted that long at our campsite.

Serves 3–4 (unless camping with Hal, in which case, serves 1)

COBBLE THIS

What's in a name? You can cobble together a cobbler by improvising the way we've done in the recipe. You could try boiling the shoe that the cobbler mended, but we wouldn't recommend it. You could rename it and call it a crisp or crumble. We certainly don't care and won't tell. But the name "cobbler" for a deep-dish dessert appears to have come from its likeness to cobblestones when baked. Ours looks more like a parking lot because we bake the dough as one big biscuit rather than in small clumps, but it'll taste as good as the one your Aunt Hermione fashions every fall when the apples are ripe. It's not the name that counts, it's the imagination.

- **Myth 1: Pizza requires tomato sauce.** False. Many pizzas use no sauce at all.

- **Myth 2: Pizza requires tomatoes.** False. They weren't even known when pizza was invented.

- **Myth 3: Pizza requires cheese.** Nope. Sicilian pizza, for one, doesn't include cheese.

- **Myth 4: Uncle Julie is a real person.** Un-unh. Check out Rick's family tree sometime.

With that out of the way, we're ready to rumble.

Rick and Hal's "We Don't Deliver in 30 Minutes" High Mountain Pizza Dough

The main difference between bread dough and pizza dough is the oil in pizza dough. It makes the dough more elastic, and gives the world's pizza chefs something to flip and twirl. Hey, if they can do it, so can you!

Top the dough with the sauce, veggies, sliced cheese, and spices of your choice. Try some of our suggestions on the following pages. Bake according to the recipe instructions.

1 packet dry active yeast

2 pinches sugar

¼ Sierra cup warm water

1 generous Sierra cup flour, plus more to dust your hands, the kneading plate, and the pot

½ spoon salt

1–1½ spoons olive oil

Up to 1 Sierra cup water

1. Proof the yeast (see Baking with Yeast, page 162) with the sugar and warm water in a Sierra cup set in the sun.

2. Mix the 1 Sierra cup flour and the salt in a large pot.

3. When the yeast is swelling and frothy, about 5 minutes, add to the flour mixture.

4. Stir in the olive oil — 1 spoon at least, 1½ if you have enough — to the flour-yeast mixture.

5. Add, in small increments, enough of the 1 Sierra cup water to make a moist, pliable dough.

6. Dust your hands and a plate with flour. Knead the dough (see page 162) on the plate till soft and pliant. Pizza dough can be moister than standard bread dough, so if it's a bit sticky, that's okay.

7. Dust a medium-sized pot with flour. Set the kneaded dough in the floured pot, cover, and let it rise in a warm place till doubled in bulk, about 20 minutes. If you've got the time, punch it down with a floured fist and let it rise again (see page 163). If not, proceed with the next step.

8. Dust the kneading plate with a little more flour. Remove the risen dough from the pot and place on the plate; knead it gently for a few minutes.

9. Press it into a flat disk and begin working it with your fingers into a larger round disk, turning it over several times as you work. The idea is to get it large enough and thin enough to cover the fry pan on its bottom and sides. When the disk of dough is big enough to drape over your fists, do just that, and then continue to expand the dough by using your knuckles gently to stretch it.

10. At this point you can begin tossing the dough in the air in a circular motion, like those guys in the pizzeria you've watched all these years. In theory, this expands the circle of dough and reduces its bulk; in practice, it's just a way of showing off.

11. Remove the dough from that over-hanging branch and try again. It doesn't matter if you fail and it falls. Just pick it up, brush off the pebbles and pine needles, and keep on truckin'.

12. Fit the dough into the fry pan, pressing it up against the sides. Let it rest 5 minutes or so as you make the final adjustments to the ingredients.

Makes 1 pizza dough (with toppings, enough to serve 4 people)

PIZZA

Somebody on the Internet claims that Americans and Canadians eat an average of 23 pounds of pizza a year. Can't be right. Rick's uncle Julie (né Jules) eats that much in a week. Uncle Julie's never been backpacking. But years ago we brought his appetite and fine Sicilian taste (cultivated in Brooklyn) to the wilderness and have been making and baking pizza ever since. We have faded photos of Hal's first attempt to flip the pizza dough. They reveal a sodden mess draped artfully over a low-hanging branch. We have later photos of Hal draped artfully over a low-hanging branch, but that's another story.

Pizza with The Works 🏠🔥

When Rick's kids were small, they would assiduously pick every mushroom, pepper, and onion off their pizza before eating it, scowling all the while. Soon, family pizzas became plain cheese varieties. Needless to say, Rick would dream all year of the pizza toppings he was missing, that is, "The Works."

½ cup sliced onions (about ⅜ inch thick)

½ cup sliced green peppers (about ⅜ inch thick)

1 cup mushrooms (slices should be about ⅜ inch thick)

2 Sierra cups boiling water, for rehydrating

½ Sierra cup Friday Night "Oh Man! I Forgot The Sauce" Sauce (see page 88)

1 pizza dough (see recipe, pages 202-203)

1 Sierra cup sliced cheese (whatever variety is at hand)

2 cloves fresh garlic, sliced thin

Pinch of salt

Sprinkling of ground black pepper

Sprinkling of oregano

Olive oil, for drizzling over toppings

at home

1. Dehydrate the onion, pepper, and mushroom slices for 24 hours, till brittle. The dehydrated yield should be about 1 Sierra cup veggies.

at camp

2. Make preparations for baking in coals or on a camping stove (see pages 217–219).

3. Rehydrate the veggies with just enough of the boiling water to cover. Soak 10 minutes. Drain and squeeze dry.

4. Spread the sauce on the dough. Follow with the remaining ingredients, in the order listed.

5. Bake for 20 to 25 minutes till the crust is brown.

Serves 4

All Mushrooms, All the Time Pizza 🏠🔥

Rick grew up thinking there was only one variety of mushroom, the common white ones from the corner grocery. Clearly, it was a sheltered childhood.

5–6 cups fresh mushrooms, sliced ⅜ inch thick (a mix of common whites and wild mushrooms: shiitake, oyster, portobello, Chinese "tree ears" [muer])

2 Sierra cups boiling water, for rehydrating

1 pizza dough (see recipe, pages 202–203)

1 Sierra cup sliced cheeses (whatever you have in your camping "larder")

2 cloves fresh garlic, sliced thin, or more to taste

Pinch of salt

Sprinkling of ground black pepper

Sprinkling of dried mint (this is not a misprint)

Sprinkling of dried Italian parsley

4 thin slices Parmesan (optional)

1 spoon olive oil, for drizzling over toppings

at home

1. Spread the mushrooms on dehydrating trays and dry 12 hours, till hard.

at camp

2. Make preparations for baking in coals or on a camping stove (see pages 217–219).

3. To rehydrate the mushrooms, drop them in the boiling water, remove from the heat, and steep 4 to 5 minutes, till soft. Drain.

4. Line the pizza dough with the mushrooms and sliced cheeses. (The theory is that you probably hike with more than one kind of cheese.)

5. Add the remaining ingredients, in the order mentioned. (*Note:* To bring out the flavor of the mushrooms, we sometimes sauté them briefly in a little oil just before placing on the cheeses.)

6. Bake 20 to 25 minutes, till crust is brown. Slice and eat.

Serves 4

Tomato Red Pizza 🏠🔥

If you combine an old left family with a new left commune, you'll get just about as many reds as are in the sauce for this conservative, right-wing pizza.

½ Sierra cup rehydrated Fastest Sauce in the West , Slowest Sauce in the West, or Look Ma, No-Oil Tomato Sauce (see recipes, pages 84–86)

1 pizza dough (see recipe, pages 202–3)

1½ Sierra cups commercial sun-dried and/or home-dehydrated tomatoes (use 10 to 12 medium-sized fresh tomatoes if dehydrating at home)

1 Sierra cup sliced cheeses of your choice

2 cloves garlic, sliced thin, or more to taste

Pinch of salt

Sprinkling of ground black pepper

Sprinkling of mixed Italian spices (oregano, tarragon, basil, thyme)

1 spoon olive oil for drizzling lightly over toppings

at home

1. Prepare the pizza sauce according to the recipe instructions.

at camp

2. Make preparations for baking in coals or on a camping stove (see pages 217–19).

3. Rehydrate the sauce of choice according to the recipe instructions.

4. Spread the sauce on the dough.

5. Top the pizza with the remaining ingredients, in the order listed.

6. Bake 20 to 25 minutes, till crust is brown. Slice and eat.

Serves 4

Pure Vegan Pizza 🔥

Sausages and cheeses have been known to slink out of camp when they hear this one's on the fire. Good. That means more for Rick and the 30-member Vestal Vegetarian Choir.

2 cups green bell peppers

2 Japanese eggplants

2 cups mushrooms

4 Sierra cups boiling water

1 pizza dough (see recipe, pages 202–3)

3 cloves garlic

  Pinch of salt

  Sprinkling of ground black pepper

  Generous sprinkling of mixed Italian spices (oregano, tarragon, basil, thyme)

1 spoon olive oil for drizzling over toppings

at home

1. To dehydrate the veggies, slice them ⅜ inch thick, spread on trays and dehydrate 24 hours, till dessicated.

at camp

2. Make preparations for baking in coals or on a camping stove (see pages 217–19).

3. To rehydrate the veggies, drop in the boiling water, remove from the heat, and steep 5 minutes, till soft. Drain.

4. Top the dough with the rehydrated veggies, then the remaining ingredients, in the order listed. (This pizza needs to be spiced heavily to bring out the flavors of the veggies alone.)

5. Bake 20 to 25 minutes, till the crust is brown. Slice and eat.

Serves 4

YOUR CALL

Okay, kids, your turn to invent a pizza. Let us know what you've come up with. Is someone in the group carrying a hot Italian sausage around the neck as a talisman? Commandeer it. Pine nuts? Anchovies? (In a can?) A wheel of provolone?

Hal and Rick's "We Deliver in Thirty Minutes" Calzone

Left the frying pan at home? Smart move, saves weight. But you want that promised pizza. You can have it as long as you've packed in a big piece of aluminum foil.

Here's what you do: Instead of lining a fry pan, lay the pizza dough on a lightly oiled piece of aluminum foil. Top half of it with your choice of toppings, fold the other half of the dough back over the toppings-turned-fillings, and pinch closed. You now have a half-moon of pizza.

Seal the calzone in the aluminum foil and bake directly on coals. In 10 minutes, flip it over so the other side can bake on coals, too. Ten minutes after flipping, call in the troops. Calzone's on.

Note: You can also bake a calzone 20 to 25 minutes in the fry pan on your stove, as if it were a folded-over pizza (see page 218 for instructions). But since it only comes out half the size of a fry-pan pizza, we usually go for the pizza instead.

Unwrapped calzone

Wrapped calzone

[Chapter 10]

Nuts & Bolts

As Rick packs up for his annual family camping trip, the neighbors scoff that he looks like he's planning a launch of the space shuttle. He appears convinced that if he could add a few rocket thrusters to the minivan, he and the brood could easily survive a couple of weeks in orbit. Some people may say that camping "ain't rocket science," but anyone who's left civilization and the frying pan behind knows that camping requires lots of preparation. After all, no one wants to run out of essentials, whether food or fuel, deep in the backwoods. This chapter will tell you all you need to know about food planning for your trip. We've even included a "how-to" guide to the cooking techniques you'll be using to create all your favorite meals — from boiling and poaching to grilling and steaming and a lot more besides.

Trip Planning

You might expect a camping cookbook to begin with a chapter on planning your trip. That's how we end our book. Not to worry. There's a method to our madness. Whether you have studiously read every page thus far or flipped your way through our recipes following your fancy, we hope we've inspired your culinary imagination. We've suggested new foods, new flavorings, new ideas. Now we want to do the same with trip planning.

We know lots of campers who are obsessive-compulsives: very organized. They fastidiously pack foods in separate plastic bags labeled "Day 1 Lunch" or "Day 4 Dinner" so that they will have just the right amount of each ingredient for each of their planned meals. You can do that with our recipes. But that's not the way we do it.

As we hike along a trail, we are more likely to ponder variations on tomorrow's noodle dish then we are to discuss tomorrow's hike. It's a game in which each player has to make the best use of the hand (s)he's dealt. We begin the trip with a full and varied "pantry." As we use up the ingredients, we try to concoct new, sometimes unheard of, ways to cook and eat the rest. Our recipes may succeed or they may fail, but the process sure is fun.

HOW MUCH FOOD PER PERSON PER DAY?

Our rule of thumb is to bring 1½ pounds of food per person per day. A day means a full day with three meals. If three of us start hiking late on a Friday morning, after eating breakfast at a roadside diner, and if we plan to hike out Tuesday mid-morning (after breakfast), then that counts as 4 full days. Three people, 4 days, 1½ pounds of food per person per day: Figure it out. That's 18 pounds of food. That's how much we bring.

To weigh the food, stand on a bathroom scale and weigh yourself. Remember the result. (You don't have to strip for this unless you like weighing food naked.) Now place all the stuff you want to take in an empty cardboard box. Pick it up and get back on the scale. Ask your partner to squat down and read the result. If you now weigh 18 pounds more than you did without the box of food, you're done. If something important is still on the counter, you need to eliminate something already in the box. When Rick's kids are going on the trip, the chocolate bars might go in first; when Hal and Steve are going, the flour and Chinese noodles are the most important items. Ed can't get started in the morning without his breakfast bars; Maureen needs her coffee. That's how you define essentials, so out go half the ginger snaps, in go the breakfast bars and coffee.

ONE PANTRY, MANY MENUS

To give you a better idea of our philosophy in action, we bring you two imaginary trips, both with 3 people, both for 4 days, both with the same 18 pounds of food. In addition to snack foods (dried fruit, cheese, crackers, cookies, snack bars, and so on), the basic cookable foods might be flour, vermicelli, bulgur wheat, sugar, eggs, tortillas, clarified butter, semisweet chocolate, dehydrated tomato sauce, dehydrated veggies (mushrooms, tomatoes, onions, peppers); small bottles of maple syrup, olive oil, lime juice, and brandy; and small baggies of powdered milk, yeast, baking powder, and coconut powder.

The original plan could be for these dinners: spaghetti with tomato sauce, a vegetable and cheese pizza, quesadillas, and trout amandine with a side order of bulgur wheat. Baking could include a chocolate cake with frosting and a Baguette in a Pot: The Generic Loaf (page 164). On a layover morning, breakfast might be crêpes, and there would be plenty of sweet stuff available for lime or coconut snow cones if there was snow nearby.

Yet with the very same ingredients, you might fashion a completely different menu. Dinners could be a veggie quiche, vermicelli pad thai (with a lime, coconut, and tomato sauce), tabbouleh/cheese burritos, and a trout and cheese soufflé. Baking might include a braided challah and a batch of chocolate brownies, and the cooked breakfast might be pancakes with maple syrup. The list of potential creations goes on and on, including chapati, chutney, cobbler, calzones, biscuits, scones, dumplings, mantou, and more.

When you're camping, your cuisine isn't limited as much by the ingredients you brought as by your imagination. It's what you do with those ingredients that counts. In a nutshell (almonds? walnuts? pecans?), that's the message of this cookbook. Tinker, substitute, create, imagine. Don't fret when you fail; everything tastes better in the open air anyway. And when you succeed, when you create a dish that your camp mates can't quite believe they're eating, when you smile and start thinking about what you can do for an encore using just the food still in your pack, that's when we'll know that this cookbook has done its job.

WHAT GOOD'S A COOLER, ANYWAY?

You've decided to be gregarious. To hell with the lonesome trail hike with a loaded pack on your back. Stuff the kids and granny and the hammock in the old VW bus, load up on fresh food and as many six-packs as will get you through the weekend, haul out the biggest cooler in your garage, fill it with ice or those gel packs, and head out to the campground (with a reservation for a campsite in the band of your hat next to the fishing flies). You're armed with a two-burner camp stove and a propane tank with enough fuel to power a small town in the Plains states. So who needs home dehydrating? You don't. Fresh fruits, veggies, meats and cheeses, butter and eggs, milk and buttermilk substitute for the dried and powered and home-prepared meals in our recipes, and you can replicate just about everything in the book at the campsite. The biggest danger will be all those neighborly folks in the next camp slot who mosey over for a taste. That's a problem we can't solve, but we can give you some tips on adapting our recipes to the luxury of a cooler full of fresh stuff.

Plan to make dishes containing meat, including chicken and fish on the first day and a half. That cooler isn't a state-of-the-art fridge, and microorganisms are tough customers.

Wherever we call for dehydrated veggies or fruits, substitute fresh. Some need to be kept cool, especially leaf vegetables like parsley, mint, basil, and spinach, as well as carrots. Others, such as tomatoes, mushrooms, avocados, and eggplants, don't need to go in the cooler.

Know your fuel supply. It's unlikely you'll want to try to simmer or bake a chicken casserole for 1½ hours (see pages 48–49, Chicken Casserole That Never Made It to the Campsite) or cook too many risottos at 20 to 25 minutes a pop (pages 113–17). Likewise, you'll settle for a quick pasta sauce rather than one that requires hours of gentle simmering (Fastest Sauce in the West [page 84] rather than Slowest Sauce in the West [page 85]).

Know your cooler's dimensions. You can make a soup or stew at home and pack it in a plastic container. But will it fit in the cooler and still allow room for all the butter and cheese and vodka? Alternative: Pack the soup ingredients in individual plastic bags, and store in the cooler only those ingredients that might spoil.

Some recipes call for puréeing (for example, Barley Soup with Mushrooms, page 30; Brazilian Black Bean Soup, page 31; Pumpkin Soup, page 38; and Pumpkin Pancakes, page 152). Unless you're traveling in one of those horizontal apartment blocks called RVs, you're unlikely to be packing an electric

blender or food processor as a sidearm. What to do? Pumpkin's not a problem; buy a can and take it along. As for the others, either make the recipe at home and find room in the cooler for it, or just skip that step and cook away as if it never existed. Nobody's going to come around with a clipboard and a checklist to see if you did it right.

If a recipe calls for roasting (Roasted Eggplant and Almond Sauce, page 87), do the roasting part at home, the rest at the campsite. The roasted veggies will last fine in the cooler.

Applesauce, apple butter, salsas, chutneys, marmalade, and jam (pages 90–105): Carry store-bought in jars (no need to store in cooler) or homemade in plastic tubs (useful to store in the cooler).

Does the recipe call for soup stock? Use bouillon cubes or canned stock. No need to keep in the cooler.

What's in a sushi roll (pages 124–25)? Instead of the dehydrated veggies, use a fresh avocado or Japanese cucumber. The cucumber needs to be stored in the cooler.

Potatoes? Toss 'em in the trunk. If you're going to make latkes (pages 158–59), bring along a small kitchen grater. Nobody's gonna snitch on you.

Buttermilk pancakes and scones (pages 151, 176–77)? Bring a quart of fresh buttermilk. Alternatively, mix the buttermilk, eggs, and melted butter in a blender and carry this batter with you in a sealed container. Make sure it's stored upright, or you're going to be eating a gel pack frosty for the rest of the trip.

For pie crust (pages 192–93), bring a small rolling pin and make the crust at the campsite. No one will believe what you're doing, and everybody will want a picture. Neat!

And the only thing Rick wishes we could have for our high mountain pizzas (pages 204–7) is fresh mozzarella; you know, the kind that comes in a little sack and drips all over the fridge. You can take it in the cooler. We can't take it in the backpack.

CAMP STOVES AND FUELS

When Rick starts talking about BTUs, Hal usually replies, "Gesundheit!" But it turns out that BTUs explain a lot about how stoves work, which one you should choose, and how much fuel you will need on your camping trip. A BTU (British thermal unit) is the amount of heat it takes to increase the temperature of 1 pound of water (about 2 cups) by

1°F. If none of the heat were wasted, it would take about 350 BTUs to boil a liter of water. Unfortunately, a typical camping stove only channels about half of that heat into your cooking; the rest floats off into the air.

The reason that there isn't a single runaway champion for fuel or stove type is that both of the cleanest-burning fuels provide about the same heat energy per pound. Propane or butane is a gas at room temperature; white gas is a liquid. Both contain about 20,000 BTUs per pound, so almost any stove you buy will be rated to boil a liter of water in 3 to 4 minutes and will be capable of boiling about 7 to 8 liters of water using 100 grams of fuel. (Other stove fuels include alcohol [only 13,000 BTUs/pound], and kerosene and gasoline [both of which tend to burn dirtier than white gas]).

Of course, there are differences. Propane and butane stoves don't require priming (prewarming); you just turn on the burner and light the stove with a match. But propane and butane gas canisters are heavy and bulky, and the gas pressure can drop drastically at very low temperatures. White gas is a convenient liquid: It is easier to measure, and you can bring just the amount you need.

How Far Does A Pound of Fuel Go?

When Rick and his family went camping recently, he figured four people, 3.5 days, 2 ounces butane per person per day should equal 1.75 pounds of butane. They brought in two 1-pound canisters. They hiked out with one empty canister and a second one that was about half gone. For the record, here's what they cooked with the single 1-pound canister (including heating water for cleanup). For the baked items below, they used an Outback Oven (see pages 218–19).

Day 1:

- Crêpes
- Small bread (baked on the Outback Oven)
- Cheese and rice burritos (includes cooking the rice)
- Ramen noodles
- Hot chocolate

Day 2:

- Crêpes
- Hot chocolate
- Brownies (baked on the Outback Oven)
- Chocolate cake with icing (baked on the Outback Oven)
- Ramen noodles

Day 3:

- Spaghetti with marinara sauce

The containers are lighter, and the same weight of white gas takes up less space than the equivalent weight of propane.

Which particular stove is for you? That's difficult to say, since more reliable, ingenious, and lighter stoves come out each year. If you don't already own a camping stove, we recommend you visit the local camping store before you buy and talk with the experts. However, we do have a few words of advice. Whatever type or brand of stove you choose, be sure that:

- It can simmer your soup or stew. Some stoves have a tendency to go out when you try to lower the flame to

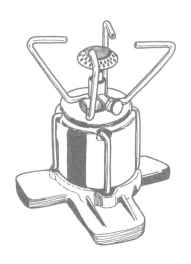

Canister stove

anything below "blowtorch." If you can get a stove that will simmer on a windy day with its windscreen in place, all the better.

- It is stable with a pot of water (or a pan of pizza) sitting on it. In fact, you might want to test it in the flowerbed out in front of the store to check its overall stability, since it is unlikely you'll have that nice flat counter to set your stove on when you go camping.

- If it's a liquid-fuel stove, you take it apart and clean it in the store or at home. Sometimes, the "special tool" that comes with the stove isn't really the only tool required to disassemble and clean the jet and burner.

How much fuel will you need? That'll depend on your own particular usage. Steve can't leave camp in the morning without his freshly brewed java. Rick and Hal indulge in complex dinner preparations that would make Julia Child glad she stayed home. If you want to use the last drop of liquid fuel to heat the washing-up water after hotcakes on your last morning in the wild, you'll need to keep accurate records of your past fuel use. Still, we can get you started. For a typical summer camping trip, figure about 1.5 to 2 ounces of liquid (white

Liquid-fuel stove

gas) fuel per person per day. If you have 4 people camping for 4 full days, figure a minimum of 24 ounces (3 cups) of white gas. Then, just to be on the safe side, throw in an extra cup.

With propane or butane, it's about 1.5 to 2 ounces of gas weight per person per day. Four people camping for 2 days can expect to use 12 to 16 ounces of compressed gas. A typical gas canister contains 16 ounces (1 pound) of gas. Be careful about underestimating with butane. With gas in the canister, it's hard to know how much fuel is left until it is nearly exhausted. That's when you shake the canister and nothing sloshes around. You can't peer inside to check the fuel level as you can with liquid fuel. Again, it's better to err on the side of caution than to miss a meal.

Cooking Techniques

In Hal's kitchen at home, he has a marble slab built into his countertop, just for working with and rolling dough; Rick has a Waring blender with enough horsepower to pull a water skier. But neither of those items can come along on their camping trips. Once you leave your kitchen behind in your rearview mirror, you'll have to make do with your knowledge, your planning, and, often, your ingenuity. Dense, dry wood will burn hotter, shortening cooking and baking times; conversely, it may take longer to heat foods on your camp stove on a windy evening than it will on a still morning. Don't even ask us to tell you about our early attempts at baking and

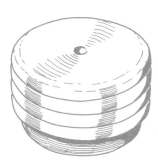

Dehydrator

steaming. They weren't pretty, or edible. Hopefully, the following sections will keep you from making some of the same mistakes we've made over the years.

DEHYDRATING

Take the water content out of food, and you've dehydrated it. That makes it lighter and thus the perfect aid to lightweight camping. And as it's unlikely you're going to be freeze-drying or vacuum-drying anything at home, you're left, as we are, with the handy home dehydrator. Imagine a toaster coil flipped on its side over a small electric fan that blows warm air up into and over a set of perforated plastic trays, all topped with a perforated plastic hood that allows most of the heat to recirculate and the water vapor to escape.

True, if you live in the desert or where the sun shines all the time, you can build yourself a sun drier (and sell us all your sun-dried tomatoes at bargain prices), but most of us need to plunk down around $80.00 for a four-tray commercial model. The Internet is

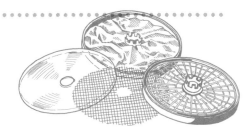

Dehydrator trays

alive with vendors willing to ship one to you. Some models allow you to expand the number of trays in use at any time; some come with fruit-roll inserts, which we find particularly useful for drying soups and stews.

Technically, of course, dehydrating isn't a cooking technique; it's more a food preparation process, but it's a step in many of our recipes, and we're calling it a cooking technique.

Here are some tips on dehydrating.

Fruits and veggies. They'll only taste as sweet as they are ripe before dehydrating. And they won't feel or look like the dried apricots or peaches or bananas or whatever you buy in the market. That's because you're not adding sulfur and other agents to the fruit.

Parboiling. Some vegetables — carrots and potatoes, for example — need to be parboiled before drying. Otherwise, they won't rehydrate in edible form. (Unless, of course, you're starving.) Don't even try tofu or avocado; the yield is shoe leather.

How long does it take? In theory, dehydrating should take just long enough to remove the moisture from a food. When the moisture is gone, food becomes tough and leathery or (depending on the food) brittle and crunchy. For example, if you stop dehydrating meat too soon, when it is the consistency of the "beef jerky" you buy at the corner convenience store, it might seem soft and tasty today, but it will begin to mold in 3 to 5 days (at room temperature). Keep dehydrating until all the moisture is gone. How long is that? It depends on what is in the dehydrator. A dehydrator with trays of ripe, moist apricots contains a lot more moisture than one with a single tray of spinach leaves; since both dehydrators have the same heater coils and fan, the apricots will take longer to dehydrate (probably 24 hours) than the spinach (1 hour might be plenty).

In practice, Rick keeps his dehydrator in the garage and never checks it more than once a day. If he loads up the trays with fresh fruit or sauces at 6 o'clock one evening, he never checks it until the following night after work, at least 24 hours later. Everything is always done to perfection. Hal, on the other hand, dehydrates in his kitchen. He checks the progress of his goodies often, mainly because each time he peeks, he can sample his wares. He often discovers that everything is completely dehydrated — also perfectly — in only 8, 10, or 12 hours. Our conclusion? If you're lazy (like Rick), leave everything 24 hours. If you're hungry (like Hal), check progress often and sample on a regular basis. It is almost impossible to "over-dehydrate"; but be sure you don't stop the process too soon, before the moisture is really removed.

Storage, at home and on the trail. Unless specified otherwise, all the dehydrated food in these recipes should be stored in airtight ("zip up") bags or containers at room temperature. As long as the food doesn't contain meat, cheese, or oil, it will easily keep at least six months. We've heard it will keep longer, but we can't make that statement from personal experience. You see, we start dehydrating each year when the strawberries first turn up at the farmers'

market in April, and whoever takes the last camping trip of the season in September invariably finishes everything off. We are more careful with dehydrated meals containing meat, cheese, or oil. Those meals are stored in either the refrigerator or freezer (wherever there is room) until we leave. Again, we assume they would keep in your fridge more than six months, but we've never had the occasion to find out. Unless we have specified otherwise in the recipes, we can vouch that everything you dehydrate from this book will keep well and taste fine for at least 10 days on the trail, because that is as long as we stay out (at one time). Considering the six-month shelf life of most items around our houses, we assume that most dehydrated foods will also keep well on month-long camping trips, or even longer. But we can't say for sure, especially for foods that contain oil or fat (from meat or cheese). If anything you bring on your month-long sojourn starts to look or smell funny, don't take a chance on it.

Prevent drips. Line trays with plastic wrap or aluminum foil to prevent drips. Line the base of the dehydrator with one of these materials as well to catch drips, but don't cover any of the air vents in the base.

Nonstick sprays. A light layer on the trays, whether lined or unlined, will prevent sticking when drying ripe fruits and vegetables and cooked foods that lack oil content. But use sparingly if you don't want to taste it. *Note:* In the recipes we use "oil" and "nonstick spray" interchangeably. You can use either, but we always use the latter.

Fruit-roll inserts. No nonstick sprays required, ever, if you use these. Anything will dry nicely and not stick. If you're oil-averse, buy extra inserts and use them exclusively.

Temperature gauges. Most models come with gauges and instructions that such-and-such foods should be dried at such-and-such temperatures. We uniformly ignore this advice and have never encountered problems. Of course, the higher the temperature the faster things will dry.

Here are some tips on rehydrating.

Color and texture. Rehydrated food won't necessarily look or feel like the original, but in camp we're after flavor, not results publishable in *Gourmet* magazine.

Meats. With rare exceptions, they will not be as soft as the originals, but long rehydrating will bring them back close to the delicacy you started with.

Stews, risottos, soups. Cover with plenty of water and let them cook down. This enhances flavor and restores thickness and bulk.

Sautéed foods, chutneys, chilies, and other schmeers. Rehydrate with a minimum of boiling water, just enough to cover. Often, letting the food sit in cool water will bring it back without putting it over heat.

BAKING IN COALS

The basic idea of baking in coals is to nestle your pot in a clearing in the dirt, pile hot coals around it, and let the coals

Pizza pan covered with inverted camping plate

Pizza pan covered with inverted camping plate and aluminum foil

Pot nestled in coals

cool as you bake. The process works best if you create a small baking area just outside your fire ring and surround it with rocks. Use a long stick to rake hot coals from the fire ring to surround the baking pot. The coals should be hot, but not flaming. If more coals are needed, they can be added later. For a pizza or a quiche (baked in a pan), invert a metal camping plate on top of the pan and cover both the plate and the outer edge of the pan with aluminum foil. Surround the pan with hot coals and, using a couple of long sticks like chopsticks, place a few hot coals on top of the foil.

It's easy to check the progress of your baking. Simply remove the top of the pot and test the content. A bread, for example, typically takes about 15 to 20 minutes, depending on such variables as weather and wind, size of pot, temperature of coals, ingredients, and your anxiety threshold. If the loaf sounds hollow when you tap it sharply, it's done. If it isn't done, add more coals around the pot and keep baking. On a windy day, you might need to rotate your pot every 10 minutes, so that a different part of the pot faces the wind. Otherwise, one side will bake faster than the other.

You can also bake food by wrapping it in foil and setting it on or under coals, as with trout and calzones.

BAKING ON A CAMPING STOVE: THE OUTBACK OVEN

The Outback Oven, made and marketed by Backpacker's Pantry (see Resources, page 224) is one of those "better mousetrap" ideas. It turns what some people think of as a portable blowtorch — your camping stove — into a real oven.

The concept is so simple that we invariably wonder why no one thought of it a long time ago. It consists of two basic parts, a "heat diffuser plate" and a "convection dome." The round stainless-steel heat diffuser plate goes over the burner of your camping stove, surmounted by metal "risers." Your covered pot sits on those risers, and the heat from the gas flame is forced out and around the diffuser plate, into the snazzy heat-retaining "skirt," grandly called a "convection dome." The convection dome traps the hot air and forces it to circulate up and around the pot. Voilà! Instant oven.

We've tested all our baking recipes on it, with three-star results. Best of all, it's fuel efficient. In fact, the operating

Outback Oven diffuser plate and Pot

manual warns against running your stove at full tilt. While the basic system will work with any pot, the deluxe kit comes with a lidded nonstick pan, and a gauge in the pan top that boasts three simple settings: warm up, bake, and burn. By adjusting the flame on your stove, you can keep the dial pointing to "bake," and the results are invariably satisfying. Thus, for example, when baking a pizza on the Outback Oven, you need none of the aluminum foil or metal plate that we use when baking in coals. Just place the pizza dough in the pan provided (or your own fry pan), top the pizza with your favorite fillings, set the filled and covered pan on the metal "ris-

Outback Oven convection dome

ers," cover it with the "convection dome," and light up. Keep your eye on the dial and peek on occasion to see if the crust is done.

Finally, a caveat. Nothing's perfect in this best of all possible worlds, and this type of oven's imperfection is its weight, ½ to ¾ pound, depending on the version you buy. If you're a backpacker and a baker, you've got decisions to make. One of them may be to leave the Outback home and head for fire-permit country.

BOILING

Boiling means cooking in boiling water. Remember that the higher the altitude, the lower the temperature at which this occurs. That's the good news, because it takes less time to get the water bubbling. The bad news is that the lower boiling temperature means you have to cook the food longer than at sea level. The chart at left indicates the differences in boiling points.

DOUBLE BOILING

If you want to heat or melt something slowly, at just the temperature of boiling water, a double boiler's just the ticket. Since you're a thousand miles from your kitchen cabinet, improvise. Here's how. Float a pot or pot top in a larger pot of water. The water below will limit the temperature of whatever food you're heating up to the temperature of the boiling water. Let the steam escape; do this by leaving the larger pot uncovered. Otherwise, the steam will condense and drip back down, soaking your supper.

FRYING OR SAUTÉING

Frying is cooking in fat in a pan over direct heat. If you do it quickly in a small amount of oil, it is often called *sautéing*. The fat may be any cooking oil — vegetable, corn, peanut, olive, canola, safflower, or sesame — or vegetable shortenings. Butter, including clarified

Double boiler

butter, ghee, and margarine are standards, of course, but watch out: They blacken and burn more easily than the others if they get too hot.

GRILLING

There's a reason cops "grill" suspects. High heat cooks their goose, and they spill the beans. You're not going to roast a goose or skewer a bean, but the grill is a camper's delight. At the local county or state park, the campsites come with built-in fire rings and grills; in the backcountry, you'll often find a battered old grill that somebody's left behind after fishing in the nearby creek. That's an environmental curse, but unless you're packing in by mule, horse, llama, or goat, it's unlikely you'll be able to carry it out. Use it, break down your fire ring, and stash the grill out of sight in a

BOILING POINT FOR WATER

Altitude	°F	°C
Sea level	212	100
2,000 ft	208	98
5,000 ft	203	95
7,500 ft	198	92
10,000 ft	194	90

BAKING OVER BRIQUETTES

Rick and Hal have never stayed at a "briquettes-only" campground, but apparently Boy Scouts and Girl Scouts set up their tents frequently in such places. They have developed a baking technique involving a cardboard box, some aluminum foil, and a briquette fire. And also, bless 'em, bolt cutters, staple guns, contact cement, knives, scissors, and other things your mama never told you about when you set out to earn a merit badge. If you're interested, you can find the instructions at the U.S. Scouting Service's Web site (see Resources, page 224).

If you're really, really set on a briquette fire, reserve a spot at the county, state, or national campgrounds. Each campsite usually has a built-in fire ring and grill.

nearby rock cave. Better, bring your own lightweight backpacking grill in its handy stuff sack. Handy because grills pick up a thick layer of pot black that will leave more evidence in your backpack than an amateur's fingerprints in a botched bank job.

If you don't mind a little extra weight and absolutely have to have a grill for your tofu burgers and stray cutthroat, there are a number of folding grills on the market that set up over a fire or sit securely on almost any camp stove. Ask to see 'em at your local camping store, or search the Internet for "backpacking grill," which will turn up a variety of options. Set a lightweight grill on rocks 6 to 10 inches over the coals or flames. If unstable, anchor it by placing small rocks on either end of the grill. Leave enough room for your cooking pot or for a piece of aluminum foil. If barbecuing directly over the coals, spread a layer of oil over the grill first to prevent sticking. If using a marinade — car campers and canoeists can bring it along in plastic containers with tight-fitting lids — there's no need to grease the grill, because marinades use more oil than a 1953 Daimler straight-eight. And if you're out in the wilds and forgot the

grill and land a trout, impale it on a green stick and "grill" it as if you were roasting marshmallows with Troop 5.

POACHING

Poaching is cooking by simmering gently in just enough water to cover. *Simmering* describes what water does just below the boiling point: Rather than bubble actively, the water moves only slightly. This point is hard to maintain on an open fire, but happily it doesn't matter. Boiling works fine instead, and the culinary police will never hear about it.

STEAMING

If you didn't bring your Chinese bamboo steamer on your vacation, you can fabricate a decent alternative. Start with your largest pot. Set a lid from a smaller

Steamer

pot in the bottom, just as if you had tried to close the pot with the wrong-sized top. Fill the bottom of the big pot with about ½ inch of water. Now cut a round piece of aluminum foil about an inch larger than the circumference of the pot and shape it to fit flat across the inside of the pot. Crimp it upwards at the edges. Use your knife to poke lots of small holes in the foil, to let the condensed steam drip back down to the bottom of the pot. Place the foil in the large pot so it just rests on the pot lid. Put the pot over the fire and bring the water to a boil. Place whatever you want to steam on the aluminum foil, and place the real lid on the large pot. Keep the water boiling in the bottom of the pot, and don't peek at the food too often. Every time you remove the top, the steam escapes.

When in America, Don't Drink the Water

- Don't believe your eyes. That indigo lake in the pristine wilderness contains micro-organisms you didn't know exist, and many of them are nasty little brutes. Even off-trail high-mountain lakes and fast-rushing streams may harbor the *Giardia* of your fondest nightmares.

- Filter, chemically purify, or boil drinking water.

- When cooking, boiling water saves the day. Most recipes in this book will get you through safely, because they get simmered or boiled for 7 to 10 minutes.

- For more information than you want (and more than you probably need), search the Internet for "backpacking water purification systems." If you use a filtration system, we'd advise bringing a spare filter, just in case.

There are drops that give adequate protection and clean-tasting water for backpackers and other lightweight hikers. Instead of using iodine as the active ingredient, they contain chlorine dioxide, a purifying agent that (believe it or not) doesn't leave your water tasting like it came from a swimming pool. Check products for Environmental Protection Agency approval indicators. (See Internet Resources, page 224, for relevant Web sites.)

Do You Need a Packing List?

Hal is of a certain age, which means that the car lights get left on until the battery's dead, keys get locked in the cellar, and homemade bouillon cubes get left in the freezer when he sets off for the backcountry. Rick forgets nothing. You might, however, want to investigate his shirt pocket on any given day to see how many "to do" lists he keeps filed there. He needs written reminders such as "take nap" and "remind Hal to check freezer." Browsing our old camping book, we find among the 16 checklists (totaling over 300 separate items) a stunning little number with its box to be checked, "Canoe *(a very hard item to forget, but we know people who've had to go back for it)."*

Moral? Foodies need lists, too. Here are a couple of examples. They're just that: examples. Look 'em over, then make up your own. Make multiple copies, one for each of the members of your party and spares for next year's trip, plus one for Hal. He needs all the help he can get. Revise as you add and subtract things from trip to trip or year to year. And remember our motto:

If it's a choice between the matches and the kiddies, take the matches.

For the seriously obsessed and compulsive, there are literally hundreds of examples of camping lists on the Net. Just search "Camping Checklists" and duck. You may be there for hours. An alternative, of course, and one we strongly recommend, is a look at our how-to camping book, *The Camper's Companion* (Avalon Travel Publishing, 1996).

COOKING AND WATER FILTRATION GEAR

- ☐ Camp stove + fuel container
- ☐ Fuel
- ☐ Matches (strike-anywhere type) or lighter
- ☐ 2 or 3 nested pots and lids
- ☐ Frying pan (optional)
- ☐ Spatula (optional)
- ☐ Pair garden gloves (to handle hot pots; to gather wood)
- ☐ Sierra cups (one each)
- ☐ Tin plates (can double as pot lids and cutting board)
- ☐ Forks or chopsticks and spoons
- ☐ Pocket knife
- ☐ Scouring pad-sponge
- ☐ Aluminum foil (2 large folded sheets for baking, steaming)
- ☐ Camp fire grill (optional)
- ☐ Water bottles (one each)
- ☐ Water filter or purification drops

FOOD STORAGE AND PACKING

- ☐ "Spice Rack" (7-day pill box + adhesive tape)
- ☐ Plastic jars, bottles (to pack liquids, sauces, condiments, butter)
- ☐ Egg containers (plastic camping cartons, for 6 or 12)
- ☐ Ziploc bags (large and small sizes; take 10 extras of each on trip)
- ☐ Check fridge and freezer for perishables and prepared dinners
- ☐ Cooler (for carrying perishables to trailhead)
- ☐ Pack containers with liquids in Ziploc bags. Store upright in pack.
- ☐ Garbage bag for car

SHOPPING LIST

Check recipes for suggested amounts of such things as flour, sugar, milk powder, cornmeal, butter, oil, and other ingredients. See chapter 10 for trip and menu planning and amounts and weights of food. Follow this commandment: *Take only what people actually like to eat.* (A preteen's list might consist of three days' worth of cookies, candy bars, marshmallows, peanut butter, and nothing else. Plan on it.)

Ingredients for meals (choose the recipes you want and shop accordingly. List all ingredients separately or you'll forget some of them).

- ☐ Flour
- ☐ Polenta
- ☐ Yeast
- ☐ Sugar
- ☐ Baking powder/soda
- ☐ Powdered tofu mix
- ☐ Powdered egg mix
- ☐ Powdered egg whites
- ☐ Powdered milk/buttermilk
- ☐ Pasta/soba/udon/rice noodles
- ☐ Semisweet baking chocolate
- ☐ Butter/margarine
- ☐ Oil (olive, peanut, vegetable, canola)
- ☐ Coffee/tea/powdered chocolate
- ☐ Brandy/port (for use in icings and desserts, too)
- ☐ Rice (arborio/basmati/sushi)
- ☐ Beans
- ☐ Nori (Japanese seaweed)
- ☐ Soy sauce
- ☐ Mirin (Japanese cooking wine)
- ☐ Rice vinegar
- ☐ Wasabi
- ☐ Maple sugar/syrup
- ☐ Lemon/lime juice
- ☐ Cheese (hard lasts longer than soft)
- ☐ Fruit/veggies for dehydrating
- ☐ Spices and condiments: oregano, thyme, cayenne, ginger, cinnamon, salt, pepper
- ☐ Cookies
- ☐ Crackers

Resources

INTERNET RESOURCES

Equipment

www.kitchenfancy.com

www.quickspice.com
Sushi rolling mat

www.equipment-camping.com
Pots, pans, and utensils for camping

www.rei.com

www.ems.com

www.campmor.com
Pots, pan, utensils, stoves, grills, water purifiers, and most any other camping equipment you might desire

www.backpackerspantry.com
Outback Ovens

http://pristine.ca/home.html

www.aerobiclife.com/aquamira.html
Water purification drops

Reference

www.foodsubs.com/Noodles.html
Asian noodle "thesaurus" with illustrations

www.chilepepperinstitute.org/pungency.htm
Scoville Heat Units Scale

http://tasteoftx.com
Chile recipes

www.foghorn.com/exhibit/homecooking.html
Rick and Hal's recipe for Beef Burgundy

http://usscouts.org/scoutcraft/oven.html
United States Scouting Service

Foods

http://importfood.com
Thai foods

www.bangkokmarket.com/home.html
Thai and Asian foods

www.thaifoodandtravel.com/mailmarkets.html
List of online sources for Thai and Asian Foods

http://importfood.com/spct5601.html
Thai coconut cream powder

www.hotchilepepper.com

www.melissas.com (click on Product Info and then Chiles)
Dried chiles

www.adventurefoods.com
Soy sauce granules

www.rainbowgrocery.org
Dry soup mixes

www. ethnicgrocer.com
Asian, Middle Eastern, and Mexican foods, oils, and spices

www.quinoa.bigstep.com/catalog.html
Quinoa

www.freshdirect.com

www.casadefruita.com
Dried cranberries and other dried fruit

www.gaines.com
Powdered maple syrup and other imaginative camping foods

www.gourmetsleuth.com/lemongrass.htm
Lemongrass

http://i-clipse.com
Asian and Mexican sauces, condiments, wrappers, seaweed, and more

Herbs and Spices

www.mvspices.com

www.groversons.com
Indian spices

www.bulkfoods.com
Spices, seeds, beans, grains, and herbs

www.americanspice.com
Hundreds of spices and condiments, alphabetically arranged

www.asiafoods.com
Asian and South Asian spices from Indian curries to Japanese seasonings

www.ethnicgrocer.com/eg/default.asp
Grains, herbs, spices, chiles, and more

www.qualityspices.com
Indian, Mediterranian, and Hispanic foods, spices

http://orientalpantry.com
Asian spices, groceries

MAIL-ORDER CATALOG

Penzeys Spices
19300 West Janacek Court
Brookfield, WI 53045
Tel: (800) 741-7787
Fax: (262) 785-7678

www.penzeys.com
Mail-order catalog with more than 250 spices, seasonings, and herbs.

EDIBLE WILD GREENS

We are not experts in the arts of survival foraging and would probably kill off the entire family if we tried to distinguish edible miner's lettuce from poisonous arrow-grass. As they say in the wild greens trade, "Contact a natural resource professional if you are unsure about a plant." We say, check out the Web sites, a few of which we list here:

www.umext.maine.edu/
onlinepubs/htmpubs/4060.htm

http://snohomish.wsu.edu/
edible.htm

www.ediblewild.com

Index

Note: Page numbers in *italic* refer to illustrations; those in **boldface** refer to tables.

Other Storey Books You Might Enjoy

Fish Grilled & Smoked by John Manikowski. Learn 150 succulent ways to cook just about anything that swims. Truly unique, this book provides step-by-step instructions for rigging a smoker streamside, operating a smoker at home, and building a backyard smoker. 224 pages. Paperback. ISBN 1-58017-502-3.

The Hiking Companion by Michael W. Robbins. Discusses hiking in various terrains, common mistakes and how to avoid them, trip planning and equipment, and basic navigation as well as Robbins's exciting, once-in-a-lifetime adventures. 136 pages. Paperback. ISBN 1-58017-429-9.

The Kayak Companion by Joe Glickman. Joe Glickman, a two-time member of the U.S. National Marathon Kayak Team, teaches beginners the basic techniques of sea, touring, and recreational kayaking, and offers expert advice to more experienced kayakers. 136 pages. Paperback. ISBN 1-58017-485-X.

Keeping a Nature Journal by Clare Walker Leslie and Charles E. Roth. Reconnect with nature by sketching and writing about the earth's beauty. Written by the woman *The Artist's Magazine* calls "perhaps the most well-known nature artist/educator in the country." 224 pages. Paperback. ISBN 1-58017-493-0.

Making & Using Dried Foods by Phyllis Hobson. Whether you use a commercial dehydrator or make one yourself, it's never been simpler to dry and store fruits, vegetables, grains, meats, and herbs. 192 pages. Paperback. ISBN 0-88266-615-0.

Nature Journal by Clare Walker Leslie. More than a blank book, this guided journal provides just the right amount of information and inspiration to record your reflections on nature. 176 pages. Paperback. ISBN 1-58017-296-2.

Picnic by DeeDee Stovel. Includes 29 seasonal picnic event ideas and more than 125 recipes — packable repasts from an informal Berry Picking Picnic to an elegant Music Festival Picnic. 192 pages. Paperback. ISBN 1-58017-377-2.

WoodsWalk by Henry W. Art and Michael W. Robbins. With enough identification information on trees, terrain, plants, and wildlife for a hundred walks in all four seasons, this book is the complete first primer for the inquisitive young naturalist. 128 pages. Paperback. ISBN 1-58017-452-3.

These and other Storey books are available wherever books are sold and directly from

Storey Publishing
210 MASS MoCA Way
North Adams, MA 01247

or by calling
1-800-441-5700.

Or visit our Web site at
www.storey.com